Copycat Cri

and

Copycat Crimi

Copycat Crime
and
Copycat Criminals

Ray Surette

LYNNE
RIENNER
PUBLISHERS

BOULDER
LONDON

Published in the United States of America in 2022 by
Lynne Rienner Publishers, Inc.
1800 30th Street, Suite 314, Boulder, Colorado 80301
www.rienner.com

and in the United Kingdom by
Lynne Rienner Publishers, Inc.
Gray's Inn House, 127 Clerkenwell Road, London EC1 5DB
www.eurospanbookstore.com/rienner

© 2022 by Lynne Rienner Publishers, Inc. All rights reserved

Library of Congress Cataloging-in-Publication Data
Names: Surette, Ray, author.
Title: Copycat crime and copycat criminals / Ray Surette.
Description: Boulder, Colorado : Lynne Rienner Publishers, Inc., 2022. |
  Includes bibliographical references and index. | Summary: "A
  comprehensive study of the nature of copycat crime, both past and
  present, and the forces that drive it"— Provided by publisher.
Identifiers: LCCN 2021051856 (print) | LCCN 2021051857 (ebook) | ISBN
  9781955055246 (hardback) | ISBN 9781955055413 (ebook)
Subjects: LCSH: Copycat crimes. | Crime—Psychological aspects. | Criminal
  psychology. | Contagion (Social psychology)
Classification: LCC HV6080 .S88 2022 (print) | LCC HV6080 (ebook) | DDC
  364.3—dc23/eng/20211025
LC record available at https://lccn.loc.gov/2021051856
LC ebook record available at https://lccn.loc.gov/2021051857

British Cataloguing in Publication Data
A Cataloguing in Publication record for this book
is available from the British Library.

Printed and bound in the United States of America

∞   The paper used in this publication meets the requirements
     of the American National Standard for Permanence of
     Paper for Printed Library Materials Z39.48-1992.

5 4 3 2 1

To my wife, Susan, my children, Tim, Paul, Jen, and Boyd, and my grandchildren, Nora and Leif: Thank you for making my life worthwhile and interesting.

Contents

Tables and Figures

Tables

Figures

Preface

ON NOVEMBER 30, 2021, A MASS SHOOTING WAS CARRIED out by a 15-year-old student at an Oxford, Michigan, high school. Within days, multiple telephone calls and social media postings threatened copycat shootings, prompting a number of regional schools to announce that they would close for a time. The Oxford school shooting is one example from a continual stream of crimes, some serious like the fatal Oxford shooting, some minor involving car stunts and pranks, through which copycat crime captures and retains public attention. But while copycat crime regularly garners media and public attention, the dynamics of this phenomenon are not understood.

In response, this book, *Copycat Crime and Copycat Criminals,* examines what copycat crime is, what theories are related to it, and what forces drive it. Imbedded in the broader public and academic interest in media and justice, copycat crime sits at the intersection of media and crime. The core of the crime and media connection is reflected in copycat crime. Despite copycat crime being uncommon, the study of the phenomenon reveals the relationship between the varied forms of media and criminality in contemporary society.

While prior popular writings and academic research provide a descriptive history of copycat crimes, and online search engines quickly deliver a rich set of anecdotal examples, neither provide an assessment of where the study of copycat crime currently stands. Despite centuries of public interest and decades of research, copycat crime remains understudied and misperceived. Paradoxically, its significance has been both downplayed in criminology and exaggerated in society. Copycat crime influences crime trends, criminal justice policies, criminal careers, and

xi

public perceptions of criminality. At the same time, these crimes do not appear to significantly raise a society's crime or violence rates. Copycat crime remains today a phenomenon with high public interest but incomplete understanding.

As social media increasingly dominate contemporary societies, interest in copycat crime has followed, making the 2020s an excellent era in which to study the phenomenon. Three trends deserve our attention. First, the relationship between media consumers and their media has changed from passive to participatory; second, criminogenic media have been suggested as playing a significant role in the launching of a number of juvenile crime careers; and third, copycat crimes appear to be increasing in prevalence.

In addition, physical separation of consumers is no longer a barrier to sharing content, and social media consumers can have multiple pseudonyms while remaining anonymous. The interactive nature of new media further encourages consumers to be participants in creating psychologically engaging, media-generated experiences. In sum, social media afford potential copycat offenders the ability to seek out like-minded crime models, both real-world and fictional, interact with them psychologically and anonymously, and virtually rehearse and plan a copycat crime.

As crimes posted for social media audiences become common, and as media cement their new relationship with their audiences, we have a new opportunity to examine closely and understand copycat crime. Seizing that opportunity, in this book I summarize the history of copycat crime, rigorously define its boundaries, characterize the theories and theoretical concepts applicable to copycat crime, and offer a way forward regarding copycat-crime-related research and public policy. Collectively, the nine chapters of *Copycat Crime and Copycat Criminals* explore both the allure and the reality of copycat crime.

Acknowledgments

THIS WORK HAS BEEN GREATLY INFLUENCED BY THE OBSER-vations of and interactions with colleagues over the years who shared their interest in the relationship of media, crime, and criminal justice. I would name them, but I know that I would forget someone and deeply regret it. Instead, I direct the reader to the text, where these colleagues are liberally cited, and to the references, where they are heavily represented. I would also like to thank the students who have taken my crime and media and my copycat crime classes, who explained what "hash tags" were and that Tiktok was the latest social media trend, and who, I hope, took away more than just a grade.

Last, I would like to acknowledge the people at Lynne Rienner Publishers. Collectively, they made writing this book smooth and stress free. The final result is enormously improved because of their efforts. Specifically, publisher Lynne Rienner was encouraging and involved in the initial conceptualization of the book, she helped focus the contents, and she was kind enough to offer a contract. Alex Holzman worked closely with me in drafting early chapters and in keeping the manuscript logical, on point, and clearly written. As senior project editor, Allie Schellong husbanded the book through the production process. Jen Kelland copyedited the entire work, correcting my lapses into wordiness and free-range punctuation. Barbara Paris closely proofread the page proofs. Sally Glover covered marketing, and Moorea Corrigan, assistant to Lynne Rienner, replied promptly to my emails and made sure that deliveries were delivered and schedules met. Thank you all for being professional, pleasant partners.

1

The Nature of Copycat Crime

Let me give you a 101 on how to ghost ride
Pull up, hop out, all in one motion
Dancing on the hood while the car's still rollin'
Stuntin', shinin', flamboastin'
Get out the way, let Casper drive
Ghost ride, go crazy
Who that drivin'?
Patrick Swayze![1]

FOLLOWING THE INSTRUCTIONS FOUND IN THE ABOVE RAP song, "Ghost Riding It" by Mistah F.A.B., a young man puts his parents' car in neutral on a slight hill so that the car can roll forward. He opens the door and, with a friend, climbs out of the car onto the roof, taking a seat and waving to a second friend who is manning a camera. The rap song "Ghost Riding It" plays and, using his arms, the man gyrates as the car begins to speed up. The screen goes blank as the sounds of yelling and a crash are heard. Another media-driven copycat crime gone bad is in the books.[2]

The goal when ghost riding is to create the impression that a ghost is driving your car, or "whip" ("Ghost Riding the Whip" n.d.; Piersa 2009). Copycats of ghost riding the whip resulted in thousands of moving-vehicle offenses, several accidents and injuries, and a few fatalities. Via YouTube clips and Google searches (see Figure 1.1),

Figure 1.1   "Ghost Riding the Whip" Google Search Popularity, January 2004 to January 2019

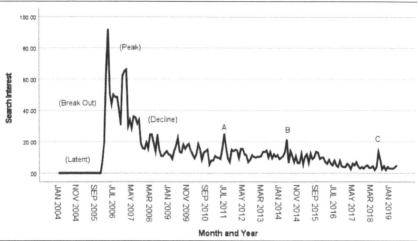

Source: Surette 2020a, 248.

Notes: Results shown for "ghost ride the whip" and "ghostride the whip" summed and divided by two (verisons correlated at .664). (A) Family Force 5 concert. (B) Marvel *Ghost Rider* comic. (C) Drake dance challenge.

detailed instructions on ghost riding spread nationwide from a minority community to the middle class (Surette 2020a). Ghost riding the whip provides a digital example of a style of copycat crime where a crime is purposely recorded and distributed to audiences by the offenders (Surette 2016c). Bolstered by media that closely follow celebrities, generate a strong need in audience members to share content, and support the idea that some crimes are acceptable, performance-style copycat crimes have seen a significant increase (Chan et al. 2012; Penfold-Mounce 2010; Surette 2012, 2016c).

Not surprisingly in this modern-day cultural environment, copycat crime has become a recurring pop culture subject found in online streaming programs like *Copycat Killers* (www.reelz.com /copycat-killers) and commercial films such as Warner Brothers' 1995 movie *Copycat*. As online and social media have supplanted the traditional media of newspapers and broadcast television, the public and academic debate about media criminogenic effects and the nature and extent of copycat crime has amplified. But the discussion remains based on rare and unusual copycat crimes, poorly documented copycat crime anecdotes, and portrayals of copycat crimes found in infotainment programming (Surette 2017). The ongoing debate reflects a backward portrait where bizarre, usually violent copycat crimes dominate, while the mundane reality of copycat crime is ignored. The central aim of this book is to clarify what copycat crime is and what it is not. To rigorously study copycat crime, it is important to be able to determine if a specific crime is a copycat. This task is not as easy as it might appear, and a first requirement for the study of copycat crime is to define it as a mutually exclusive set of criminal events separate from other crimes.

Defining Copycat Crime

In this book the term *copycat crime* refers to a crime whose cause lies in an offender's exposure to media about a prior crime.[3] Whereas a homicide requires only one crime and one victim for study, copycat crime is unique and problematic in the necessity that two crimes be validly tied together via the media. In a copycat crime pairing, the media chronologically yoke two crimes together. The crimes share a unique criminogenic connection, with the first serving as a generator for the later crime. Although the crimes can be separated by time and geography, the media are linking mechanisms, and the removal of the media would eliminate the occurrence or form of the subsequent copycat crime. In sum, calling a crime a copycat indicates that a unique criminological and psychological media-linked dynamic is operating.

Hence, for a crime to be a valid copycat crime, it must have been inspired by an earlier, media-publicized or -portrayed crime. The perpetrator of a copycat crime must have been exposed to the media content of the original crime and must have incorporated major elements of that crime into their offense (Helfgott 2015). At a minimum, a copycat crime requires a crime dyad, with at least one generator and one copycat crime. A generator crime can be a real crime covered in the news or portrayed in infotainment media or a fictional crime created in entertainment media. Generator crime content can be delivered by print, visual, audio, or new-media channels. Additionally, copycat crimes can range from detailed rote copies of a crime to composite crimes created from multiple media models, to amorphous adoptions of criminal personae (for example, when the 2012 Aurora, Colorado, movie theater shooter assumed the movie role of "The Joker"), to broadly motivated targetings of specific types of victims (Helfgott 2022, forthcoming). Anecdotal reports of examples include copycat bank robberies (Livingstone 1982; Schmid and de Graaf 1982); race, school, and political disturbances (Hamblin, Jacobsen, and Miller 1973; Ritterband and Silberstein 1973; Spilerman 1970); and military coups (Li and Thompson 1975; Midlarksy 1970). A copycat crime can be committed by an individual, a small group, or a large collection of people and can encompass a range of criminal behaviors, including collective acts like rioting (Bohstedt and Williams 1988; Myers 2000), small-group crimes such as sniper and school shootings and hate crimes (Coleman 2004), individual acts such as suicide (Phillips 1979, 1982; Phillips, Lesyna, and Paight 1992), and lone-wolf terrorism (Nacos 2007; Phillips 2013; Tuman 2010; Weimann and Winn 1994). Copycat crime thus encompasses the full range of criminal activity from the trivial to the homicidal, and it is not the criminal behavior but the associated media dynamics that generate copycat crime and separate it from noncopycat crime.

In this conceptualization, most crimes are not copycat crimes, and as defined, a copycat crime can involve broad types of criminal behavior. However, for rigorous study, copycat crimes must be mutually exclusive from noncopycat crimes, and defining the basic elements required for a particular crime to be part of a copycat crime dyad is a necessary first step. A copycat crime pair will contain, at a minimum, the following:

1. A generator crime—an account or portrayal of a crime in a media product that is the precursor to a subsequent crime.
2. Criminogenic content—media content that encourages the committing of an emulated crime.
3. A copycat criminal—an individual who commits a crime after being influenced by criminogenic media content.
4. A copycat crime—a crime whose occurrence or form is shaped by criminogenic media content in a generator crime.

In the basic copycat crime process, fictional or real-world generator crimes are distributed via the media to create a threshold level of accessible criminogenic media content in society. The criminogenic content interacts with other social and individual factors to create a pool of potential copycat criminals who, when given the opportunity in the proper environment, commit copycat crimes. While a crime dyad is a minimum requirement—at least one generator and one copycat crime are needed—some copycat crime family trees involve multiple generator crimes where a set of crimes contribute unique individual elements to a single copycat crime. Along the same lines, a heavily publicized generator crime can spawn multiple copycat derivatives and recurring waves of copycats so that one generator copycat crime, like a heavily publicized school shooting, can generate second- and third-generation copycats.[4]

Difficulties Studying Copycat Crime

The complicated and unique nature of copycat crime has rendered rigorous study of the phenomenon difficult (Langman 2017, 2018), and although there exists today a sizable amount of research on violent media's relationship to aggression, research on copycat crime has lagged. A leading reason for this deficiency is the difficulty in examining copycat crime levels (Landsbaum 2016). Whereas other crimes are comparatively easy to quantify and are routinely tallied, copycat crimes are not counted systematically, and debate about the extent of a copycat effect persists (Clarke and McGrath 1992; Stack 1987, 2000).

The invisibility of copycat crime is further exacerbated by its multicrime nature. Studying copycat crime first requires that a media link between two crimes be correctly recognized. A media-portrayed crime and its subsequent copycat crime can be so separated in space and time that an unknown number of copycat crimes invariably go unrecorded. As parodied by the online satire site *The Onion*,[5] the reality of false positives is a research concern when crimes that appear similar are incorrectly labeled as copycat crimes (see Coleman 2004 for a list of presumed copycat events).

Copycat Criminals Continue to Mimic Liquor Store Robbery from 1822
    Noting the similar circumstances surrounding all of the cases, sources confirmed that countless copycat criminals continue to imitate the infamous Blackjack Collins' robbery of a liquor store in 1822. "We still see thousands of individuals each year who have clearly patterned their heists after Blackjack, an early American criminal who masked his face in cloth, walked into Johnsons' Spirit and Tobacco Shoppe brandishing a firearm, and screamed at the clerk, 'Give me the money!'", said criminal profiler Paul Gorman, adding that the meticulously recreated homages are typically executed by those—just like Collins—who seek to quickly increase their personal wealth. "And just as Blackjack fled the scene on horseback, we find that nearly every modern-day culprit uses some form of transportation to make their getaway, a hallmark of the initial crime that has repeated itself for nearly 200 years."

Hence, what is currently thought about copycat crime has been surmised from anecdotal, often haphazard, post hoc reports of crimes labeled as copycats. Although *The Onion's* 1822 copycat-generator criminal, Blackjack Collins, is fictional, the satire highlights the issue of research difficulty and leads to the question of why bother to study copycat crime.

Why Study Copycat Crime?

A small but steady stream of crimes described as copycat crimes can be easily found by search engines (Surette 2015b; Surette et al. 2021). Public concern connected to copycat terrorism, school shootings, mass and serial murderers, and suicides is now common. An irony of copycat crime is that the imitation of crime is perceived in criminology as both common and rare. Beginning with Italian criminologist Gabriel Tarde, since the late 1800s some criminologists have argued that the basic nature of crime is imitative, and this perception has led to the conclusion that much crime is copied from other perpetrators. Copycat crime is both common and uninteresting. Others see media-linked copycat crime as rare and applicable to such a small proportion of crime as to be unimportant.

There is some truth to both views. On the imitative-crime-is-common side, social learning theory has established that much crime is based on real-world crime models (Akers and Jensen 2003; Bandura 1973; Sutherland 1947). It is generally conceded in criminology that exposure to real-world crime models is important in the genesis of criminality and that a substantial proportion of crime is influenced through physically direct person-to-person modeling. Juveniles, in particular, are thought to model criminogenic parents, older siblings, and neighborhood offenders, especially when launching their criminal careers (Akers 2011; Sutherland, Cressey, and Luckerbill 1992). When queried, about one-fourth of adult offenders report that they have attempted a copycat crime, and many copycat offenders state that they attempted their copycat crime as teenagers (Surette 2013a; Surette and Chadee 2020; Surette and Maze 2015). Youthful copycat crime appears to be a jumping-off point for a substantial number of delinquents.

On the copycat-crime-is-rare side, it is true that media-generated criminality likely makes up only a small portion of all criminality and that the majority of crimes are not linked to media content. When asked, three of four offenders report that none of their crimes were copycat crimes

(Surette 2014; Surette and Maze 2015). If most crime is not generated by the media, and the imitation avenue that has received the most support in criminology is not the media but other people (Sutherland, Cressey, and Luckerbill 1992), why worry about media-generated copycat crime?

The answer is three pronged: recent changes in the nature of the media/audience relationship (Grodal 2003b; Surette 2020a), research suggesting the genesis role of media in the launching of juvenile criminal careers (Surette and Chadee 2020; Surette and Maze 2015), and evidence indicating that copycat crimes are increasing (Helfgott 2022, forthcoming) all raise the importance of studying copycat crime. Copycat crimes may be rare, but they influence crime trends, criminal justice policies, criminal careers, and public perceptions of criminality.

From the public's point of view, an ability for media content to generate real-world criminality has been a leading public concern about media effects on society for over 150 years (Surette 2015b, 2017). The question of the extent of the media's ability to generate crime lies at the crux of public concern regarding pernicious media effects. If, as many believe, the media are producing copiers of serial killers, terrorists, and other serious criminals, the public has reason to worry, while, ironically, being simultaneously fascinated by the copycat crimes they worry about.

Lastly, for social scientists in the fields of criminology and mass media, understanding the extent and dynamics of media-linked crime would help to explain the broader media effects on crime and justice and the media's relationship to noncriminal social behaviors. The study of copycat crime also has relevance for several criminology theories, including social learning, subcultural, cross-cultural, and life-course theories of crime. Copycat crime research would be additionally helpful in the study of the media's role in cognitive processing, the influence of the media on the adoption of behaviors, and the impact of media immersion on individuals. As crime's association with media has a unique history, copycat crime can provide an untapped reservoir for understanding broader media, crime, and social behavior questions.

Copycat Crime's Cultural History

Historically, the verb *to copy*, denoting the hand duplication of printed material, is thought to have appeared in 1580 (Surette 2015a).[6] The profession of copyist was recognized in the 1700s. Over the eighteenth century, the term *copyist* evolved, and by 1814 the derivative *copyism* began to refer to the negative behavior of imitators. Thereafter, the word *copyism* was frequently used to disparage actors and artists (Siegelberg 2011). In parallel with the etymology of the word *copying*, references in popular culture to the media as a source of crime imitations can be traced to the 1600s. Sharpe (1999, 228–229)[7] noted that from the end of the 1600s, it was widely accepted that entertainment media accounts of crime encouraged real crime, a belief repeatedly expressed throughout the 1700s. For example, a 1728 pamphlet claimed that an honest young man was led to become a highway robber after seeing the play *The Beggar's Opera*. By the 1760s, newspaper reporting in the United States was being criticized for amplifying crime waves (Sharpe 1999). Widespread public acceptance of media-generated crime continued into the nineteenth century, as shown in an 1828 newspaper editorial:

> We deem it of little benefit to the cause of morals thus to familiarize the community, and especially the younger parts of it, to the details of misdemeanor and crime. . . . [I]t suggests to the novice in vice all the means of becoming expert in its devise. The dexterity of one knave, arrested and sent to State Prison, is adopted from newspaper instruction by others yet at large. (Bleyer 1927, 157, citing the *Evening Post,* June 6, 1828).

Based on several heavily covered anecdotal examples, by the latter half of the Victorian era, weekly print periodicals known as penny dreadfuls were widely characterized as drivers of juvenile crime (Dunae 1979; Springhall 1994).

> It is almost a daily occurrence with magistrates to have before them boys who, having read a number of "dreadfuls", followed the examples set forth in such publications, robbed their employers, bought revolvers with the proceeds, and finished by running away from home, and installing themselves in the back streets as "highwaymen." This and many other evils the "penny dreadful" is responsible for. It makes thieves of the coming generation, and so helps fill our gaols (Springhall 1994, quoting Alfred Harmsworth 1893).

This early public acceptance of a media-crime link was succinctly summed up in the 1886 British magazine *Punch* (quoted by Dunae 1979, 138): "The Boy Pirate and The Boy Brigand of fiction soon becomes the boy burglar and the boy thief of fact." The notion of crime generated as the result of media content has thus been popular for 300 years, but the labeling of the media-crime connection as "copycat crime" did not happen quickly.

Box 1.1   **First Media Reference to Copycat Crime**
Murdered Man's Diary Found: "Copycat" Inquiry
Daily Telegraph Reporter

A diary belonging to George Gerald Stobbs, 48, of Mansfeldt Road, Chesterfield, who was found murdered in a hedge at Clodhall Lane, Baslow, Derbyshire, on Wednesday, was found yesterday by Mrs. Frances Adlington, wife of a Chesterfield businessman. She was out with her two dogs at the time.

She found it in a wood 300 yards from the main drive of Stubbing Court, Wingerworth, where the murder is believed to have been committed. Following this, police investigating the "copycat" murder found a track over a quarter of a mile long, made by Stobbs' dragged body.

A police spokesman said last night: "We think it unlikely that one man could have dragged the body the whole distance. It would have taken at least two powerful men. One or both might well have been concerned in the killing of William Elliott, 60, in the bubble car murder nine months ago."

Elliott, of Haddon Road, Bakewell, was found murdered not far from where Stobbs was found. Their cars were abandoned in the same road in Chesterfield, nine miles away.

Source: "Murdered Man's Diary Found" 1961.

It was not until the late 1800s that the words *copy* and *cat* were united and the disparaging of social acts as "copycat behavior" appeared.[8] It took another seventy years before the words *copycat* and *crime* were combined. Reproduced in Box 1.1, the first documented reference to a copycat crime occurred in the United Kingdom in April 1961 in a *Daily Telegraph* newspaper story ("Murdered Man's Diary Found" 1961). Eight months later the phrase *copycat criminal* appeared in a December 1961 *New York Times* article by David Dressler, "The Case of the Copycat Criminal." Once born, the expression *copycat crime*, together with general acceptance of its social impact, steadily increased.

From its popular culture roots and under different names, media-generated copycat crime became a phenomenon widely acknowledged by the public and slowly began to attract serious academic attention. In the twentieth century, research in two areas began to empirically explore copycat effects. The first area of research involves copycat suicides. Sociologist David Phillips called the media-generated copycat effect on suicides the "Werther Effect," so named for the main character of Johann Goethe's 1774 novel *The Sorrows of Young Werther*, who commits suicide when faced with unrequited love. The second copycat research area deeply examined is copycat terrorism, characterized as having a "contagion effect" in the terrorism research literature (Poland 1988; Tuman 2010). Within the terrorism research literature, there are few doubts about the media's ability to motivate copycat terrorism. Numerous anecdotal descriptions of media-linked terrorist events, including kidnappings, hostage-taking bank robberies, airline hijackings employing parachutes or altitude bombs, suicide bombings, and online beheadings of hostages, are available (see Poland 1988; Tuman 2010). The early anecdotal copycat crime cases, in combination with research on media-copied suicides and terrorism, established public support for the proposition that media-linked copycat crimes occur at a significant rate.[9] Despite impetus from these two research streams and the availability of a large set of anecdotal historical examples, criminology remained reluctant to study copycat crime.

Criminology Discovers Copycat Crime

With the popular notion of media-generated crime already in circulation among the press and the public, in the late 1800s criminologist Gabriel Tarde applied the idea of imitation to the study of crime and legitimized, at least for a short time, the concept of copycat crime in academia. Tarde coined the phrase *suggesto-imitative assaults* to describe copycat crimes and provided anecdotal examples, the best known being murders he linked to Jack the Ripper (Tarde [1912] 1968, 340):

> What more striking example of suggesto-imitative assault could there be than the series of mutilations of women, begun in the month of September 1888 in London in the Whitechapel district! Never perhaps has the pernicious influence of general news been more apparent. The newspapers were filled with the exploits of Jack the Ripper, and, in less than a year, as many as eight absolutely identical crimes were committed in various crowded streets of the great city. This is not all; there followed a repetition of these same deeds outside of the capital and very soon there was even a spreading of them abroad. At Southampton attempt to mutilate a child; at Bradford horrible mutilation of another child; at Hamburg murder accompanied by disemboweling of a little girl; in the United States disemboweling of four negroes.

In addition to making imitation the main crime engine, Gabriel Tarde was the first criminologist to consider the media as an important source of crime ideas. His best-known quote explicitly pointed to a strong media influence: "Infectious epidemics spread with the air or the wind; epidemics of crime follow the line of the telegraph" (Tarde [1912] 1968, 340). Although Tarde's ideas about crime quickly fell into disfavor in criminology following criticism of his research, other academic references to copycat crimes began to appear in the 1920s (see, for example, Bleyer 1927).

The idea of media-linked imitation as a crime-causing process flourished for only a short time with Gabriel Tarde but survived more permanently within psychological theories and within a focus on face-to-face imitation in criminology. Popular use of the word *copycat*, academic thought about imitative crime, and media influences on deviant behaviors were to remain separated for another sixty years. Outside academia, media-linked crimes continued to be identified by the public as a concern from the nineteenth into the twentieth centuries, despite academic abandonment of Tarde's advocacy of media-generated criminogenic imitation.

In twentieth-century criminology, imitative crime was subsumed within Edwin Sutherland's criminological theory of "differential association," where face-to-face interactions were felt to trump media influences. For the public, however, the plausibility of media-driven imitative crime never lost popularity and continued to influence public policy. From the Victorian-era penny dreadfuls, to the dime novels and yellow journalism of the 1890s, to the radio programs and movies of the 1920s and 1930s, the media remained commonly perceived by the public and policymakers as sources of criminogenic imitation. The first serious effort to study media effects on society, the Payne Fund studies in the United States, led to the adoption of the Motion Picture Production or Hays Code in the 1930s, a set of voluntary rules and guidelines meant to make movies safe for the public (Hays 1932; Surette 2015a). The code clearly reflected the belief that media crime models generate criminal imitators, stating,

> Crimes Against the Law. These shall never be presented in such a way as to throw sympathy with the crime as against law and justice or to inspire others with a desire for imitation.
>   1. Murder:
>   a. The technique of murder must be presented in a way that will not inspire imitation.

      b. Brutal killings are not to be presented in detail.
      c. Revenge in modern times shall not be justified.
   2. Methods of Crime should not be explicitly presented:
      a. Theft, robbery, safe-cracking, and dynamiting of trains, mines, buildings, etc., should not be detailed in method.
      b. Arson must be subject to the same safeguards.
      c. The use of firearms should be restricted to the essentials.
      d. Methods of smuggling should not be presented.

Following the Payne Fund studies and the Hays Code, media-generated imitative crime continued to remain accepted by the public through the 1940s and generated a brief crusade against comic books as a cause of juvenile delinquency in the early 1950s (Nyberg 1998; Sparks and Sparks 2002).[10] However, the media as a crime generator was not reintroduced as a source of serious study in criminology until the age of television.

In the 1950s, criminologist Daniel Glaser (1956) reformulated Sutherland's theory of differential association to include media influence and reintroduced to criminology the media as a significant crime source. A second major push in the reintroduction of media as a crime generator was the development of social learning theory pioneered by Albert Bandura (1973), who expanded the ideas of behavioral psychologist B. F. Skinner (1988) from the behavior-modification lab to everyday society. The social learning perspective sees behavior as acquired from watching others and learning what to expect from imitating their behavior. In addition, heated public debate about media effects and a large body of research on media and aggression were triggered by government hearings in the 1960s on possible negative social effects from media; a cluster of airline hijackings widely credited to copycat effects in news media coverage; a 1966 fictional commercial film, *The Doomsday Flight*, about an airline hijacking; and the first television-raised generation entering their teenage prime delinquency years.

These divergent forces all contributed to the academic acceptance of media-linked copycat crime in the 1960s. Based on the theoretical efforts of Glaser and Bandura, newsworthy copycat crimes, and popular culture portrayals, by the end of the 1960s a criminogenic role for the media was present in criminological theory, and the phrase *copycat crime* began to appear in the popular media. By the end of the 1970s, the idea of copycat crime had been widely popularized, as reflected in dialogue from an October 27, 1977, episode of the ABC television comedy *Barney Miller* (Episode 6, Season 4, "Copycat"):

DETECTIVE YEMANA: Mr. Boston here was robbed by a guy who used the same M.O. as he saw on TV last night.
CAPTAIN MILLER: Another copycat crime! That's the fifth in the last two weeks.
DETECTIVE YEMANA: Yeah. There's a lot of good things on. It's the new season.

Copycat crime's time had come; thereafter it was a widely accepted, easily recognized criminological concept. Pop culture references to copycat crime and periodic real-world media-linked crimes kept copycat crime in the public mind through the 1980s. Two impactful sets of crimes in 1983—the poisoning of over-the-counter medicines mimicking the poisoning of Tylenol headache medicine (see Box 8.1) and a wave of antigovernment protest bombings—dramatically brought copycat crime home to the public and marked the beginning of a significant increase in the use of the term and interest in its study.

By the end of the twentieth century, copycat crime was a concept available to quickly describe, categorize, and explain selected crimes. The year 1995 was a watershed for the concept. For the first time, the term *copycat crime* was employed in the public debate about media criminogenic effects as stories were published about a crime labeled as a copycat of a crime portrayed in the movie *Money Train* (see Borg 1995; Holloway 1995). The film depicted a scene in which a New York City subway toll booth was doused with gasoline and set afire by a psychotic criminal. Following the film's release, a similar crime was committed in the New York City subway system. While the film character was saved, the real-world toll collector died from his burns. The timing and similarity of the movie crime and the real-world crime launched a debate about the criminogenic effects of media in general and movies in particular. In the same year, the film *Copycat*, about a psychologist who lectures on serial killers and finds herself pursued by a serial killer who copies prior serial killers, further cemented the idea of media-generated copycat crimes in the public's mind. By the end of 1995, the idea of copycat crime had become so engrained in the public psyche that it began to appear in stories about sports and fashion (Surette 2015b).[11]

Mediated Crime

The technological evolution of media enabled the cultural acceptance of copycat crime as a social phenomenon. Examination of the historical development of the media reveals a persistent trend. Each advance in media technology brought the mediated experience, the experience that an individual has when experiencing an event through the media, closer to what it would be like to experience the event in the real world. As the first mass media, print media provided narratives and factual information but left to readers the generation of visual imagery and emotional reactions. In the late 1800s, artists' drawings and then photographs initially moved print media a small step toward imaging the real world, but the phonograph and radio, which provided sound, and home radio, which added live coverage and emotional dialogue, nudged the mediated experience substantially nearer to a real-world experience in the early 1900s. In the next media evolution in the 1920s, full-length commercial films provided continuous visual action and eventually sound, which again moved the media-based experience closer to a real-world one. Movies became more graphic and realistic through the 1930s and 1940s, until the 1950s television networks provided the first mediated experience combining easy access, live coverage, sound, moving images, and home delivery (Surette 2015a). Over the second half of the twentieth century, media technology evolved further to create delivery vehicles that increased access to media content and broader content choices for consumers. The late-twentieth-century introduction of electronic interactive games and computer-generated images poised the mediated experience via virtual and augmented reality to be truly competitive with and sometimes preferable to real-world experiences. Importantly, by the twenty-first century, technology changes moved the media audience from passive consumers to active content-creating participants (Surette 2017).

In terms of crime, individuals today can experience crime through the media and have the sensation of undergoing an actual crime experience. A media consumer can be a crime fighter, crime victim, or criminal in a way that realistically mimics each role. The cumulative result for copycat crime is that currently a multimedia environment ubiquitously presents realistic, graphic, and instructive crime models that can be interactively test-driven by potential copycat offenders. While the experience of real-world crime is concentrated among the poor and socially vulnerable, the experience of realistic mediated crime is a potentially universal experience. We live in a time where criminogenic media are parsed, recast, and filtered through a digital, visually dominated, multimedia web. In addition to the glut of crimes found in entertainment media, some real-world crimes have their images shared in real time in social media and become crime news. Their reenactments appear in entertainment films and television programming and audi-ence-produced YouTube videos. Through such avenues, mediated crime is realistic and influential, is repeatedly recycled, and cumulates in the popularity of social-media-driven copycat performance crimes (Surette 2016c). More than ever, crimes in the media are both culled for instruc-tions on how to commit them and emulated for the attention they garner.

Contemporary media influence how the public perceives crime and justice, and criminology concedes that peer-to-peer imitation plays a role in many crimes. However, the goal of this book is not to explore either dimension. Other works discuss the general portrait of crime and justice found in the media and the role of the media in people's beliefs about crime and support for criminal justice policies, as well as the media's impact on criminal justice (see Surette 2015a for an overview). Similarly, the process of direct person-to-person imitation of crime, par-ticularly among delinquent peers, has been a significant element of criminological theorizing since the 1930s, with Sutherland's theory of differential association. In contrast, this work focuses on the set of crime influences generated through media-provided criminal models. As such, it explores copycat crime as it is commonly perceived—as a result of criminogenic media—and not the result of real-world crime models, such as a neighborhood delinquent gang leader or the influence of a criminal parent or sibling. If the media have important social effects on crime, it is through the media-generated emulation of crimes that the strongest effects will appear. Media-generated copycat crime marks the nexus where the media's criminogenic influences are determined, where public fears reside, and where calls for public policies arise.

Despite the social drivers and copycat crime's long evolution from a marginal concept largely ignored in criminology to its current embrace, copycat crime remains sparsely researched. It is erroneously, albeit com-monly, portrayed in the media in an inverse manner that creates a per-ception that is the opposite of reality. For copycat crime that means that bizarre, violent, rare crimes, such as school shootings and terror attacks, are put forth as representative, while more mundane copycat crimes such as moving vehicle offenses and vandalism are ignored. In addition, a major issue in the study of copycat crime remains the continued lack of coherent, interdisciplinary theoretical discussion. The discussion that is readily available tends to be more descriptive than explanatory (Surette et al. 2021). Capping off the importance for studying contemporary copycat crime is the development of new interactive social media and the accompanying heightened audience participation in the creation and distribution of content. The balance of this book strives to correct the misconceptions circulating about copycat crime within the contemporary new-media environment, to develop theoretical perspectives for understanding the generation of copycat crime, and to provide directions for needed policies and research.

Copycat crime exists today as a phenomenon with high public interest but little public understanding. Reports of horrific crimes labeled as copycat crimes regularly peak interest in the relationship between media and crime, but despite periodic attention and expressions of concern, specific research-based information about criminogenic media effects is not readily available. Instead, rare violent copycat crimes have dominated the literature, few copycat criminals have been studied or interviewed, little scientifically adequate research has been conducted, and, not surprisingly, well-grounded generalizations about copycat crime have been sparse. Although the phrase *copycat crime* appeared more than half a century ago, researchers still largely rely on anecdotal reports from journalists to gauge the extent and nature of copycat crime, with the result that many crimes are labeled as copycats without thoughtful assessment. While debate over pernicious media effects continues, with the most recent revolving around video games and social media, a discussion is lacking about copycat crime set in a broad array of scientific disciplines. A coherent summary of current knowledge, theories, and speculation about copycat crime in the contemporary digital, social media world is needed. As a response, this book explores the relevant current copycat crime research, theories, and knowledge.

Organization

The following chapters discuss copycat crime in terms of the following: evidence of its existence and prevalence; what we currently know about copycat crime; types of offenders, crimes, and media; models of the dynamics of copycat crime; and research that needs to be pursued and policies that are indicated. The text draws from research conducted in multiple disciplines, including criminal justice, criminology, sociology, political science, law, public administration, journalism, biology, psychology, and communications. Examples are drawn from the popular culture media sources of magazines, newspapers, music, video games, films, and the internet. Both the allure and the reality of copycat crime are explored, with a focus on social media. The work is offered as an entrée into the extant research and unaddressed research questions regarding copycat crime for interested individuals, researchers, and policymakers.

Chapter 2: Copycat Crime in Theory

Chapter 2 introduces five theoretical perspectives that are applicable to copycat crime. Starting with imitation and the disciplines of biology and psychology, a foundation for understanding copycat crime is laid out. Ideas regarding imitation are followed by descriptions of research on social contagion and the diffusion of innovations. The fourth area of discussion covers social learning theory; the fifth and last area describes the relevant media studies concepts. The basic causal processes, theoretical concepts, and working hypotheses underpinning each theoretical pillar are introduced, setting up their application to copycat crime in Chapters 5 and 6.

Chapter 3: Copycat Effects in Practice

The existence of media-induced copycat effects has been questioned and their importance disparaged by, among others, Clarke and McGrath (1992), Stack (1987, 2000), Torrecilla and colleagues (2019), and Sutherland, Cressey, and Luckerbill (1992). Chapter 3 reviews the research concerning pernicious media-generated copycat effects not associated with crime. It addresses the question of what evidence there is for media effects on noncriminal behavior. There does exist good evidence of copycat effects in noncriminal behaviors, and a substantial set of research has been conducted on media-induced copycat suicides and on the effect of violent media on socially aggressive behavior. Research on advertising also contributes to belief in media-induced effects on social behavior. As a whole, this research provides evidence and support for a substantial media behavioral effect on consumers and the potential importance of copycat crime as a social phenomenon.

Chapter 4: Measuring Copycat Crime

In the same manner that the association between two weakly related variables may be statistically significant but substantially irrelevant, copycat effects may occur in the world but be so infrequent as to be unimportant. As the substantive importance of copycat crime is some-times questioned, a review of the estimates of its prevalence is included. Chapter 4 therefore looks at the empirical methods employed concern-ing the determination of copycat crime waves and the measurement and identification issues that have retarded the study of copycat crime, along with historical approaches for studying crime waves and crime clusters. The first issue—the prevalence of copycat crime—has been estimated with a set of surveys that asked respondents if they had com-mitted a copycat crime in their lifetime. The next issue—how to objec-tively assess evidence for copycat crime clusters and distinguish a valid copycat crime cluster from a random distribution of criminal events—has been examined by researchers using time-series crime data and var-ied quantitative approaches.

Chapter 5: Imitation, Contagion, and Diffusion

Having established reasonable grounds for the existence of a persist-ent copycat effect, Chapter 5 begins the two-chapter task of applying each theoretical perspective to copycat crime, with Chapter 5 cover-ing imitation, contagion, and diffusion. First, a biological impetus for the imitation of crime is proposed, followed by a discussion of the psychological drives to imitate crime. Next, moving from an empha-sis on individual copycat offenders, processes that encourage the con-tagion of crime in large social groups and the diffusion of new behav-iors in social networks are detailed. The contagion and diffusion perspectives share an interest in how the adoption of new behaviors works in social settings. They differ in that social contagion research is more focused on negative group behaviors like riots, while the dif-fusion research is focused on the spread of positive social innovations such as healthy habits.

Chapter 6: An Interdisciplinary Perspective

Chapter 6 first applies the most directly relevant criminological theory, social learning, to copycat crime, then applies research in media stud-ies that is pertinent for copycat crime. The chapter then culls all five theoretical areas to offer an interdisciplinary perspective for researching and understanding copycat crime. The proposed interdisciplinary copy-cat crime approach considers both individual-level and aggregate-level processes. The aggregate level includes the cultural, social, and media factors and the dynamics that generate copycat crime waves. At the individual level, a family of suggested factors determine an individual's risk of copying a media-modeled crime.

Taken together, Chapters 4 through 6 cover current theoretical ideas and concepts regarding copycat crime and lay the groundwork for discussions in Chapters 7, 8, and 9 about the current state of copycat crime knowledge, the research that needs to be pursued, and the social policies that warrant consideration.

Chapter 7: Crime, Criminals, and Environments

Drawing from the literature on the five foundational theories, Chapter 7 extracts the characteristics that are hypothesized as linked to copycat crime. The media characteristics regarding crime models and criminogenic content associated with copycat crime are examined first, followed by review of the personality traits and exposure settings that have been associated with copycat crime. From these characteristics a set of untested propositions related to media, at-risk individuals, and copycat crime acquisition are pulled. Last, a copycat crime typology that dichotomizes the various copycat crime types and motivations suggested in the foundational theoretical literature is offered along the copycat crime dimensions of spontaneous or planned crimes, genesis or metamorphic crimes, and risk-reduction or media-attention crimes.

Chapter 8: Copycat Crime Across the Media

Much as Chapter 7 separates copycat crime and copycat offenders into subgroups, Chapter 8 breaks down the common perception of the media as a monolithic entity and examines copycat crime across constituent parts of the mass media. The first section of the chapter focuses on the historical relationship between copycat crime and print, sound, and visual legacy media found within books and newspapers, popular songs and radio programming, and television and movie content. The subsequent section examines the media by types of content and covers entertainment, news, advertising, and infotainment content's relationship to copycat crime. How these media differ in their delivery of content and portraits of crime and the implications of those differences for copycat crime are discussed. The dynamics of copycat crime are next contrasted with legacy media in a discussion of the various types of new digital media and copycat crime.

*Chapter 9: What We Know—and
Don't Know—About Copycat Crime*

Chapter 9 begins with discussions of two models of copycat crime. The first model presents aggregate paths that describe how copycat crime rates are generated depending upon the pool of potential copycat offenders available and the nature of the media and the cultural conditions in a society. The second is a multiple-path model that individuals traverse on their way to committing copycat crimes. This model's paths determine whether or not an individual will choose to commit a copycat crime and determines what type of copycat crime they commit. Following the introduction of the aggregate and individual copycat crime paths, the causal role of media in a society either as a direct causal trigger for crime or as a crime-molding rudder is discussed, with evidence presented for the media more often being a rudder for crime than a trigger.

In closing out the book, Chapter 9 discusses social policies related to copycat crime and criminogenic media that are supported by research and current knowledge. Acknowledging the persistence of a reversed portrait of copycat crime influencing public perceptions of the phenomena, three policy-related questions are considered: What do we know about copycat crime? What do we need to know to act? What policies and practices make sense now? A set of policy recommendations and the implications of copycat crime case law are considered. Yet-to-be-addressed research questions are discussed, and speculations about the future of copycat crime, its media portrayal, trends in copycat performance crime, and the live-streaming of copycat crimes are offered as calls for future research.

Notes

1. Excerpt from "Ghost Ride It" (2006) by Mistah F.A.B. from the album *Slappin' in the Trunk Vol. 2*. The discussion of "ghost riding the whip" draws on Surette 2020a.

2. To view the ghost riding the whip video, visit "Ghost Riding the Whip Gone Wrong," video posted to YouTube by daboo760, November 1, 2007, https://www.youtube.com/watch?v=r36PUoWDyog.

3. The discussion in this section draws on material from Surette 2016a.

4. An overview of the copycat crimes linked to the Columbine shootings provides an example of a multiwave copycat crime sequence. See zyopp, "Columbine Iceberg," scifiaddicts.com, http://scifiaddicts.com/p/IcebergCharts/comments/owo44n/columbine_iceberg.

5. The full satire can be seen at "Copycat Criminals Continue to Mimic Liquor Store Robbery from 1822," *The Onion*, January 5, 2015, https://local.theonion.com /copycat-criminals-continue-to-mimic-liquor-store-robber-1819577324.

6. The section on the cultural history of copycat crime draws from Surette 2015b.

7. Citing *Thievery a la Mode: The Fatal Encouragement* (London, 1728).

8. The first recorded print use of the word *copycat* was apparently in the 1887 novel *Bar Harbor Days* by Constance Harrison; the next was in Sarah Orne Jewett's 1890 novel *Betty Leicester: A Story for Girls*.

9. For initial discussions of the copycat crime rate, see Helfgott 2008; Pease and Love 1984a; Schmid and de Graaf 1982; Surette 2002; Wilson and Herrnstein 1985.

10. See also Wertham 1954 for advocacy of censorship of comic books as causes of juvenile crime and delinquency. Sparks and Sparks 2002 criticizes Wertham's link between comic books and violent delinquency as based on unscientific studies with biased samples and anecdotal testimony obtained from boys who were being treated for a wide range of psychological problems.

11. For example, the term appears in the sports pages in 1995: "Certainly, a late hit on Young Saturday, courtesy of Chicago safety Shawn Gayle, has the Cowboys thinking about a copycat crime" (*New York Times*, January 10, 1995, B9); again in 2001: "Before it gets to be a copycat crime, the teams should exercise their powers the way the New Orleans Saints sent guards into the stands Monday night to break up bottle-throwing" (*New York Times*, December 19, 2001, S1); and in a 2008 entertainment story: "In its homeland there have been efforts to duplicate it, the most recent example being the IT Crowd, a half-hour tribute to workplace shenanigans that can only be considered a copycat crime" (*New York Times*, September 30, 2008, E7).

2

Copycat Crime
in Theory

COPYCAT CRIME IS A PHENOMENON WHERE PUBLIC BELIEF outpaces scientific knowledge. As with UFOs, much information about copycat crime is based on a small amount of mostly indirect evidence. There are, however, theories that apply to copycat crime and can be used to guide research. The foundation theories introduced in this chapter provide plausible explanations for copycat crime. Many of the theoretical ideas that will be applied to copycat crime match beliefs about individual offenders and a criminological search for a "criminal man"—the prototypical offender historically thought to be fundamentally different from the law abiding (Rennie 1978). More than a century of research has shown, though, that the assumption of significant differences between law-abiding and criminal individuals is questionable. Instead, there are reasons to believe that the opposite is true and that offenders and the law abiding are more similar than different along most dimensions (Rennie 1978). However, people also generally believe that the media negatively affect others more than themselves (Perloff 2002). In 1983, W. Davidson named this perception the "third-person effect." The term *third person* is derived from the expectation that the media will have its greatest effect not on me (the first person) or on you (the second person) but on him or her (the third person). Belief in a third-person effect is common and more pronounced when the behavior is undesirable. Hence, when asked, individuals see crime content as having a larger impact on others than on themselves (Perloff 2002). Extending to perceptions about copycat crime, when asked, offenders will often state that they are not influenced by media content to commit crimes but that other offenders are so influenced (Surette 2002). It is a short leap from a third-person effect to the wider belief that media-attuned offenders are fundamentally different from the rest of society. Driven by this common perception, the expectation is that copycat offenders will differ innately in some fashion from noncopycat offenders, and explanations of copycat crime often focus on exploring for statistically significant differences. As yet undeveloped in this historical search for innate differences are coherent theoretical bases to guide the study of copycat crime.

In response, a survey of the research applicable to copycat crime reveals five theoretical perspectives that have brushed up against copycat crime. The theories overlap so that similar concepts and processes have acquired different labels within the different theories, and similar events can be explained differently depending upon which theory is applied. The five theoretical arenas further differ in their basic research questions and how much their associated theorists have considered the spread of crime or the importance of the media. Irrespective of their differences, as a group the theories provide several anchoring concepts and processes that can be used to construct an interdisciplinary perspective for studying copycat crime. The balance of this chapter introduces each theoretical area. Chapters 5 and 6 will focus on their copycat crime applications.

The first theoretical area focuses on general imitation from the biological and psychological perspectives. Research in these perspectives has looked at the biology and psychology of imitation in both animals and humans. The second theoretical perspective, social contagion, has focused on human collective behaviors across a broad set of social acts. In this perspective, behaviors usually spread and die relatively rapidly and are represented by unusual social behaviors committed by large groups of people. The contagion of violent crowd behavior, such as riots and lynching, has been one focus (Fagan, Wilkinson, and Davies 2006; National Research Council 2013; Stovel 2001; Sullivan 1977). A third useful theoretical perspective examines the diffusion of social innovations. A convenient way to differentiate contagion from diffusion is to consider contagion as behavior within a social group, while diffusion operates between social groups. Social diffusion theory takes a deep interest in how useful behaviors, termed *innovations*, are introduced into a new social group. The fourth theoretical pillar relevant for copycat crime is social learning theory, which focuses on how individual humans acquire new behaviors. Unlike proponents of the three prior perspectives, social learning theorists have extensively studied the acquisition of criminal behaviors. The fifth theoretical area is media studies. This field broadly focuses on how people and societies interact with media and how varied media content influence attitudes and behaviors. Detailed overviews of each theoretical field follow.

Imitation—Offender See, Offender Do

Imitation as a biological and psychological phenomenon has been recognized as a common human characteristic since antiquity. Aristotle (350 BCE) observed, "Man is the most imitative of living creatures and through imitation learns his earliest lessons. The instinct of imitation is implanted in man from childhood [and] imitation is in our nature." An early definition offered by social psychologist Edward Thorndike in 1898 remains apt: imitation is learning to do an act from seeing it done. Nineteenth-century animal psychologist Conwy Lloyd Morgan (1896) and other early naturalists considered imitation to be a low-level cognitive characteristic of women, children, savages, the mentally impaired, and animals, all of whom were believed to have little ability to reason (Galef 2005a). While disparaging of the behavior, this early attention to imitation did bring it under the umbrella of biology and set the stage for the latter, less misogynistic and less racist study of imitation.

The Biology of Imitation

If imitation is a basic common human trait, what are its biological roots? Today the dominant biological view of imitation in humans is that the translation of the perception of behavior into corresponding physical imitation of that behavior is a consequence of the way humans are neurologically wired (Dijksterhuis and Bargh 2001). Early support for an innate predisposition to imitate can be found in the nineteenth-century concept of induced movement, sometimes referred to as ideomotor action (see Carpenter 1874; James 1890; Lotze 1852). An example of induced movement would be when audience members watching a film of a person walking along the edge of a cliff find themselves minutely moving their bodies and displacing their body weight to one side as if they were on the cliff. These movements are induced by the situation of the person they are observing. The implication of induced movement is that people unconsciously tend to mimic actions they see being performed by others and that humans are biologically predisposed to imitate (Prinz 2005). True imitation occurs when an animal imitates a behavior that it has never done before and the behavior is unusual for that species (Mazur 2002, citing Thorpe 1963). An animal using a tool to obtain food after watching tool use would qualify. This ability to imitate behavior following observation of a previously unknown behavior has been observed in primates, birds, and rats. In humans, research on imitation has focused on the acquisition of language (Flanders 1968; Kymissis and Poulson 1990).

If imitation is innate, the unresolved biological question is the translation problem (Rizzolatti 2005). Sensory and muscle systems are classically considered to be separate biological systems, so the question is what bridges the observation of an act with the generation of the muscle commands to replicate that act. The contemporary neurological answer is mirror neurons—a diffused system of brain cells where visual input is processed to drive the muscular motor system.[1] Through mirror neurons, seeing is translated into doing.

Why would mirror neuron systems evolve? The first part of an answer argues an evolutionary advantage. It has been recognized since the 1940s that imitative behavior must be genetically adaptive to survive evolutionary culling and the best human survival response in unfamiliar situations is to copy others who understand the situation (Miller and Dollard 1941, citing Fortes 1938). The second evolutionary advantage of imitation is shown by the comparison with its opposite, invention of new behavior through trial-and-error learning. Invention of new behavior by an individual is difficult, time-consuming, and error prone. In contrast, imitation is easy, fast, and economical, as the newly acquired behavior is lifted directly from others. Imitation is an enormously efficient technique for learning new behavior and avoids the sometimes fatally incorrect errors produced in imitation-free trials (Miller and Dollard 1941). Learning if a mushroom is safe to eat by eating one is a dangerous trial-and-error process; it is enormously safer to eat a mushroom only after seeing one eaten by others. Being able to imitate is therefore a particularly strong evolutionary advantage for social animals. Mirror neurons would be selected as a means for quickly learning helpful actions performed by others, and individuals and groups of individuals who imitated better and quicker would have survival advantages. For example, being able to imitate a troop member using a new food-gathering technique, such as gathering termites using a stick, would give a powerful survival advantage over individuals who could not imitate. Imitation is so useful a biological trait that convergent evolution of imitation appears in varied phyla. Birds, gorillas, chimpanzees, rats, humans, and probably dolphins and orangutans all appear to imitate (Galef 2005b).

Mirror neuron research suggests an automatic biological tendency to imitate exists in humans, but as the mythical legend of lemmings following one another over a cliff reflects, oftentimes it is not healthy to automatically imitate (Kinsbourne 2005). For social creature such as humans, automatically imitating a behavior that results in being attacked or banished would not be evolutionarily beneficial, so unconsidered, fully automatic imitation would not be genetically encouraged. The evolutionary response apparently is that humans automatically mentally model behaviors first. As induced movements suggest, we imitate in our minds and preset our muscles to mimic as a first step. We then either copy or inhibit copying of the virtually modeled behavior as a second, usually consciously considered step. In many situations the potential imitated behavior is suppressed as dangerous or inappropriate, and although we have learned the behavior steps, we do not execute them. In other situations, the potentially imitated behavior is deemed advantageous, and we behave as we have seen others behave.

In terms of undesirable or aggressive behavior, many will cognitively learn the behavior as an automatically generated mental model, but most will inhibit the real-world expression of that behavior (Decety and Chaminade 2005). Imitation is thus performed at the abstract neurological level far more often than it is observed as overt motor system behavior (Kinsbourne 2005). In sum, we think about imitating far more than we actually imitate.[2] Accepting the existence of a biological foundation for imitation, the psychology of human imitation follows in interest.

The Psychology of Imitation

A biological capability to imitate appears in a number of species, but humans additionally evolved flexible imitation in their behavioral repertoire (Harris and Want 2005). The psychology-of-imitation literature uses the term *mind reading* (or *theory of mind*) to explain imitation. In this perspective, mind reading does not refer to a psychic ability but rather describes how humans understand others' intentions and emotions by observing their behaviors, gestures, and speech to deduce their mental state—or read their mind (Hurley and Chater 2005). The capability of humans to "know" what is being felt in another person's mind is seen as strongly tied to both the ability to imitate others and the ability to infer emotions and intentions that allow individuals to properly function socially (Meltzoff 2005). A capacity to imitate is therefore felt to be necessary for individuals to develop a theory of mind and for human social groups to form and cooperate (Goldman 2005). For example, the human emotion of empathy and the ability to mentally take the role of others depend on an ability to see the world as others see it. In turn, this psychological capacity is seen as evolving from the biological ability to imitate observed behavior.

From this stream, a useful concept for copycat crime related to child development is role play—the imaginary imitation of a social role (Claxton 2005). Role-play imitation contributes to the development of adult-level mind-reading capabilities when, for example, a child takes on the role of a doctor or astronaut in imaginary play (Goldman 2005). In this process, sets of behaviors, rather than specific modeled behavior, are imitated. When role playing, a child imitates by embellishing upon a social prototype. This free-range imitation forces the child to duplicate in his or her mind the supposed mental states of another and frees imitation from its original rote biological boundaries. The behavioral lessons of imitation can then be applied to new, never-observed situations. Humans are therefore uniquely able to imitate not only what we observe but also what was intended by an action (Tomasello and Carpenter 2005). Humans can infer the behavioral outcome that a model intends to achieve even when the model's actions fail (Heyes 2005; Tomasello and Carpenter 2005). Humans have thus evolved to be able to distinguish between simply being observed (actors) and being observed by others who wish to imitate us (instructors) and between simply observing the behavior of others (audience members) and observing with the intention to imitate (students), to learn but suppress a new behavior (potential copiers), or to imitate and perform observed behavior (copycats). Humans psychologically and biologically react to each scenario differently (Decety and Chaminade 2005).

With mirror neurons providing a biological base and role playing socially encouraging imitation, through what psychological mechanism does media content get translated into criminal behavior? Priming has emerged as the leading psychological candidate. The concept of priming was first used in cognitive psychology to study the use of information within network memory models. In this application, a memory node for different concepts such as "criminal," when activated, primes other associated nodes ("police," "arrest," "jail," or "victim") to be activated more easily and more quickly than when this prime is absent (Dijksterhuis and Bargh 2001). Priming provides individuals with ideas and beliefs that encourage a particular social reality—the perception that the world is such that a particular type of behavior is appropriate, justified, and likely to be successful (Roskos-Ewoldsen, Roskos-Ewoldsen, and Dillman 2002, 2009; Shrum 2002; Wyer and Srull 1989). More specifically, priming research refers to the effect of a preceding stimulus or event on how subsequent stimuli are reacted to; a prime puts a behavioral boundary around reactions to the world (Roskos-Ewoldsen, Roskos-Ewoldsen, and Dillman 2002, 2009). The concept of priming was therefore used by imitation theorists Jean Piaget in the 1920s, Neal Miller and John Dollard in the 1940s, and Albert Bandura in the 1960s to expand the process of imitation in humans from a rote "copy-and-paste" process to one where behavior observed and behavior enacted could significantly differ (Baer and Deguchi 1985; Kymissis and Poulson 1990).

Applied to the media, priming has been related to the effects of media content on behavior and judgments (Smith and Donnerstein 1998; Yi 1990). For example, watching a violent film can prime hostile or aggressive thoughts in viewers. These hostile thoughts subsequently trigger in some viewers other hostile thoughts, feelings, and behaviors (Roskos-Ewoldsen, Roskos-Ewoldsen, and Dillman 2009). When primes are linked to a behavior, the probability of that behavior is thus increased. Because priming can be linked to a broad set of constructs associated with a social stereotype (violent criminal is a far-reaching media prime, for example) and is not necessarily tied to specific behavior, the concept also provides a psychological explanation for altered imitation in which the imitated behavior is related but not identical to the observed behavior.

Another psychological concept found in communications research, scripts, is related to priming in that a prime can result in a preestablished behavioral script coming into play. Psychological scripts are preexisting directions that, when triggered, individuals cue up and follow (Anderson et al. 2004; Farrar and Krcmar 2006). A script lays out the sequence of events that one believes are likely and the behaviors that one believes are possible or appropriate in a particular situation (Huesmann 1998). L. Rowell Huesmann (1986) offers a pair of time frames through which media can create new scripts. One is a long-term script-creation process needed to acquire new behaviors. The second is the quick activation of preexisting scripts in which recent media content primes the retrieval of already learned behaviors.

In summary, research from 1900 to 1940 rescued imitation from its nineteenth-century reputation as a lower cognitive ability and positioned it as a core element in normal human development that plays a crucial role in personality development. In the 1940s, imitation was connected to operant conditioning to provide a bridge to modern social learning theory. In keeping with the adage "When in Rome, do as the Romans," imitation is considered the default social behavior for humans, who are biologically wired and psychologically primed to imitate (Dijksterhuis 2005). Selective imitation—copying only what one thinks will work—is today seen as a crucial cognitive ability that humans develop around age three (Whiten, Horner, and Marshall-Pescini 2005). The contemporary view is to see selective imitation as a powerful psychological mechanism in the copying of crime (see Chapter 5).

Social Contagion—Following the Crowd

Concerns with political mobs and social riots in the 1800s led to the study of how behaviors spread within crowds. The study of collective behavior emerged in the writings of Charles Mackay and Gustave Le Bon. Mackay (2012) popularized the subject in his 1841 book, *Extraordinary Popular Delusions and the Madness of Crowds*, which, through a set of editions, described a diverse, sometimes humorous collection of crowd behaviors, including homicidal poisonings, the Crusades, tulipomania, alchemy, and viewing highway men as celebrities. Gustave Le Bon, in his 1895 book, *Psychology of Crowds*, produced the first social science–based effort to study collective behaviors. Le Bon hypothesized that each person has an amount of animal instinct that can be activated within crowds and causes individuals to atavistically revert under a crowd's influence (Lochner 2002). Le Bon (1895, 24, 26) felt that crowds erased the rationality of their members: "People are less likely to check themselves because a crowd is anonymous and, as a consequence, irresponsible. The sentiment of responsibility which controls individuals disappears entirely. . . . An individual in a crowd is a grain of sand amid other grains of sand, which the wind stirs up at will." Le Bon's writings popularized the two questionable but still popular concepts of collective mind and mass hysteria, which portrayed crowds negatively and as inherently violent.[3]

Historically, discussions of crowd contagion first employed the idea of "evolutionary regression" to explain copying of criminal behaviors within crowds. In this early perspective, crowds caused people to throw off civilization and revert to more primitive and violent impulses. The "maddening crowd" was thought to cause previously law-abiding crowd members to transform into a lawless mob. There is, however, little supportive research for the existence of this mechanism. The subsequent refinement of the theory abandoned the transformation of crowd members and shifted to proclivity or convergence, explaining crowd behavior in terms of "birds of a feather flocking together." Crowds were theorized as enhancing the preexisting proclivities of their members. The idea was that individuals in a crowd behave just as they will alone, only more so (Blumer 1939; Park 1904). In this process, crowds assemble like-minded people (for example, persons prone to vandalism and violence as in the 2021 US capitol insurrection), who then act according to their predispositions (Allport 1924; Miller and Dollard 1941; Turner and Killian 1957). Contagion theorists began a search to detail the contagion mechanisms that set off these proclivities, with processes like milling behavior and circular reactions forwarded to describe hypothesized collections of like-minded people assembling, mixing, and circulating until, like a simmering pan of water, a crowd came to a violent boil.

Neal Miller and John Dollard made the most comprehensive statement of the proclivity perspective in the 1940s. They focused on the negative collective behaviors of riots and lynching and hypothesized a "deprivation → frustration → aggression" causal chain. In this chain, members of a crowd are first deprived of some reward or goal, which generates increased levels of frustration, which in turn results in group aggression. However, as with the transformation theory, subsequent research found little empirical evidence for a "deprivation → frustration → aggression" relationship or for the proclivity perspective in general. However, before the proclivity perspective waned, an increased view of the importance of media was introduced. Miller and Dollard (1941, 223) observed, "In the past, the size of a crowd was limited by the range of a human voice and the reports of it, or by the span of sight of a man from a hill or tower. Modern crowds may be world-wide and may receive stimuli which initiate crowd reactions with almost the same effectiveness as they can be received when within actual earshot." For the first time, the power of virtual crowds created by electronic media was recognized. The worldwide protests in 2020 against police use of lethal force following the deaths of African Americans in police custody stand as recent examples.

Subsequent research conceptually carved out social contagion as distinct from other parallel social behaviors such as obedience, compliance, and conformity (Cook and Goss 1996; Levy and Nail 1993). Diverse collective behaviors, such as mass hysteria, claims of UFO abduction, political protests, and fashions, have been studied, but the focus in this literature has been on "bad crowds" exemplified by rioters and lynch mobs. The benign nature of much collective social behavior was overshadowed by an assumption that, given the opportunity, most crowds will behave violently. Crime and other negative behaviors have been perceived as more contagious than law-abiding behaviors due to the hypothesized mechanisms of contagion, which are seen as weakening normal social constraints (Cook and Goss 1996). Social contagion is usually perceived as the unintentional spread of a behavior typically suppressed by embarrassment, norms, or punishment. While contagious behavior is not necessarily criminal (singing, dancing, praying, and other behaviors sometimes break out in social contagion waves), the contagion of violent riots and hate crimes has attracted the most interest.

Differing from imitation, which involves the learning of new behavior, contagion pertains to the release of perceived innate behavior that is already learned but suppressed (Milgram 1977). In contagion theory, behavior is not imitated as much as freed. While not particularly interested in studying a media role, contagion theorists did conceptualize two contagion mechanisms, approach/restraint conflict and deindividuation, which are useful for understanding copycat crime. The term *approach/restraint conflict* describes the psychological tension experienced when one is deciding whether to copy a crime. *Deindividuation* refers to anonymity within a crowd and is related to how the anonymity of social media can encourage copycat crime.

Other various mechanisms have been proposed as transmission avenues for contagion effects. Modeling and suggestion have been argued to play a role, as have identification with and physical closeness to the behavior model. Contagion literature often refers to situations where observing a model reduces preexisting moral conflict about copying an observed behavior (Wheeler 1966). The neutralization of normal inhibitions against deviance through anonymity within a crowd is seen as particularly powerful and necessary concerning the emergence of deviant behaviors (Turner 1964). An individual in a rioting crowd may want a new television but will abstain from stealing one until seeing others looting lessens guilt about stealing and raises confidence that crowd anonymity will prevent arrest.

While explanations of the contagion of behavior within large groups did not garner supporting research evidence, it was discovered that the number of people engaging in a crowd behavior assumed an S-curve distribution (Miller and Dollard 1941). Collective crowd behavior is taken up slowly at first by a few individuals; imitation speeds up rapidly as other individuals in the crowd see more behavior models and the apparent social acceptance of the behavior; imitation finally slows and plateaus as all those who are going to copy the behavior have done so. The graphs of the spread of swastika vandalism in the United States in the 1960s shown in Chapter 5 provide examples of these distributions.

In contrast with the weakly supported research on contagion within large crowds, the study of collective behavior in small groups did make progress, at least in terms of better empirically describing individual actions. The best-known early researcher of small-group behavior, Muzafer Sherif (1936), produced sound, empirically based studies in the 1930s on social contagion. Sherif advanced the concept of emergent norms, which he hypothesized influence an individual's perceptions of the world and regulate behavior in small-group settings. In these settings, a social norm emerges through social-psychological interactions among the group members and becomes a tacitly agreed-upon behavior rule (Sherif 1936). The emergent norms set the boundaries of the acceptable and expected behavior for that small group in that specific setting. An example in crime and justice would be symbolic legitimation steps taken during vigilante actions, such as holding kangaroo courts prior to a lynching. The special setting of a vigilante trial and symbolic mimicking of a legitimate judicial proceeding was thought to create an emergent social norm that allowed a collective crime to be committed, legitimized the lynching, and spread social responsibility among the crowd (Miller and Dollard 1941). Ralph Turner and Lewis Killian continued research into the process into the 1970s, forwarding as key concepts milling behavior and rumor, through which norms might emerge within and spread beyond small social groups.

However, while collective norms are applicable to small groups in unique situations, there has been no empirical evidence for them emerging in large groups. Instead, the contemporary view is that large groups are heterogeneous and composed of many homogeneous small groups of family, friends, and acquaintances that act independently (McPhail 2017). Not everyone at a riot is rioting; many are peacefully participating, simply observing, or attempting to leave. Individuals in large groups are more influenced by the members of the small group they identify with than by large group dynamics (Aveni, A. 1977; Green, Horel, and Papachristos 2017; Papachristos et al. 2015; Wilkinson and Carr 2008). In sum, a gang member is more likely to copy the behavior of other gang members than that of a large number of strangers.

Such findings led to another reformulation of contagion theory in the 1970s and the embracing of rationality as the core explanatory concept for collective behavior by Richard Berk (1972, 1974), Carl Couch (1968), and Charles Tilly (1978). Crowd members were subsequently seen as a collective only in the sense of being physically in one place. Each individual's actions were determined by rational choices tied to each individual's goals. Similar actions do not necessarily reflect similar causes and people may act alike in a crowd but not for the same reasons. A television may be looted to punish a store owner, to do something exciting and illegal, to sell later for money, to present as a gift, or to furnish an apartment. Unfortunately, like prior theoretical explanations of contagion, rationality was quickly found to have its limits, so that emotions and the complexity of decisionmaking were added as playing significant roles in the copying of behavior within a crowd. Limited rationality became the explanatory concept of choice in recognition that individual decisions within a crowd are usually limited by incomplete information and time demands. Decisions to copy or not copy crime in a large, dynamic crowd setting are often spontaneous, hurried, and not well thought through (Tilly 1978). "Let's steal the TV, hope for the best, and worry about the consequences later" describes a commonly accepted contagion thought process.

From this theoretical history, the research on contagion has emphasized the study of the direct physical exposure of imitators to initiator models in variously sized social groups. The contagion setting has usually focused on the transmission of a contagion effect that mirrors a medical epidemic process (Slutkin 2013). This body of research contains several contradictions but overall reflects that people do not simply contagiously behave in herd-like crowds.

For example, the impact of behavior-model status differs across studies. In some, a model's high status increased copying; in others, low status did (Cook and Goss 1996). In hysterical contagion, where a psychosomatic illness spreads through a population, initiators are more likely to be social isolates and hold lower group status (the explanation offered is that the copied behavior, an illness, is not attractive or desirable, so a low-status model can more easily set off the contagion wave). In contrast, models associated with copying behavior that results in rewards, looting for example, are more likely to be high status

A second contradiction is that the impact of demographically similar or dissimilar models varies in effect. Dissimilar models have more influence on copiers who are conflicted over copying a behavior but desire the rewards from copying. Demographically similar models, in contrast, are more influential in the contagion of unattractive behaviors (Levy and Nail 1993).

Similar behaviors in crowds may also be generated in widely different ways; some of the behaviors may be contagious, some self-generated. Small-group dynamics and individual characteristics are more important than large-crowd-level processes for what gets copied, when, and by whom (Green, Horel, and Papachristos 2017; Papachristos et al. 2015). Varied universal mechanisms of contagion were proposed and rejected in turn, leaving the aggregation of individual-level processes and characteristics as key to the generation and understanding of large-crowd copycat acts, such as the 2010 Arab Spring protests and the 2011 UK riots (National Research Council 2013). The factors most often perceived as central were those that lifted the social constraints against deviant behaviors, but the detailing of the copying of criminal behavior is not found in social contagion research. While contagion theory focused on large-group criminality and thus is applicable to copycat crime, the copying process was more effectively described in research that focused on the spread of positive social behaviors and research on the social diffusion of innovations.

Social Diffusion—Sharing the Good News

In contrast to the study of social contagion and its focus on negative social behaviors, social diffusion research has historically focused on the spread of positive social behaviors such as new technologies or health habits. Coming largely from a business and social policy orientation, social diffusion theory says little directly about crime. Nevertheless, social diffusion research offers useful, empirically supported concepts for understanding copycat crime. With historical roots in Gabriel Tarde's laws of imitation, diffusion theory describes the process by which an innovation is communicated through a society and adopted over time. Before the 1943 publication by Bryce Ryan and Neal Gross of their seminal study on the use of hybrid seed corn by Iowa farmers, the diffusion of innovations had been largely dormant as a subject of serious study. Contemporary research is now found across a wide range of disciplines. As described by the theory's main proponent, Everett Rogers (2003), a decision to copy an innovation has four conceptual elements: the innovation (the behavior or practice whose copying is encouraged); communication channels (the social mechanisms through which information about the innovation is transmitted); time (involving both the adoption rate of an innovation and when in a diffusion cycle individuals adopt); and the social system (the community and environment in which diffusion occurs). Six research questions frame this perspective.

The first research question asks what characteristics of a successful innovation determine why some innovations are more successful and diffuse more rapidly than others. For copycat crime, the analogous question would ask what the characteristics are of crimes that become successful generator crimes. The most important characteristic for likely success is an innovation's value as perceived by a potential adopter, which is in turn linked to five attributes of an innovation (Rogers 2003).

The first attribute, relative advantage, entails any improvement in the eyes of potential copiers over past practices. According to Rogers, relative advantage can include economic profitability, lowered initial costs, decreases in discomfort, increases in social prestige, saving of time and effort, and quick rewards. Attribute two, compatibility, relates to how well an innovation matches an individual's existing values, past experiences, and needs. Attributes three and four are complexity and trialability. Complexity refers to the difficulty of employing and understanding an innovation (for crimes that require unique skills or equipment, even when innovative and successful, diffusion would be hindered). Related to complexity, trialability refers to a possible copier's ability to try an innovation on a limited pre-adoption, low-risk basis. Lastly, the attribute of observability is the degree to which results of prior copying by others are visible to potential copiers. Collectively these five attributes set the likelihood that an innovation will diffuse. Innovations that have the optimal combination of high relative advantage, trialability, observability, and compatibility and low complexity have a diffusion advantage; those that do not are hindered in their diffusion potential. All five attributes are useful for predicting successful copycat-generator crimes.

The second research question asks how the knowledge of an innovation is distributed. In diffusion theory, distribution is addressed via communication channels through which knowledge of an innovation is passed from an innovator to an adopter. Communication channels can involve either face-to-face interactions or the mass media. A problem noted in the diffusion research on socially desirable innovations and pertinent for copycat crime is that potential adopters are usually socially separated and their communications limited (Rogers 2003). The media, however, can reduce information blockage by providing communication channels that overcome social differences and allow dissimilar individuals to interact. Regarding the positive innovations focused on in diffusion research, mass media channels are reported as usually more efficient at spreading factual knowledge about an innovation, but interpersonal channels are more persuasive and effective in generating final adoption decisions. The media can spread the word, but colleagues drive the final decision to copy.

Under the third diffusion element, time, three questions are involved. First, what steps do individuals take in deciding to copy an innovation? Second, following awareness of an innovation, what determines the time span it takes for an individual to adopt? Third, what factors are related to the rate of adoption in a society?

Concerning the first time-related question, adopters have to transverse five steps in deciding to copy an innovation: knowledge, persuasion, decision, implementation, and confirmation. The crucial time span involved is the time it takes an individual adopter to go from step 1 to step 4 and to make and implement the adoption decision. The diffusion research reports that concerning the two early decision steps of acquiring knowledge of the innovation's existence and functions and being persuaded that adoption might be a good idea, individuals want to know what the innovation is and why it works. Rogers (2003) reports that media can effectively transmit such information, and the media's role is seen as important. In step 3 (decision to copy or not) and step 4 (implementation), individuals seek information to reduce uncertainty about the consequences of adoption. The availability of a trial adoption, where full commitment and risk are avoided, significantly increases decisions to adopt. At this stage, the media are not as important as face-to-face interpersonal networks for socially advocated innovations. Innovations that can be modified to better fit individual situations and needs are additionally more likely to be implemented. Step 5, confirmation, refers to postadoption consequences and the availability of successful adoption anecdotes that influence others still traversing the prior four decision steps. If confirmation of the expected results from an adoption occurs, the innovation decision is reinforced, and further diffusion buoyed. If it does not, then postimplementation discontinuance follows.

Adopters decide to copy an innovation at different times during a diffusion lifespan. In the same manner that the attributes of an innovation influence diffusion, the characteristics of potential copiers influence when they adopt. Rogers (2003) describes five types of individuals who adopt at different times in a diffusion cycle depending on their level of innovativeness. Rogers calls the first adopter group the innovators; they have the greatest level of innovativeness and are the earliest adopters. They launch new ideas into their social settings by importing them from outside. Many copycat offenders are expected to reside in this group. Those in the next group to adopt, the early adopters, react quickly to the successful modeling by the innovators. The third group, the early majority, makes up a large adopter group, but being less innovative, these individuals will wait a substantial period before adopting and will do so only after a number of successful trials of the innovation are available for review. The fourth adopter group, the late majority, will adopt only after most others in their social system have done so and an innovation is well established. While an extensive set of characteristics differentiate early from late adopters, the most relevant for copycat crime is the level of innovativeness: the inherent attraction to innovations present in an individual (Rogers 2003).[4] The more innovativeness individuals possess, the more quickly they will copy. The final adopter group, the laggards, are not innovative and are the isolates in their social systems. They adhere to past, long-established practices and fall in line with Gabriel Tarde's conception of custom-dominated cultures. Some will never adopt even a proven beneficial innovation such as a vaccine.

In the diffusion literature, the media's roles differ among innovators and early adopters as compared to the early and late majority groups. Media are felt to be more important for earlier adopters than for later adopters because early in a diffusion cycle there is little experience with an innovation, and the likely consequences of adopting are not well known. The group characteristics forwarded in the diffusion research are that generally innovators are psychologically oriented outside their group and are risk takers.

The third diffusion time span question involves the rate of adoption of an innovation in a society. While the first two time-related questions involve individual-level decisions—the steps involved in deciding to copy or not and the characteristics of early versus late adopters—the third examines the aggregate adoption rate. How the spread of an innovation through a population is described depends upon how the adoption rate is plotted. The typical adoption rate (which mirrors the pattern found for collective behaviors in the contagion literature) forms either an S-curve (if the cumulative number of adopters is plotted) or a normal bell curve (if adoption is plotted over time as a frequency—see Box 5.1). The lead edge of the typical diffusion S-curve reflects that after the initial 10 to 20 percent of adoptions, the diffusion process for innovations is driven by peer rather than media influences. Suggesting that media play their most significant role early in the process for socially encouraged innovations, once the 20 percent tipping point is achieved, additional media promotion is less necessary and will not significantly affect the adoption rate (Rogers 2003).

Again harkening back to Gabriel Tarde, the last diffusion theory research question asks what characteristics of social systems encourage innovation diffusion. Diffusion research describes two social roles as helpful for successful diffusion. The first is the opinion leader, an individual who occupies the center of an interpersonal communications network, functions as an information clearinghouse, and provides successful demonstrations of new innovations. The second is the change agent, a person who actively champions an innovation. A common social interaction described for socially encouraged innovations in the diffusion literature is for a potential adopter (a local farmer, for example) with a specific problem (low yield due to crop disease) to seek out a known change agent (the local government agriculture agent), who recommends an innovation (a new hybrid seed) as a solution (Rogers 2003; Ryan and Gross 1943). Social systems that provide open communications across overlapping social groups with credible opinion leaders and accessible change agents maximize the speed of innovation adoption. Significantly for the diffusion of crime techniques, aspects of contemporary social media can fulfill these social system requirements in societies otherwise lacking these diffusion enhancers.

While descriptive of the traits of innovations and the individuals who adopt them, the decision steps and time frames associated with adoption, and the media's role in diffusion, social diffusion research does not adequately address copycat crime. Focused on technology adoptions and socially encouraged behaviors, social diffusion research details the steps needed to encourage adoption of socially championed, highly visible innovations. While some social diffusion research has looked at the diffusion of crime and is discussed in Chapter 5, the bulk of the research has aimed to explain how new positive behaviors spread and how to encourage them. The research findings can be partially reverse-engineered for plausible copycat crime insights, but the details about how new socially negative behaviors like crime diffuse have not been heavily explored. Theorizing about how new negative and positive behaviors are acquired fell to social learning theorists.

Social Learning—Hey Everyone, Watch This!

While they are sometimes someone's last words, "Hey, everyone, watch this" can also describe how most social behavior is transmitted. A major pillar for the study of media and crime within criminology, social learning (also known as observational learning) expanded B. F. Skinner's ideas from the lab to society. In social learning, behavior is acquired from watching what happens to others and developing expectations of the likely results of copying. It follows a basic causal premise: Watch what happens to me. If you behave the same, the same thing will happen to you. Known for his Bobo doll experiments on media and aggression, Albert Bandura first detailed the tenets of the copying of social behavior with Richard Walters (1963), before subsequently developing them fully (Bandura 1973, 1986, 2001). For Bandura, copying is most likely when three things happen: detailed instruction combined with demonstrations are provided, positive consequences are observable, and guided practice is available. Social learning theory argues that the same learning process produces both conforming and deviant behavior. Combining principles of classical and operant conditioning plus observational learning, Bandura (1973) provided a basis for the copying of behavior at the individual copier level.

> Step 1: Exposure to behavior models. Models come from three places: family, neighborhoods, and media. Models from multiple sources can be blended together into a composite model.
> Step 2—Copier creation of a composite model. As observers can create a composite model from multiple sources, the final behavior copied need not bear exact likeness to any of the individual models. And while the success of observed models is important for imitation, the models need not portray directly observed rewards to encourage copying.
> Step 3—Acquisition of necessary skills. A copier acquires the ability to perform the observed behavior (memorizing the sequence of behavior steps, for example). Acquisition happens via four subprocesses: attention, memory retention involving symbolic coding and rehearsal, physical ability, and reinforcement. The first two subprocesses frequently happen (many learn the modeled behavior), subprocess three is limited by preexisting copier capabilities, and subprocess four depends upon receiving rewards for copying behaviors.
> Step 4—Performance of the behavior. First, the social setting of a potential copier is crucial for whether opportunities for performance are present. Second, if a new behavior is preformed, real-world consequences and social effects come into play.
> Step 5—Generation of consequences for the copier. What happens to the copier, whether copying is reinforced, rewarded, or punished, sets the future for the performed behavior.

Step 6—Effects on society. The final step in social learning is the effect of copied behavior on the social environment of potential copier. Environmental changes from copied behavior can enhance further copying (society becomes more tolerant of the copied behavior and provides more instruction models and copying opportunities) or suppress it (society reduces the availability of models, decreases copying opportunities, and punishes copying).

The six steps describe a cycle that begins with the social environment's ability to provide models, descends to the experiences of the individual copier, and returns to the copier's social environment. In the social learning perspective, it is important to note that it is not necessary to observe a model being rewarded for a specific behavior for observational learning to occur and copying to follow. It is the expectation of eventual reinforcement on the part of the copier that is essential for copying.

Regarding steps 1 and 2 and the exposure to and creation of composite models, early social learning theorists emphasized real-world, proximal models; later ones saw the media as outstripping reality as model sources. Bandura eventually gave the media multiple roles. First, the media expand the reach and number of available models. Second, the media can provide direct instructions. Third, the media can create a permissive social environment for the modeled behavior (Bandura 1973). As model features are taken from multiple sources and combined, media immersion by copiers is important, and multiple viewings, emotional content, and rehearsal maximize social learning. The copier's decision to copy is also encouraged by the observation that a model's life history reflects rewards as opposed to punishment. Usually this comes across in terms of characteristics of the composite models such as prestige, competence, high status, and power. Therefore, models who "look" like they have been rewarded increase imitation, and the existence of a media model's material possessions will encourage imitation without the modeled behavior being directly rewarded. The key to Bandura's social learning process is the transition from his third step, acquisition, to the fourth step, performance. Step 3 is attained by many observers in a society; step 4 is performed by only a few. The research of Bandura and Walters (1963) showed that when rewards for demonstrating modeled behavior were varied, every one of their child subjects acquired the knowledge and learned how to perform the modeled behavior. The children differed, however, in copying until all were offered rewards. All learned the modeled behavior, but until rewarded, few performed it. As argued in the imitation research literature, the performance of a socially learned behavior is far from guaranteed and is often suppressed.

The characteristics of potential copiers are important, therefore, for step 4, performance, to happen. The most important characteristic in social learning theory is self-efficacy—the self-judgment of one's capability to perform the modeled behavior (Bandura 1986). Although not as important as self-efficacy, copier demographic characteristics that are similar to the behavior models further encourage copying. However, Bandura argued that when predicting the performance of modeled behaviors, copier characteristics, with the exception of self-efficacy, were less important than "predisposing conditions." The culture, local environment, and other social-setting characteristics in which potential imitators find themselves after exposure to a behavioral model determine performance more than their individual traits. Thus, dedicated video game players will learn SWAT team and sniper tactics without ever applying them. According to Bandura and Walters (1963, 290), many things that people learn are not revealed behaviorally either because the appropriate situations do not occur or because the equipment needed to execute is lacking. Thus, viewers of television programs may learn gun-fighting skills that are never exhibited because they do not have access to guns or the occasion to use them. For Bandura (1973, 67) social conditions that increase the permissibility and value of a behavior override personal dispositions, and it is primarily types of social inducements rather than types of people that predict who will put into practice what has been learned. As previously discussed in the imitation literature, neurological mechanisms cue many behaviors for imitation; however, most are inhibited by other cognitive and social restraints. Similarly, social learning research finds that many learn, while few perform.

Regarding the fifth step, consequences, Skinnerian behavior modification theory predicts that consequences will be the most important factor in determining the persistence of copying. However, when actions are guided by anticipated consequences that are not accurate— for example, when punishment is seen as unlikely when it is actually probable—copying will be weakly controlled by actual consequences until cumulative experiences produce more realistic expectations. That is, until punitive results erase the faulty expectation of rewards, copying will continue. The media are also strong sources of vicarious reinforcement and can serve as motivators to copy by raising expectations of similar rewards and by weakening copying-suppressing inhibitions.

Social learning theory also predicts that when new behaviors have become cemented through reinforcement, they become habitual even though they are not always successful. As operant conditioning research shows, reinforcement can be inconsistent and even randomly punitive without eliminating a copying response. In sum, once a behavior is performed, even if haphazardly rewarded, it becomes resistant to elimination. Regarding the media's role in consequences, social learning theory proposes that the groups and individuals who comprise or control the major sources of social reinforcement for the individual will have strong influence on behavior. Usually these are peer and primary groups (Megens and Weerman 2012; Young et al. 2013), but they can include imaginary or virtual persons found in media content (Akers 2011). Thus, in some circumstances for some individuals, the media can not only serve as the behavior model source but provide reinforcing praise to the copier after performance of the behavior. In the last step for social learning, the eventual social effects set the cycle of copying as short- or long-lived, bounded or extensive. Social incentives or external reinforcements can be tangible rewards like material goods or intangible rewards such as social praise and status gains (Bandura 1973; Rosekrans and Hartup 1967). Copycat crimes can bestow both.

In summary, five derived social learning tenets are relevant for copycat crime. First, media compete with reality as a source of models, and modeling sources have expanded from live models to include media ones. In technologically developed societies, behavior is usually modeled from a variety of encounters with individuals, written accounts, and visual portrayals. Second, multiple viewings, emotional content, and rehearsals that provide detailed instruction, combined with demonstrations and guided practice followed by rewards, ensure more or less permanent retention of modeled activities and maximize media-generated copycat effects. Third, visual media are more influential than non-visual media, and behavior is learned more thoroughly from observing actions than from hearing or reading descriptions. Fourth, portraits of successful models are more important than whether models or their behaviors are portrayed as good or bad; rewards for behavior models outweigh assessment of their moral values. Last, social setting is more important than the copier's characteristics, and predisposing social conditions outweigh predisposing personal characteristics.

As the media are a required element of the definition of copycat crime employed herein but have disjointed roles in the four theoretical perspectives covered thus far, direct research on media is of extreme interest. What does the body of research that places the media as central and required contribute to an understanding of copycat crime?

Media Studies—What Constructs Your World?

The importance of studying media and society is best explained from the theoretical perspective of social constructionism. In this perspective what people believe is real is a socially negotiated idea determined by a mix of personal experience, conversations with others about their experiences and beliefs, and media portrayals (Surette 2015a). Under social constructionism, people socially construct what they think worldly conditions are and behave based on the information they receive directly from personal experiences and indirectly from significant others and the media (Gergen 1985). A view of reality need not be tethered to actual conditions in the world, and for crime, behaviors can be criminalized or decriminalized independent of changes in victimization or offense rates (Spector and Kitsuse 1987). The ability of media-generated social constructions to drive social behavior has been long recognized, and the development of social media in the twenty-first century has heightened the effects of the media on the social construction process.

The single most important change between old and new media lies in the relationship between the creators of media content and its consumers. In legacy media, content was created and distributed by distant businesses and delivered to dispersed consumers. One side created legacy media content; the other side consumed it. Feedback loops between audience and creators were weak, slow, and haphazard, and there were clear distinctions between writers and readers, speakers and listeners, performers and audiences, and producers and consumers. New media, however, have an inherently different creator-consumer relationship. With new media, consumers can also be producers of self-generated mediated content and assume the role of content distributors. Legacy media's top-down content flow has been replaced by audience creative participation, peer-to-peer distribution, and the proliferation of user-generated content (Yar 2012).

The result is that, with new media, the delivery of content is determined by the consumer, and mediated attendance and the sharing of experiences are easier to achieve. New-media consumers can be active participants in the development, distribution, social assessment, and ultimate social impact of their content. New media have both mass-market ability to reach large audiences and the ability to link individuals who see themselves as sharing interests, socioeconomic status, education, or ideology. Partway between mass media and interpersonal communication, new media provide unique one-to-many communication avenues similar to the mass media but with the capacity for personalization for and by individuals. By providing a two-way exchange of information, new-media internet-based blogs and chat rooms, along with social media platforms, can substitute for direct face-to-face communications. When physically near peers are not available, new-media-based relationships can substitute (Valente and Saba 1998). And because audience members are not as psychologically isolated as with legacy media, individuals can communicate anonymously but intimately. The rise of mediated over directly experienced reality means that today many spend more time in a media-constructed reality than in a directly experienced one. Increased exposure to criminogenic models is one result, and for copycat crime, social constructionism implies that contemporary media can play a central function in whether people see a crime as appropriate to copy (Surette 2020b).

Research on social cognition has been employed by media studies researchers to study the mental processes that occur when judgments and attitudes are influenced by media content. Social cognition studies led to the examination of how people process media-supplied information and how information processing impacts subsequent imitation. The cognitive-response approach contends that individuals are active, not passive, participants in a media-based persuasion process. In this perspective, people's cognitive responses to media-supplied information, rather than the information per se, determine the extent and nature of media influence so that similar content can have extremely different impacts across individuals. The detailing of two social cognition paths has resulted from this research.

Reflecting more considered interaction with the media, a central systematic cognitive path is followed by individuals who are motivated and able to evaluate media-accessed information. Reflecting a second, more hurried, shallower media interaction, a heuristic peripheral path is followed when individuals are not motivated or are unable to evaluate media information (Kahneman 2011). These two paths, however, are not felt to adequately cover the possible ways that media affect behavior. A third pathway, narrative persuasion, has been forwarded based on research on media-based entertainment-education efforts (De Graaf et al. 2012; Singhal and Rogers 2012). Derived from research on the use of entertainment-formatted media to invoke social change, this third path reflects the psychological engagement with media content that negates consideration of cognitively evaluating media-supplied information—a media narrative is consumed but not consciously evaluated by the consumer. The goal in media narrative persuasion is to subtly change behavior through stories and characters, not facts and arguments.

Importantly, narrative persuasion offers an explanation of media influence on consumers initially resistant to change through the use of empathetic transitional characters (Green et al. 2006; Slater and Rouner 2002). Initially espousing contrary beliefs, transitional characters model the process of attitude and behavior change for the media consumer. Thus, individuals initially unlikely to change their behavior would be persuaded to do so by observing an empathetic media model who was also initially unwilling to change but underwent a transformation in the narrative in which a change in behavior was portrayed in a positive light (Polichak and Gerrig 2002). In this transitional process, a copycat crime can become a positive act.

Together, the three paths help to explain the general impact of media on attitudes and behavior and, by extension, on copycat crime. The systematic and heuristic pathways are related to how much thought and reflection is expended on a decision. More cognitively demanding, the systematic decision path is followed when a decisionmaker can determine the validity of media-provided information and is motivated to expend energy to systematically access and consider a substantial amount of information before reaching a decision (Shrum 2002). In this path, media consumers are thought to counterargue the information provided in the media content and compare conflicting information regarding its reliability and validity. In sum, when the motivation to evaluate media-supplied information is high, the information is available, and there is time to review it, such as when the consequences of a failed crime attempt are viewed as serious (Should I rob a bank?), a systematic decisionmaking path would be followed (Petty, Priester, and Brinol 2002). On the other hand, when a potential offender is not motivated to closely search for and evaluate information, the heuristic path would be followed (Shrum 2002). In this decisionmaking path, a shallow, abbreviated search for information is conducted, and a decision is quickly reached when choices are perceived as trivial, information is not available, and time is limited (Should I steal this magazine from the waiting room?).

The narrative persuasion path captures the phenomenological experience of reading, hearing, or viewing dramatic media content and relates to the deep psychological involvement with media content that can develop in consumers. Narrative persuasion was developed to address the reality that most media consumed are narrative and formatted as stories. The mental processing of media narratives is qualitatively different from the cognitive processing of informational media. Transportation, engagement, and absorption have been used to describe this level of media involvement, where media information is not evaluated in any way but simply absorbed (Singhal and Rogers 2012). Following this pathway, people get lost in a book, cry during a movie, and are made happy or sad by a song. Narrative persuasion is more likely followed if there is interest in the narrative genre (for copycat crime, the consumer enjoys crime stories) and if the content is well crafted and has realistic special effects (Slater and Rouner 2002).

In addition to the three pathways, three additional concepts with links to the psychology of imitation have been employed in media studies research to understand media effects on attitudes and behaviors. Collectively, the concepts of priming, exemplars, and scripts involve the impact of specific elements of media content on the psychological state of media consumers and their social construction of the world. In this application, priming, as previously described, refers to the effects of media content on people's subsequent behavior or judgments by activating mentally linked phenomena. Exemplars focus the priming process to describe powerful media-supplied primes (Petty, Priester, and Brinol 2002). A typical media-generated exemplar involves a highly newsworthy event that is portrayed as an iconic example of a larger set of similar events (Zillmann 2002). For example, a particularly heinous murder of a child might be presented in the media as exemplary of child victimization. How easily recalled and how influential exemplars will be relates to how recently and how frequently they have been activated. Media exemplars are hypothesized to have effects on both worldviews and social behaviors. Scripts, also introduced earlier, further contribute to understanding media-generated copycat crime via the rapid cueing of already-learned scripts and the long-term acquisition of new behavioral scripts from repeated exposure to media content (Huesmann 1986). Hence, already-learned criminal behavior can be activated and new criminal behaviors can be copied from the media. Collectively, media studies provide ways to perceive how media can play significant roles in the perception of the real-world and how media consumers can interact with media content in different cognitive and psychological ways. The implications for how copycat crimes come into existence are developed in Chapter 6.

Conclusion

Each theory contributes a piece to the overall understanding and study of copycat crime. Rooted in the disciplines of biology, genetics, and psychology and a focus on general imitation processes, imitation theory employs the concepts of mirror neurons, selective imitation, primes, and scripts to provide a biological basis, genetic reason, and psychological processes for the capacity to copy behavior to evolve and persist (Flanders 1968). Imitation theory investigates two main research questions: What are the evolutionary benefits of imitation and how is imitation cognitively processed? Imitation theory's inferred causal chain translates as follows: behavior is observed → mirror neurons translate visual behavior into muscle commands → behavior is assessed as likely beneficial → behavior is imitated. The primary limitation of the imitation research in terms of copycat crime is that social processes and a media role are minimal in imitation theory; however, it does provide a foundation for why dysfunctional imitation like copycat crime may be common.

Rooted in social psychology, social contagion theory begins to address the inattention given to social processes found in the imitation research. Usually studying large crowds, contagion theory's main research question asks how shifts to new behaviors happen within social groups. Employing a set of shifting, sometimes debatable concepts, such as fads, mass hysteria, the collective mind, evolutionary regression, transformation, proclivity, and emergent norms, social contagion theory focuses on the copying of behavior within groups of people. While there is extensive research on social contagion, it is better at describing social contagions than explaining them. Except in small-group studies, social contagion theory has not delivered strong empirical support for its contagion mechanisms, and, crucially for copycat crime, the media are largely absent in the contagion literature. Despite deficiencies, social contagion does offer two concepts, approach/restraint conflict and deindividuation, that are useful for conceptualizing copycat crime, and initial research quantitatively described the spread of social behavior.

Based in the sciences of marketing and organizational psychology, diffusion theory focuses on socially endorsed behaviors and the fundamental research question of how the adoption of socially positive behaviors spreads. Diffusion's basic causal chain is as follows: a problem needing a solution exists → a change agent/opinion leader champions an innovative solution → innovators enact initial adoptions and trials → rapid increase in adoptions for successful innovations occurs. Diffusion's most relevant copycat crime concepts include innovations, innovators, innovativeness, early adopters, relative advantage, communication channels, change agents, and trialability. In diffusion theory, the media's role is mixed; it is initially high, then moderates as the diffusion of an innovation plays out. The theory of social diffusion better describes the social interactions that underlie the copying of behaviors than contagion and has produced more research-based empirical support for its concepts and mechanisms. Its primary limitation concerning copycat crime is its emphasis on the adoption of socially endorsed, innovative behaviors. The likelihood that sanctioned criminal behavior will diffuse differently and that media will have a unique role in copycat crime is high.

The combination of social learning and media studies offers the best theoretical perspective for explaining the decision steps that occur between exposure to a generator crime and commission of a copycat crime. Social learning theory is based in behavioral psychology and operant conditioning and employs the concepts of efficacy, composite models, rewards and punishments, and acquisition. How humans acquire new behaviors in social settings is its primary research question. Social learning shares with media studies conceptual interest in scripts, primes, and cognitive pathways. The basic social learning steps are (1) modeling of behavior to a capable learner, (2) acquisition of the knowledge of how to perform the modeled behavior, (3) practice and rehearsal by the copier, (4) performance, and (5) reward or punishment for copying and (6) assessment of results. The role of media in social learning was conceived as low early in the theory's history; more recently the media are seen as having moderate to strong effects.

Starting from a science base of social psychology and social cognition, media studies have focused on how individuals interact with media content. In combination with social learning and sharing some theoretical concepts, media studies address the question of how the media influence behavior. The concepts of social cognition, social construction of reality, scripts, primes, exemplars, heuristic and systematic decisions, and narrative persuasion are employed to address this research question. Unlike in the other theoretical perspectives, a media role has consistently been seen as crucial but also as widely varied, depending upon consumer characteristics and consumption settings.

While social learning and media studies have contributed a well-developed conceptual model for copycat crime, the major limitation remains the lack of direct empirical research. Before these five theoretical perspectives can be brought to bear on copycat crimes, basic methodological and existential questions concerning copycat crime need to be addressed. Specifically, what research exists to support a general media copycat effect? Therefore, Chapter 3 asks what the research that does not examine crime but involves media-induced copying of other behaviors states. Another copycat crime methodological concern is how to decide when a copycat crime is present. The prevalence of copycat crime and the measurement of copycat crime are two methodological issues that present unique research problems not found in the study of other types of crime. These questions are addressed in Chapter 4. With the five theoretical perspectives and their concepts as a base and the research considerations in Chapters 3 and 4 in mind, the application of the theoretical ideas and concepts to copycat crime becomes the focus of Chapters 5 and 6.

Notes

1. For additional discussions of mirror neurons and imitation, see Iacoboni and Geffen 2013; Kasten 2020; National Research Council 2013; Rizzolatti 2005; Rizzolatti and Fogassi 2014; Solis 2020.

2. This raises the question of why it would be adaptive for a human to expend cognitive resources to continually prime and then suppress imitation. The answer found in the imitation literature is that automatic imitation evolved first and provided many survival benefits. It eventually needed to be suppressed to avoid the automatic copying of punished behaviors and the negative social consequences of inappropriate imitation when surviving in dynamic social groups became crucial. Prinz 2005 hypotheses a rudimentary behavioral inhibition system in humans that functions to suppress the rote imitation of behavior.

3. Although there has never been evidence of a "collective mind," the concept maintains popular support and is used regularly as a plot element in science fiction and horror tales. Stephen King's 2006 novel *Cell* is an example.

4. According to Rogers 2003, early adopters tend to be more educated and more literate; have higher social status and greater upward social mobility; display greater levels of empathy, ability to deal with abstractions, rationality, and intelligence; favorably view change; have higher aspirations; cope better with uncertainty and risk; and have lower levels of fatalism and higher perceptions of self-efficacy and control. Early adopters also have more exposure to mass media. A key difference is how venturesome innovators are when compared with the skeptical late adopters and laggards.

3

Copycat Effects
in Practice

A MAJOR QUESTION HOVERS OVER THE STUDY OF COPYCAT crime: how to determine if copycat crime persists at a significant level in society. This question has been indirectly examined in research on copycat behavior that is not related to crime. Research on advertising and public service ad campaigns, hysterical behaviors, suicide clusters, and violent media suggests that significant copycat effects from criminogenic media are plausible. This chapter briefly reviews evidence from each regarding a general media-induced copycat effect.

Advertising and Public Service Ad Campaigns

The first noncriminal areas with implications for the potential of media to have significant copycat behavioral effects are advertising and public service information campaigns, sometimes referred to as PSAs. Advertising in general aims to change consumer purchasing behavior, while public service information campaigns aim to change specific social behaviors in a positive way. Research on advertising has created a massive, powerful behavior-influence industry generally referred to as "Madison Avenue" and has bolstered belief in the media's ability to significantly influence behaviors. The bulk of research on advertising has examined buying behavior, and research on how ads influence product purchases and other social behaviors has a long history (for overviews, see Arrington 1982; Nelson 1974; Tuten 2008; Vaughn 1980; Wells et al. 1989).

Recent research, though, has noted negative (but not criminal) effects from advertising on consumer behavior, including alcohol consumption (Kinard and Webster 2010; Weintraub and Knaus 2000), tobacco use (Kinard and Webster 2010), and eating disorders (Folkvord et al. 2016; Harris, Bargh, and Brownell 2009). Throughout, this literature concedes significant media-generated behavioral effects, usually attributing them to the mechanisms of customer identification and product priming (Fennis and Stroebe 2016). Those who see benign rather than pernicious social effects from advertising argue that the behaviors targeted for influence in ads are economic in nature, socially endorsed, and set within content that does not encourage crime (Kotowitz and Mathewson 1979). Therefore, in their view, it is an inappropriate leap to extend advertising effects to crime or violence in society as the desired behavior changes strived for in ads are qualitatively different from the negative behaviors associated with crime that generate social concern. In this way, advertising is perceived as analogous to the diffusion of socially positive (or at least neutral) innovations. Regardless of whether advertisements have positive or negative behavioral effects, the research on advertising has established a media-based ability to substantially influence social behavior. The research, however, does not establish that advertising similarly influences socially prohibited criminal behaviors.

Historically, media have also been successfully utilized to affect consumer behavior through prosocial television programs and ad-like public information campaigns. These campaigns work to produce the opposite of copycat crime effects and are designed to use the media to reduce and solve crimes. Such media campaigns are not new and are historically rooted in government media campaign efforts to raise public support during World War I (Surette 2015a). The "Wanted Dead or Alive" posters on the Western frontier and the FBI's "Most Wanted" list are two additional historical examples. Following these early campaigns, government efforts to positively influence public behavior using media information campaigns took hold in the 1930s, and by the 1960s, media-based campaigns aimed at changing social practices in health and other areas regularly appeared. By the 1970s, it was generally accepted that properly designed television programs could generate beneficial social effects like crime reduction (Greitemeyer 2011).

Utilizing advertisement-styled formatting, three types of media anticrime campaigns were subsequently developed in the 1970s. These efforts targeted crime victims and witnesses and were geared to increase cooperation with authorities, encourage people to better protect themselves, and get offenders to stop committing crime (Surette 2015a). To produce the opposite of copycat crime effects, one type of campaign employed anticrime advertisements to deter offenders from committing crimes. A second type, aimed at citizens, contained victimization-reduction messages and relied on the persuasiveness of celebrities to encourage audience crime-prevention behavior (Engle 2012). The third type used media reenactments of unsolved crimes and advertised monetary rewards to increase witness cooperation with law enforcement investigations (O'Keefe et al. 1996). Collectively, these efforts established a media ability to influence attitudes and sometimes behaviors in carefully designed media products.

Hysterias

Described by Elaine Showalter (1997) as imitative disorders socially constructed to manifest culturally acceptable symptoms, outbreaks of hysterical waves of odd behaviors provide another well-substantiated area of media-generated copycat behaviors. Evidence of localized contagion of hysterical behaviors and cross-cultural diffusion of hysterias is found in a history of waves of noncriminal copycat behaviors associated with illnesses, bizarre experiences such as UFO abductions, and beliefs in secret political conspiracies (King et al. 2007). Hysterical behavior waves have been portrayed as copycat outbreaks triggered by shared social stress (Showalter 1997). Such waves have erupted within different cultures and periods of history, with the turn of each century appearing to be especially fertile times for them to appear (Showalter 1997). During the hysterical waves, public debates about the reality of underlying real-world causes for illnesses and behaviors associated with the waves have been common. Skeptics have viewed them as purely psychological in nature and as having no basis in fact or science. In contrast, sufferers have provided anecdotal reports of shared symptoms and experiences that have been presented as evidence of real underlying biological causes and as proof of the real-world factual validity of the hysterical outbreaks. High-profile advocates of hysteria waves tied to physical symptoms and medical syndromes have often been doctors or scientists who developed treatments for the hysterical illnesses. These advocates have frequently used the media to argue the reality of concrete physical origins for the sudden wave of sufferers and presented pseudoscientific explanations for a hysterical behavior's social explosion (Showalter 1997).

In an early example of a psychological hysterical condition, in the early twentieth century W. Fletcher (1908) reported on the spread of *latah*, defined as abnormal exaggerated behavior in reaction to sudden, unexpected sensory stimulus. A similar phenomenon related to crime is amok (as in "to run amok"), a state in which an individual falls into a violent, uncontrolled rage sometimes resulting in a murder spree (Schmidtke, Schaller, and Müller 2002; Westermeyer 1973). Examples of copycat hysterical waves of illnesses include nineteenth-century female hysteria and, more recently, recovered repressed memories of child abuse, chronic fatigue syndrome, gulf war syndrome, and multiple personality disorder (Showalter 1997). Claims of satanic ritual abuse and alien abduction are two of the more bizarre recent hysterical waves, as is belief in secret conspiracies and political cabals popularized by Q-anon renditions of CIA, FBI, and other deep state efforts to control and mislead the public. In her history of hysteria, Showalter (1997) argues that some cultures are more prone to hysterical waves than others and that the United States has a history of hysterical waves appearing regularly. She points out that US news, infotainment, and entertainment media habitually provide supportive content, outlets for those who champion hysterical conditions, distribution avenues for anecdotal victim narratives, and behavior models to copy the appropriate symptoms from.

Emulating the cycle of crime waves (Sacco 2005), while the behaviors expressed within different hysterias vary widely, the cycle that hysterias follow is consistent. Initial cases catch the attention of media, and an advocate champion emerges (often the advocate is a doctor, scientist, or celebrity), the hysterical symptoms and evidence acquire a label, the number of persons diagnosed with a syndrome or events offered as proof of the reality of the condition grows rapidly and spreads geographically, the cycle peaks and then declines, and the hysteria disappears as both a diagnosis and social movement. The pattern for the "chronic disease syndrome" hysteria in the 1990s is exemplary. After emerging, the physical symptoms linked to chronic disease syndrome expanded, and an extensive search for a biological cause was undertaken. The number of persons diagnosed grew rapidly, and advocates championing the reality of the condition attacked contrary research findings and prescriptions for nonbiological therapies and counseling. A decline in the number of diagnoses followed over time, and the fading of the hysterical wave eventually resulted (Wessely 1994).

Irrespective of any reality of underlying physical causes or evidence, social hysterias show that copycat behavior can be widespread and that the media are able to affect large numbers of disconnected people. Hysterias are more somatic than antisocial and are not usually violent or criminal, however. Most often people come to believe that they are being harmed by something in their environment or by some mysterious outside force (King et al. 2007). Hysterias establish that positively presented media models can urge susceptible individuals to emulate illnesses, but they do not provide strong evidence of a copycat criminal effect. Research on violent media and social aggression moves a step closer to that point.

Violent Media and Social Aggression

The most discussed body of parallel copycat crime research involves media violence as a cause of social aggression, as it receives the most media attention. A review of this extensive body of literature is beyond this book's scope, but, collectively, this research reveals a consistent pattern in favor of the notion that exposure to violent media increases the risk of aggressive behavior for some individuals through the direct imitation of observed violent acts (Surette 2015a). However, questions about the general soundness and quantity of the research on violent media and human aggression aside, aggression is not the same as crime. Although they overlap, aggression is not necessarily criminal; nor is most crime aggressive. Rudeness, insulting speech, unfair hording, and loud and obnoxious behavior can all be aggressive without violating the law. Similarly, fraud, bad-check writing, and most property crimes are not physically aggressive. Therefore, media-generated copycat crime is not expected to present in the same way as media-generated social aggression, and violent copycat crimes are expected to follow unique pathways. An assessment of violent media effects on aggression offered half a century ago remains valid: For some children under some conditions, some media is harmful. For other children under the same conditions, or for the same children under other conditions, it may be beneficial. For most children under most conditions, most media are probably neither particularly harmful nor particularly beneficial (Schramm, Lyle, and Parker 1961).

In summary, while the large body of research on human aggression and the embedded research on media and aggression are helpful in some ways in the study of copycat crime, the two phenomena are not syn-onymous. Although experimental studies confirm that visual and inter-active media violence can lead to short-term imitation, researchers do not know exactly how and to what extent the media cause long-term changes in aggressive behavior. A multifactor approach, in which expo-sure to violent media is one of a set of factors that facilitate or inhibit aggression, has been seen as reasonable (Gentile and Bushman 2012). The problem in applying "violent media causes social aggression" research to the "media causes copycat crime" hypothesis is that the validity of extrapolating from research on aggression to draw a conclu-sion about media and crime is questionable (Coyne 2007; Savage 2004, 2008). Even if media do foster aggressive behaviors, whether their influence extends to criminal behavior is a separate question. A focused area of research that does support the perspective that media might be generating copycat crimes is found in the study of copycat suicides.

Copycat Suicides

A substantial amount of empirical research on copycat effects has come from the examination of copycat suicides (Notredame et al. 2017). Public acceptance of the notion of media-generated copycat suicide followed a 1978 commercial film, *The Deer Hunter*, which was con-nected to a number of incidents (Coleman 1987; Ramsland 2011). Aca-demic interest was affirmed in the early 1980s when sociologist David Phillips (1982) labeled a copycat suicide effect the "Werther effect," for a fictional character in a 1774 Johann von Goethe novel. The link-age between the story and suicides was strong enough that the author added a disclaimer to later editions of *The Sorrows of Young Werther* to dissuade copycats (Minois 1999).

Beginning in the late 1800s, media-sourced imitation of suicide became a long-standing social concern, and periodic calls for restric-tions on the publication of suicide instructions in news and entertain-ment followed. Contemporary research on suicide clusters is rooted in a 1910 Viennese Psychoanalytical Association symposium whose pro-ceedings included a section devoted to whether newspaper reports of suicide engendered suicides among school children (Schmidtke and Schaller 2000, citing Unus 1910). Soon after, Edward Phelps (1911) described both suicide and crime as imitatively influenced by newspa-per coverage. Subsequently, suicide clusters were regularly noted, and starting with print media, links between suicides and media reports of suicides surfaced soon after the emergence of each new medium. Across the twentieth century, references to suicide epidemics among school-children, adolescents, the institutionalized, and specific ethnic groups regularly appeared.[1]

In the late 1970s and early 1980s, sociologist David Phillips researched imitative suicides linked to media news coverage and entertainment portraits. His research provides examples of some of the methodological and measurement issues faced when studying copycat crime. In his 1974 study on newspaper coverage of suicide and subsequent suicides, Phillips used national data on suicides and newspaper front-page stories to estimate a copycat suicide effect. His technique was to simply estimate the number of suicides above the expected number if no copycat effect was operating. To measure the presence of an effect, he estimated the expected number of sui-cides in the absence of a copycat effect during a month with front-page coverage of a suicide and compared that expected no-copycat-effect number with the number of suicides observed. If the observed suicides significantly exceeded the expected no-copycat value, Phillips attributed the overage to a copycat suicide effect. Phillips found that suicides increased after twenty-six front-page suicide sto-ries and decreased after seven of them, a difference he reported to be statistically significant. He concluded that suicides increased signifi-cantly for a brief period after a suicide story only after the story was published, not before; that the more publicity, the more the national sui-cide level increased; and that the increase occurred primarily in the geo-graphic areas where the suicide story was published.[2]

In a subsequent study, Phillips (1979) extended the Werther effect to automobile fatalities using data about California daily motor vehicle fatal-ities and front-page suicide stories from five California newspapers. In this study, Phillips found that three days after a publicized suicide (see Figure 3.1), automobile fatalities increase by 31 percent after each sui-cide story. The more a suicide was publicized, the more automobile fatal-ities increased, with the age of the drivers significantly correlated to the age of the suicide victims. In keeping with his 1974 study, Phillips in 1979 concluded that motor vehicle accident fatalities increased markedly just after publicized suicide stories and only after the publicized story; that single-vehicle crashes increased more just after suicide stories; that the more publicity, the greater the increase in motor vehicle fatalities in the area where the suicide story was publicized; and that suicide stories

Figure 3.1   Automobile Fatalities Following a Publicized Suicide

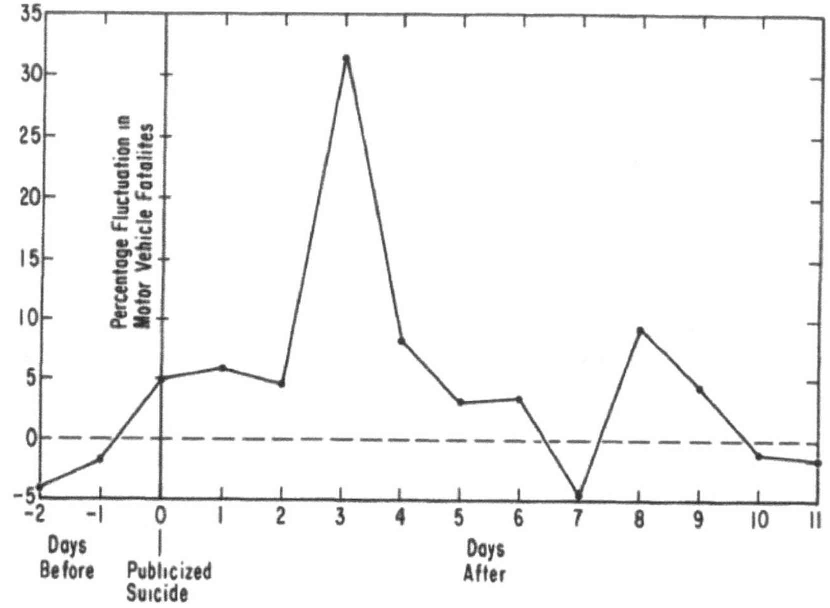

Source: Phillips 1979, 1157.

about young persons tended to be followed by single-vehicle crashes involving young drivers.

In a third copycat suicide study, Phillips (1982) looked at suicides portrayed in television soap operas and subsequent real-world suicides. He speculated that increases in suicides apparently occur because soap opera suicide stories trigger imitative suicides and suicide attempts, some of which are disguised as single-vehicle accidents. In this study, Phillips corrected for linear trends in suicide deaths by calculating the slope of a linear regression line fit to his time series data. Thus, given the null hypothesis of no copycat effect, the number of expected suicides on a specific day following a soap opera suicide equals the number of suicides on that day of the week during a comparison control period, plus the weekly trend increment. Limited to the statistical methods available in the 1970s (neither autoregressive integrated moving average (ARIMA) based time series analysis nor time series data were widely available), Phillips's methodology subsequently came under criticism (see Hittner 2005; Jonas 1992; Wasserman 1984). Irrespective of the strength of his evidence, Phillips demonstrated the need for empirical testing for copycat effects, time series data, examination of time trends, and valid measures of media attention and copycat events that are accurately time-stamped. Since the final decades of the twentieth century and through the beginning decades of the twenty-first, suicide clusters have subsequently been regularly reported (Blood and Pirkis 2001; Gould, Jamieson, and Gould 2003; Hassan 1995; Marzuk et al. 1993; Stack 2000).

In terms of copycat crime, the common takeaway from the literature on copycat suicide is the argument that if suicide can be media generated, less fatal acts such as crime should also be open to influence. The suicide research also addresses the concern raised about similar repeat crimes being mislabeled as copycats but actually being due to a single repeat offender (discussed in Chapter 4). Successful suicides can be copied but not repeated. The counterargument to the conclusion that copycat suicides provide unarguable evidence for copycat crimes is that suicide is a unique behavior resulting from extreme stress and carried out by either mentally or physically pained individuals, so a media copycat effect reasonably can be substantial for suicides while insubstantial for crime (Diekstra 1974). As the motivations for crime and suicide differ so significantly, media influences on imitative suicide have been argued to operate differently than those connected to copycat criminality.

With those caveats in mind, copycat suicide research does indicate that demographics are not predictive of suicide waves, but the widespread availability of suicide models in the media are. Supporting this contention, the copying of specific methods of suicide has been studied in some depth. Crosby, Rhee, and Holland (1977) reported research on self-immolation (suicide by fire) that provides evidence of copycat suicides tied to political protest following news coverage of prior self-immolation victims. The authors concluded that news media coverage provided dignity and significance to this suicide method and influenced the choice of method for persons already determined to commit suicide. In a second self-immolation study, Ashton and Donnan (1981) describe a similar cluster in the United Kingdom in the late 1970s. Other suicide methods have also been observed to cluster. Examining asphyxia suicide by placing a plastic bag over one's head in the United Kingdom, Church and Philips (1984) reported that a news-media-reported plastic bag suicide significantly increased the likelihood of subsequent plastic bag suicides. Similarly, Marzuk and colleagues (1993) found evidence of plastic bag asphyxiation increasing after the publication of a book,

Final Exit, that described the suicide method in detail while presenting suicide in a positive light. They did not find that the overall suicide rate shifted, however, indicating that suicide methods were copied but not that more suicides were triggered.

Additionally, the matching of suicide-generator models to suicide copiers has been reported. Schmidtke and Hafner (1988) looked at train suicides in Germany and found a significant increase in suicides among young males who matched suicide-generator model demographics but not for young females or elderly males. Concerning celebrity suicides, Gundlach and Stack (1990) examined suicides after front-page coverage in early-twentieth-century New York and found that noncelebrity suicides did not appear to increase copycat suicides but that after a minimum level of coverage was reached (at least three front-page stories), celebrity suicide coverage generated suicide clusters. Jonas (1992) also found celebrity suicides in Germany were associated with significant increases in copycat suicides, and alternative explanations for the observed increase in suicides were not supported. In a summary of this research, Pirkis, Burgess, and colleagues (2006) state that the greatest imitation effects are found when the copier is similar in age and sex to the media suicide model and the model was revered in some way, a celebrity being the most common. Most recently, Niederkrotenthaler and colleagues (2020) concluded, after conducting a meta-analysis, that the reporting of celebrity suicides had meaningful impacts on total suicides.

In addition to the above methods of suicide, different types of media have been studied for their ability to encourage suicide. Regarding print media, Marzuk and colleagues (1993) found support for imitative suicides, while Thorson and Oberg (2003) found no evidence of a suicide epidemic after the publication of Goethe's *The Sorrows of Young Werther*. Thorsen and Oberg (2003) did find evidence of a small number of imitative suicides but not enough to generate a true cluster in their view. However, as Hemenway (1911) found a century ago, a number of studies report a linkage between newspaper coverage of suicide and imitative suicides.[3] Similarly, the study of visual media, television, and film has produced linkages between media suicide portrayals and copycat suicides.[4]

The imitative suicide literature is not unanimous in its conclusions, however, and some studies did not find evidence of a copycat suicide effect. Williams and colleagues (1987) found no evidence for an effect of the portrayal of suicides by soap opera characters on real-world suicides. Following a BBC television show, *EastEnders*, about a drug overdose by a main character, analysis of data from two local emergency rooms after the broadcast concluded that no imitation effect emerged. Kirch and Lester (1986a), after examining suicide jumps in the 1970s from the Golden Gate Bridge, also reported no evidence of clustering. Using a similar empirical method, Kirch and Lester (1986b) reported mixed results for plastic bag suicides across various time frames in a reanalysis of Church and Philips's (1984) data.[5] Plastic bag suicides did appear to cluster 90 and 150 days after a publicized suicide, but no ready explanation was offered for why these particular time lags rose to significance.

Regarding unexplained copycat effect time lags, Kirch and Lester (1986a) point out that at a recurring problem with the copycat suicide research is a disconnect between the time of a suicide and the next similar suicide. Even when the time between events is not random, no theoretical or logical explanation for the amount of time lag or the presence of inconsistence lag times across studies is found in the literature. Kirch and Lester state that a copycat effect seems to manifest itself in an unexplained time sequence of nonrandom bursts. Without an understanding of the underlying operating dynamics, attempts to use the media as a suicide deterrent have, unsurprisingly, not been fruitful. Holding (1975) found no prophylactic effect on suicides from an antisuicide television program. In contrast, Mercy and colleagues (2001) found that exposure to the suicide of a friend or a media portrait of suicide decreased suicide risk but only after a substantial period of more than a year. Based on such inconsistent results, Mercy and colleagues (2001) concluded that exposure to the suicidal behavior of real or media models was not a risk factor after controlling for subjects' depression, alcoholism, and immigration history. One speculation about the ambiguous findings is that possibly counteracting media-induced Werther effects are media suicide-prevention effects, termed *Papageno effects* after a character in Mozart's opera *The Magic Flute*, who is talked out of committing suicide (Niederkrotenthaler 2017; Scherr and Steinleitner 2017). Evidence of a significant Papageno effect has not been presented though.

The consensus from this mixed research is that a copycat mechanism makes a haphazard appearance, but when it does appear, it seems to work through social learning and contagious imitation processes.[6] Overall, the copycat suicide research suggests a media-molding over a media-causing effect that operates through a restraint reduction mechanism. Schmidtke and Schaller (2000) concluded that there is substantial evidence for an imitative effect, and Pirkis, Burgess, and colleagues (2006) state that media coverage as a cause of suicide meets the criteria of consistent findings (observed across different designs and populations), statistical significance, and expected direction (more media attention relates to stronger copycat effects) and aligns with known facts about suicide and its susceptibility to imitation. A media-based copycat suicide effect is conceded, but beyond that simple agreement, little is understood.

Conclusion: Noncrime Copycat Effects

Evidence of a media-generated copycat effect on noncriminal behaviors ranging from product purchases to health, diet, and exercise routines, hysterical illnesses, social aggression, and suicide supports the plausibility without proving the existence of a media-linked copycat crime effect. Although these behaviors range from beneficial to fatal, it is felt that copying a crime is a qualitatively different decision and act. Most crime involves direct harm to others and risk of formal criminal justice sanctions. Due to these considerations, copycat crime may happen but be rare. Additionally, the majority of the noncriminal copycat events were openly committed and socially tolerated, whereas, with some exceptions, much copycat crime will be hidden and, upon discovery, punished. The surreptitious nature of copycat crime makes answering three basic questions regarding copycat crime necessary for serious study. First, how prevalent is copycat crime? Second, how does a researcher determine whether a specific candidate copycat crime is a true copycat crime? Third, how are clusters of similar crimes determined to be imitative or random? These questions involve methodological and measurement issues that are not normally confronted when studying other types of crime but are central in the study of copycat crime. They are taken up in Chapter 4.

Notes

1. There is extensive research and literature on media and suicide. A 2017 compilation of articles edited by Thomas Niederkrotenthaler and Steven Stack provides a recent overview. For additional historical studies of copycat suicide, see Strahan 1893; Oppenheimer 1910; Unus 1910; Phelps 1911; Hemenway 1911; Rost 1912. For additional examples, see Ward and Fox 1977; Coleman 1987; Gould, Jamieson, and Gould 2003; Rubinstein 1983; Schmidtke and Hafner 1988.

2. Phillips 1974 used the suicide of Ku Klux Klan leader Daniel Burros, who committed suicide on November 1, 1965, as an example. In the month after Burros's death, 1,710 suicides were recorded, whereas there were 1,639 suicides in November of the previous year and 1,665 suicides in November of the subsequent year.

Phillips took the average of the prior and subsequent year suicides (1,652) as a linear estimate of the number of suicides expected in November 1965 under the null hypothesis of no suicide copycat effect on national suicides. He then subtracted the null estimated number from the observed suicide number (1,710) and argued that the 58 extra suicides were imitative.

3. For research linking newspaper coverage to suicide clusters, see, for example, Blood and Pirkis 2001; Crosby, Rhee, and Holland 1977; Etzerdorfer, Sonneck, and Nagel-Kuess 1992; Gundlach and Stack 1990; Jonas 1992; Pirkis, Blood, et al. 2006; Schmidtke and Schaller 2000.

4. For examples of research on film and television programing content and copycat suicides, see Hawton et al. 1999; Holding 1975; Schmidtke and Hafner 1988; Pirkis, Blood, et al. 2006; Schmidtke and Schaller 2000; Thorson and Oberg 2003; Williams et al. 1987.

5. Kirch and Lester 1986b uses a mean rate change to measure a copycat suicide presence. From 1976 to 1977 there were forty-six suicides on the Golden Gate bridge. The researchers' null hypotheses assumed a Poisson distribution with an average rate of 46/729 suicides per day (0.0631). Their reported analysis lacks details, but they concluded that jumpers from the Golden Gate Bridge were randomly distributed over time and that no discernible clustering effect was apparent.

6. For recent discussions of copycat suicide mechanisms, see Blood and Pirkis 2001; Church and Philips 1984; Diekstra 1974; Eisenberg 1986; Etzerdorfer, Sonneck, and Nagel-Kuess 1992; Gould and Olivares 2017; Gundlach and Stack 1990; Ji et al. 2014; Jonas 1992; Niederkrotenthaler and Stack 2017; Niederkrotenthaler et al. 2020; Pirkis, Burgess, et al. 2006; Pirkis et al. 2007; Schmidtke and Hafner 1988; Schmidtke and Schaller 2000; Ueda, Mori, and Matsubayashi 2014.

4

Measuring
Copycat Crime

A VEXING QUESTION CONCERNING COPYCAT CRIME IS HOW
to decide if a specific crime is a copycat crime. This question has been
addressed through varied mathematical approaches to evaluate whether
a crime can be validly labeled as a copycat crime, a crucial step for conducting research on the phenomenon. Mathematical approaches range
from early simple methods to recent sophisticated mathematical modeling. All assume that a crime sharing characteristics with a prior crime
is more likely due to imitation than randomness. The initial step toward
measuring copycat crime is determining its prevalence.

Copycat Crime Prevalence

The most common method to estimate how much copycat crime exists
relies on self-report measures and directly asking people if they have
ever attempted a copycat crime. Estimates of copycat crime prevalence
are summarized in a 2014 meta-analysis of ten surveys involving
nearly 1,500 incarcerated adults and at-risk youth (Surette 2014). The
ten surveys were conducted between 1975 and 2011 and were generated from seven separate research efforts. Samples were drawn from
four US locations and one foreign country. The majority of the respondents were incarcerated adult males; two samples included females,
and six sampled teenage youth. All respondents were asked if they had

ever attempted a copycat crime in their lifetime. The combined result was that one in four reported a personal copycat crime attempt. The proportion of respondents reporting a copycat crime history across the surveys ranged from 13 to 46 percent (Surette 2014). An additional 2015 survey of incarcerated inmates by Surette and Maze (2015) reported a copycat crime attempt prevalence of one in three respondents. Copycat prevalence is not evenly distributed, however. A recent examination of copycat crime prevalence reports significant differences by gender, incarceration status, and age (Surette 2020b).

Based on these surveys, a copycat crime attempt appears as a characteristic of a substantial number of offenders and a small but nonzero proportion of nonoffenders. Copycat crime does not comprise a substantial proportion of the total amount of crime. It remains a rare criminal occurrence, and the majority of crimes are not copycat crimes. Copycat crime is indicated as being both rare in frequency and common as a criminal career trait. The importance of copycat crime lies in its commonality in the criminal life course of a significant number of offenders, not in its impact on overall crime levels. When copycat crime is part of a person's criminal history, it frequently appears at an early age (Surette 2002, 2020b; Surette and Chadee 2020; Surette and Maze 2015). As will be discussed in detail in Chapter 7, copycat crimes are thought to be committed most often by criminally oriented youth. Its criminological importance emerges as a factor not in aggregate crime rates but in the origins of criminal careers. The next research issue is how to determine if a particular crime is a copycat crime.

Assessing Candidate Copycat Crimes

Crimes usually come to be labeled as copycat crimes by journalists in a subjective, haphazard manner that undermines rigorous research. To counter this fault, a seven-factor procedure can be used to score individual crimes as substantiated or unsubstantiated copycat crimes (Surette 2016b).[1] The seven factors considered when deciding if a crime is a copycat crime are time proximity, theme consistency, scene specificity, repetitive consumption, self-editing, offender statements, and second-party statements.

The first factor, time proximity, is the time span between the generator and proposed copycat crime. Logically, a generator crime must precede a copycat crime in time, but how close in time must a generator crime fall to indicate a copycat crime link? For example, should a crime in the twenty-first century that resembles a crime in a movie from the 1930s be considered linked by time proximity? The applied operational assumption is that without evidence of recent exposure to the media-portrayed crime by the offender, the greater the time separation between two crimes, the weaker the likelihood of a copycat link. A time gap of less than five years was chosen as a sufficient cut-off based on the argument that the portrayal of generator crimes would still be present in the available popular culture and readily accessible to potential copycat offenders during the five-year period following a generator crime. To be considered as proximal, generator crimes older than five years require supplemental evidence of offender exposure, such as ownership of a film or book or reliable statements of recent exposure.

The second and third score factors relate to the correspondence between the candidate generator and the copycat crime. At a general correspondence level, theme consistency is present when common lifestyle elements that the offender and the media crime model share are found. Indicators of theme consistency are similar patterns of thought, feelings, or behaviors, where the offender parallels the model in a broad sense. An example would be if an offender dresses in a unique manner, such as wearing a black trench coat like that worn by a film character. The next copycat crime score factor, scene specificity, relates to the details of the generator crime that match the candidate copycat crime. Scene specificity is indicated when an offender acts out a specific scene from media-delivered content by using the words, gestures, dress, or behavior portrayed by the media crime model. An example would be when an offender quotes lines from a movie while committing a similar portrayed crime.

The next two scoring factors relate to the interaction between the possible copycat offender and the copycat-crime-generating media. Together they reflect how psychologically deeply an offender is involved with generator crime content. Following the logic that exposure to a media rendition once is less persuasive of a copycat effect than repeated exposure to the same media product, repetitive consumption before the commission of a candidate copycat crime is seen as evidence of deeper psychological engagement. In parallel with repetitive consumption, the presence of self-editing, where an offender repetitively consumes selected generator crime media content and ignores the balance of the media content, is a heightened indicator of a copycat effect.

For visual media, the use of freeze-frame or slow motion to detail and study crime-relevant scenes is an additional indicator of self-editing.

The last two factors refer to statements about the role of the generator crime media in the commission of the candidate copycat crime. Available only for cases where an offender is available or has left relevant messages, statements attributing a significant role to the generator crime are given extra weight. Offender statements that the crime was not media linked would reduce the copycat crime likelihood, while offender statements that point to a significant media role would increase a crime's copycat likelihood. The final factor is statements from second parties. Given less weight than offender statements, comments from investigators, friends, or relatives that link generator media to a crime augment a crime's copycat validity. Due to their less-than-rigorous application history, journalist statements would not increase a crime's copycat likelihood.

Based on these seven factors, initial copycat crime score points are calculated as follows: time order and proximity (one point), theme consistency (one point), scene specificity (two points), repetitive viewing (one point), self-editing (one point), offender statements (plus two points when an offender credits the media as their crime source or minus two points when the offender discredits the media as a crime source), second party statements (plus one point when media credited as an influence, minus one point when the media is discredited). In cases with no arrest or offender death, the maximum points would equal seven; otherwise the maximum score is nine. A crime's score can be divided by its potential maximum score for a final copycat score that ranges between one and zero, with divisions at .33 and .66 distinguishing between unsubstantiated, possible, and substantiated copycat crimes.

An example of an unsubstantiated copycat crime is the 1995 Oklahoma City bombing by Timothy McVeigh, linked to the movie *Red Dawn*. This crime gets one point for time order and proximity and one point for repetitive viewing (McVeigh rented *Red Dawn* four times prior to the bombing). There are no points for self-editing or offender statements as McVeigh did not personally connect the movie to his bombing (Kifner 1995). However, a point is awarded for theme consistency as McVeigh shared several attitudes with lead characters in the film. Finally, no points are awarded for copying a specific scene from the movie or for second-party statements. In total, McVeigh's Oklahoma City bombing receives a total of two out of nine possible points, or a .222 copycat crime likelihood score.

An example of a possible copycat crime is the 1997 school shooting by Michael Carneal, which has been linked to the 1995 film *The Basketball Diaries*. Several media outlets described the film as the reason why the teenage Carneal went on a shooting spree, killing three female classmates (Thompson 1997). Copycat crime scoring awards a point for time order (the 1995 film preceded the 1997 crime). In the movie, the main character dreams of walking into a classroom in his high school and shooting several students and a teacher. Carneal's crime was similarly in a school setting, earning one point for theme consistency and two points for scene specificity. There is evidence that he had watched the movie but no evidence of self-editing or repetitive viewing. According to CNBC, when asked where he had seen a similar shooting, Carneal named the film (Thompson 1997). Carneal's initial comments would have resulted in two points for offender statements, but he recanted and later denied that his crime was connected to *The Basketball Diaries* (Tillotson 1997). The conflicting statements cancel each other out, and no points are awarded for offender comments. However, the film was held responsible for the crime by second parties and earns a point for second-party comments (Thompson 1997). Carneal's shooting spree totaled five out of nine possible points, garnering a copycat crime score of .556 and a label as a possible copycat crime.

An example of a substantiated copycat crime is connected to the 2002 vampire movie *Queen of the Damned*. The offender, Alan Menzies, killed his friend, Thomas McKendrick, in 2002. In the weeks before the murder, Menzies believed that the heroine in the film, vampire Akasha, was ordering him to kill someone (King 2002). He stated that an insulting sexual remark by McKendrick regarding Akasha had made her unhappy. Menzies believed he could not allow McKendrick to insult Akasha and that she would not turn him into a vampire if he did not kill someone. He subsequently murdered McKendrick, drank McKendrick's blood, partially ate his head, and buried him in a shallow grave (Robertson 2003a, 2003b).

Following the film's release by less than a year, Menzies's crime scores one point for time order and proximity. As Menzies was on a quest to become a vampire, the crime also receives a point for theme consistency and two points for scene specificity (Robertson 2003a). Menzies was obsessed with the film and had watched it over one hundred times, earning a point for repetitive viewing. There is no evidence of self-editing. Offender statements earned two additional points, with Menzies saying, "After I had seen the tape so many times,

I wanted to go out and murder people." He also said, "I should have never watched that movie. It sent me mad" (King 2002). Lastly, a point for second-party statements is awarded as friends stated that Menzies was obsessed with vampires and the *Queen of the Damned* film (Robertson 2003b). The murder receives a total of eight out of nine points, a copycat crime score of .889, and a substantiated copycat crime designation.

An initial copycat crime score can be combined with Bayes's theorem to calculate the final probability of a specific crime being a copycat crime. Bayes's theorem is a probability-based estimation method that incorporates new knowledge as it becomes available to estimate the probability of an event occurring. For copycat crime, the application of Bayes's theorem works as follows. First, a candidate copycat crime happens—a crime thought to be similar to an earlier crime is noted. Using Surette's (2016b) seven-factor copycat crime scoring and Bayes's theorem, a probability regarding whether the second crime is a copycat crime can be calculated. Given the crime's prior probability of occurring based on the rate of past occurrences of similar crimes and the addition of new information, Bayes's theorem combines qualitative and quantitative information (Silver 2012). To calculate the probability of a crime being a copycat crime, three probabilities (x, y, and z) need to be estimated and plugged into Bayes's formula:

$$\frac{xy}{xy + z(1 - x)}$$

Probability x is based on the crime's historical rate and the probability of a similar type of crime occurring in the past. For copycat crime, this is an initial estimate of how likely it is for a similar crime (but not a copycat crime) to occur based upon how often that type of crime has occurred historically. Using robberies of taxi drivers as an example, this probability is simply the probability of one taxi robbery being followed closely by another taxi robbery. The probability (and value of x) can be determined by looking at the taxi robbery crime rate over time (for example, the number of crimes per year divided by 365 provides the probability of a crime type occurring on any particular day). In a community with ninety taxi robberies in the prior year, the probability of a taxi robbery occurring on any specific day is .246.

The value of y, the probability of the candidate crime being a copycat crime, is based upon Surette's (2016c) seven-factor copycat crime score.

The estimate of y provides the probability of a new taxi robbery being a copycat given the additional knowledge provided by a crime's copycat crime score (a recommended conservative approach reduces this score by .10 to account for scoring subjectivity). In the taxi robbery example, the adjusted y value would be .678 (Surette's seven factor copycat score applied to the taxi robbery example equals $(7/9) - .10 = .678$).

The value of z is the probability of the candidate crime not being a copycat crime despite its similarities to prior crimes. The value of z is not simply the inverse of y and is instead based on the estimation of the individual probabilities for each of the seven copycat crime scoring factors being a false indicator. For example, time proximity may be present, but the candidate crime could still not be a copycat crime. Likewise, scene specificity could be observed without the candidate crime being a copycat, and so on through the seven factors. The task is to assign a logical estimate to each factor's being present but the crime not being a copycat crime. Assuming that each factor is independent of the others, the value of z is the product of the seven separate probabilities (if a factor is not present, it cannot be a copycat crime indicator, and its probability is set to 1.0).

In estimating Z in the taxi robbery example, each of the seven copycat score factors is separately approximated (designated as lowercase z). For time order and proximity, an initial conservative z estimate of .90 would be reasonable in this example based on the logic that many similar crimes appear in the one-year time span. Similarly, for crime theme consistency, a z estimate of .90 could be argued as types of robbery victims vary significantly without influence from media models. For scene specificity, a z estimate of .50 makes sense on the logic that the likelihood of an exact robbery location, a taxi, appearing independently is felt to be smaller. As both repetitive viewing and self-editing are not applicable, the z estimate of both defaults to 1. Assume for this example that a taxi robber has been apprehended and falsely states that he got the idea from news accounts. As he is unlikely to lie and the majority of offenders would not bother to falsely nominate themselves as copycat criminals, the estimate of offender statements being false indications is assigned a low z of .33. Along the same logic, second-party statements connecting the taxi robberies to media accounts provide an initial z estimate of .50 in the belief that such statements might be wrong about half the time. The taxi robbery example estimate of the probability of a crime having its specific combination of factors and not being a copycat crime becomes the product of the seven individual z estimates for each factor (in this example, $Z = .9 \times .9 \times .5 \times 1.0 \times 1.0 \times .33 \times .5 = .067$). In the example taxi robbery, the overall value of Z and the probability that a crime with these characteristics is not a copycat crime is estimated to be low.

Based on the three probability estimates ($x = .246$, $y = .678$, $Z = .067$), the final Bayes's theorem value is the revised estimate of how likely it is that a candidate crime of interest is a copycat crime; in this taxi robbery example, that value is .77. Given the available knowledge about the candidate copycat crime and about how often these types of crimes happen, it would be a reasonable conclusion that about three-fourths of the time the candidate copycat crime is an actual copycat crime. If additional knowledge becomes available—for example, evidence of repetitive viewing of taxi robberies in the media is forthcoming from an arrested taxi robber (and given an individual z estimate of .75 for the report of repetitive viewing being a false indicator)—the probability of copycat crime validity would increase to .815 or about four out of five times.

The point of this probability-driven assessment of candidate copycat crimes is to raise researcher confidence when studying copycat crime that actual copycat crimes are being studied. Other empirical approaches for validation are possible, and the described approach relies upon some admittedly subjective decisions. Irrespective of its deficiencies, however, an ability to make grounded assessments of the likelihood of a proposed crime being a copycat crime is important. The pursuit of useful research on copycat crime depends upon studying, to the best of a researcher's ability, actual copycat crimes. It is a crucial minimum requirement that researchers validate the crimes they argue are copycat examples before offering analysis results, conclusions, and policy recommendations.

Time Series Crime Sets

In addition to evaluating crimes as media-linked copycat pairs, assessing aggregate sets of crimes to determine clusters and waves has been a second empirical task. Crime-clustering research looks at the occurrence of similar crimes within a narrow time frame in one geographic area. As crimes within a crime wave need not be physically close or occur in a tight temporal sequence, crime wave research, in contrast, focuses on similar crimes occurring over long time periods across wide geographic areas. The two phenomena share the methodological challenge of empirically distinguishing a random grouping of similar crimes from nonrandom crime clusters and waves.

Crime Clusters

Research on crime clustering has focused on neighborhood contagion effects usually within lower socioeconomic neighborhoods. Teenage pregnancy and school dropout clusters are examples of noncrime clusters that have been studied. This body of research has generally reported evidence that includes the potential for contagion but does not eliminate the possibility that the observed clusters are due not to imitation but to similar inclinations among individuals living in the same community. As Philip Cook and Kristin Goss (1996) note, nonrandom clusters are not proof of contagion, as a tendency of people with similar dispositions to live, go to school, or work together may mimic a contagion effect. Harkening back to the "Birds of a feather flock together" adage, a crime cluster may result when people with similar proclivities simply behave similarly rather than copy one another. A second noncontagion explanation for a crime cluster is the impact of an outside shock that produces copycat-like crime clusters, such as a drug turf war increasing homicides in a neighborhood. As with correlations not proving cause, the ebbs and flows of crime clusters may be due to noncopycat causes.

The research on crime clusters has focused on near-repeat crimes or crimes that are near in time and space to one another based on the hypothesis that similar crimes committed sequentially in close proximity have a nonrandom connection. In general, the research indicates the likely rarity of copycat crime while not eliminating its possibility. As initial successful crimes are thought to result in later similar crimes, the possibility that copycat effects may be operating is attractive, and near-repeat research initially looked promising for understanding copycat crime.

A number of near-repeat researchers have recently studied violent crime, including shootings and gang violence.[2] The near-repeat hypotheses that crimes occurring close together in both space and time are not independent has been consistently supported (Bowers and Johnson 2004). Near-repeat patterns have been found to vary considerably across crime types and time spans though (Youstin et al. 2011). In one study, similar houses close to each other (next-door in particular) in affluent areas on the same side of the street showed significantly greater crime risk within one week of an initial crime (Bowers and Johnson 2005). Burglaries were reported to cluster in close proximity (300 to 400 meters) in one- to two-month groupings by Johnson and Bowers (2004) and within up to ninety days by Zhang and colleagues (2015). In a third study, the effect range was found to be 200 meters and involved a two-week time span (Johnson et al. 2007). In addition, the type of crime matters. A near-repeat pattern found effect range varying from one day within two to four blocks for robbery to four days within zero to six blocks for auto theft (Youstin et al. 2011) and up to six days and a quarter of a mile for robbery (Zhang et al. 2015). Zhang and colleagues (2015) also found that for assaults, the repeat range was seven days and slightly more than a mile. Youstin and colleagues (2011) speculated that the near-repeat pattern for robbery was driven by spree crimes committed in short time frames likely by the same offender.

The empirical assumption in the near-repeat research is that the distribution of random crimes will be reflected in the average time elapsed between the crimes (Johnson 2008). In less convoluted language, 100 crimes in 300 days would equal a 3-day average (300/100) between crimes. The research question associated with near-repeat research is whether patterns of repeat victimizations were generated where crime was the result of stable risk factors and crime clusters were produced by a random process or whether an enhancing nonrandom mechanism such as a copycat effect was generating a nonrandom crime pattern.

Research studies on near-repeats address whether the clustering is random or not, but the research does not address possible differing causal relationships between the crimes (Ornstein and Hammond 2017). This research, therefore, does not directly address the copycat crime question, as burglary clustering, for example, can be due to various mechanisms such as a serial criminal committing a string of burglaries in one area over a brief time span, the characteristics of houses or victims attracting a set of separate independent burglars, or copycat offenders consciously copying the success of prior criminals. Theoretically, all three mechanisms could be operating simultaneously. As only the third mechanism involves a copycat effect and distinguishing between the three options is not possible in the aggregate time series data used in this research, determining whether a set of crimes is random or not is possible, but determining when one has a set of copycat crimes is not empirically possible.

Instead, two theories have been argued as explanations of near-repeat crime clusters, neither of which requires a copycat effect. The first, boost theory, states that crime clusters occur when the risk of crime is raised for a short time by the impact of an initial crime. The boost hypothesis is that an initial crime raises area risk for a short period, and a residence transforms from a presumed suitable crime target to a known suitable crime target (Youstin et al. 2011). Empirically, a boost effect has been found more likely when the same offender commits a cluster of similar crimes (Johnson and Bowers 2004). The offender's success in their initial crime is perceived as boosting their confidence or criminal self-efficacy to repeatedly commit the same crime in the same neighborhood.

Countering boost theory is flag theory, which holds that crime clusters occur because victim homes share characteristics that make them attractive targets for multiple unconnected offenders (Youstin et al. 2011). Row houses with low back windows not visible from the street, for example, might generate a cluster of home burglaries. In the flag hypothesis, crime targets that share crime-attracting characteristics are targeted by different offenders. Flag theory suggests that a copycat process is unnecessary as the offenders are attracted to their crime victims by victim characteristics independent of the actions of other offenders (Johnson and Bowers 2004; Johnson 2008).

Empirical findings offer support for both theories. For example, Johnson's (2008) analysis suggested that a boost process was unable to generate patterns of repeat victimization in line with a pure boost theory expectation; instead a mixed boost and flag model was argued. Target attractiveness in specific areas can generate spatial concentrations of crime (supporting flag theory) and contagion-like processes (supporting boost theory). Despite the empirical evidence for nonrandom crime clustering, neither theory requires an operating copycat crime effect. Therefore, like the research on social aggression, hysteria, and suicide, the near-repeat research does not confirm the existence of copycat crime but does not exclude it as an empirical possibility.

Reducing the probability of a large-scale copycat effect, the near-repeat research reports evidence in favor of the same offenders repeating crimes, not new offenders copying crime. Johnson and Bowers (2004), for example, conclude that among five possible explanations for the appearance of burglary clusters, the most likely engine is the same offenders committing the clustered burglaries, followed by a group of co-offenders working an area together. They give less credibility to an offender network discovering that good crime opportunities exist in an area, discussing these opportunities among themselves, and implementing prior observed successful crime methods. Along the same lines, Ratcliffe and Rengert (2008) attribute near-repeat shootings to retaliation, escalation, or coercion, not to copycat effects. The media as a source of crime knowledge are seldom considered important in the near-repeat research. A media-generated copycat crime process, where the media serve as the social network base, is not suggested.

The near-repeat boost theory tends to dissuade against a copycat crime–based explanation where offenders are mimicking the success of prior offenders. Instead, boost theory forwards a crime spree process where the same offenders commit a series of crimes after locking onto a specific type of victim. In the near-repeat research, crimes such as burglary are most often seen as not directly copied by one offender modeling another, in the sense that copycat crime is herein perceived, but as outgrowths of community factors that increase the risk of victimization or decrease the risk of apprehension (Townsley, Homel, and Chaseling 2003). A copycat crime cluster, by definition, would involve multiple offenders (one model, one copier at a minimum), whereas a crime spree would involve one offender committing multiple similar crimes over a short time frame. Speaking to the comparative rarity of copycat crime, burglaries committed in close spatial and temporal proximity are more often seen as involving the same offender repeating a crime as opposed to multiple offenders or a copycat crime effect. Youstin and colleagues (2011) cite support for this conclusion in other research reporting that solved near-repeat burglaries are committed by the same offender about 98 percent of the time and that, when interviewed, three of four career home burglars reported that they returned to the same set of houses.

The problem, therefore, in identifying true copycat crimes in near-repeat data is distinguishing one offender using the same crime method and committing a cluster of crimes, from two offenders operating in the same neighborhood because attractive crime targets are common, from a copycat crime offender pair, one of whom is mimicking the other. Empirically all three possibilities would present the same crime time series data. Additionally, near-repeat research uses both time and space to determine clusters, whereas for copycat crime, time is the only important factor, as spatial proximity is irrelevant due to widespread access to media, an effect heightened by the rise of social media (Surette 2017). Social media further allow clustering effects to be independent of spatial proximity so that a copycat crime set could occur close together in time but not physically near to each other, a situation that heightens the likelihood of copycat crimes going unidentified (Lewis et al. 2012).

In sum, regarding copycat crime, confounding factors not related to copycat crime can be hidden within near repeat data. It is possible to have an offender initially be a copycat offender and then become a serial offender, particularly if the copycat crime technique is successful. In the absence of specific information from offenders, there is a difficultly in distinguishing copycat crimes from repeat crimes in time series crime data, and copycat crime cannot be determined empirically from the analysis of time series crime data. A nonrandom cluster may not include copycat offenders, and a true copycat dyad may be so separated as to appear in separate data sets or substantially separated time periods. In the end, the research on near-repeat crime is not directly related to copycat crime, but the methods developed under the near-repeat umbrella are useful for examining crime clustering along time dimensions. One characteristic both copycat crimes and near-repeat victimizations do appear to share is that risk of victimization decays at an exponential rate so that both copycat effects and crime clusters decay quickly (Johnson 2008; Wooditch and Weisburd 2016). The bottom line from near-repeat research is that even in crime clusters, copycat crime appears to be rare and distinct from typical crime clusters.

Crime Waves

The empirical issue regarding copycat waves is that similar crimes will sometimes appear grouped together in any random-walk data series. What is needed is a means of determining whether a group of crimes observed over time is the result of a copycat effect or just a random set of crimes that happen to have occurred together. Crime waves present the empirical question of whether the waves are due to a random background Poisson process, in which independent events randomly appear in groups, or the crimes are appearing together because they are somehow causally linked.

The quantitative approaches for addressing this question have ranged from simple to complex. All share the logic of determining the probability of a group of similar crimes appearing randomly in a time series data set. This has been assessed based on the data's temporal pattern and what is already known about the crimes. An example problem would be whether a half dozen taxi robberies in a six-week period signal a true set of linked crimes or a random group of independent robberies. In the literature, the empirical goal is described as distinguishing a self-exciting process from a random Poisson process in a crime series data set. Additionally, conceiving copycat crimes as criminal innovations, the Bass model from the diffusion literature and the adoption rates of innovations have been utilized.

Non-Poisson time series sequences are called self-exciting when the appearance of an event results in the increased probability of another similar event following. In this perspective, copycat crime may be self-limiting if a copycat crime surge is followed by increased law enforcement and failed crimes become more common, generating a suppression effect. As argued in the near-repeat research, self-excitation isn't necessarily a direct copycat crime process, as one crime need not serve as a model but could function as triggering a nonimitative process, where an initial crime increases the likelihood of similar crimes without serving as a generator crime. Like copycat crime, self-excitation crime processes are usually thought to be self-limiting in the sense that an excitation effect is thought to decay over time in the range of two to six weeks (Johnson 2008; Lewis et al. 2012; Short et al. 2009).

To assess the possibility of a copycat crime wave, a Poisson process helps to differentiate random from nonrandom crime sequences. For example, random rolls of a die would create clusters of similar numbers through a random Poisson process. Thus, a string of threes in rolls of a die would not be due to contagion (where a roll of a three would boost the likelihood of a following roll also being a three). However, given enough die rolls, long strings of threes, and of every other digit, would be statistically expected, but with longer sequences of the same outcome (threes, for example) becoming less probable, but not impossible, in a random set of die rolls. A noncopycat series can be mathematically and operationally defined as a Poisson process where the occurrence of a crime does not affect the appearance of the next similar crime; by definition, the observed crimes are independent of each other. In a Poisson process, crimes appear in a known average amount of time; for example, over a selected time period the average number of events that will happen is a known value—usually based on the overall mean of the data. Therefore, in a Poisson data series, a crime may occur immediately after another crime or there may be a long time lag between crimes due to their randomness. However, over a sufficient time frame, the crimes will appear on average at a known rate (i.e., a taxi robbery might occur an average of every four days in a hypothetical city's crime data). The empirical dilemma is how to decide if a cluster of events falls within reasonable random expectations or signals a non-Poisson dependent relationship between crimes, where an earlier crime raises the probability of a subsequent one. This decision is based on the probability of the observed clustering occurring within a longer sequence of truly random events. Putting this as an empirical question, one might ask what the probability is of eight taxi robberies occurring in two days in a city that averages a taxi robbery every four days. Box 4.1 provides an example.

Box 4.1   The Poisson Process and Crime Waves

In a randomly distributed set of crimes, the probability distribution of the waiting time between crimes is the expected number of similar crimes that occur per time unit. The null hypothesis is that crimes are independent, not copycats. The number of crimes occurring in any interval of time is therefore independent of the number of crimes occurring before or after. An example adapted from Stat Trek follows.[3]

Over a selected year, the average number of a type of crime is two crimes per day. What is the probability that three crimes will be committed tomorrow?

Poisson formula [$P(x; \mu) = (e^{-\mu}) (\mu^x) / x!$] (read as the probability of three crimes given an average of two crimes per day)

$\mu = 2$ (two crimes of this type are committed per day, on average)

$x = 3$ (we want to find the likelihood that three similar crimes will be committed tomorrow)

$e = 2.71828$ (the natural e constant reflects an exponential distribution)

Applying values to find the probability of $P(3; 2)$, or seeing three similar crimes in a day given that these crimes previously averaged two per day, results in a probability of .18. One can expect a day with three crimes about once every five days. Confidence that the number of similar crimes is unexpected and not a random Poisson distribution increases as the probability lessens. Applying the standard social science confidence level of .05 or less, in this example, having three crimes on one day is not rare enough to conclude a nonrandom distribution. However, a day with four similar crimes has a probability of .045 and suggests that something nonrandom is happening. A random five-crime day would be highly unusual, with a probability of .009, and would demand exploration for a nonrandom explanation.

A real-world application of the Poisson process is given by Hayes (2002) regarding the contagion of war. He assumed a null hypothesis that wars are independent, random events and that, in any given year, there is the same probability that war will break out. If wars are truly random, the average number of new wars per year should obey a Poisson distribution where each occurrence of war is unlikely. If p is the probability of a war starting over the course of a year, then the probability of seeing an observed number of wars in any year equals e^{-p} p^n/n! When p is small, most years will have no wars followed by years with a single war. As the number of wars (n) grows, the likelihood of a year having that number of wars declines steeply, so it would be extremely rare for ten wars to occur in the same year. Applying the Poisson formula, Hayes (2002) found that the presence of an ongoing war significantly increased the probability of another war starting; he concluded that unfortunately wars were contagious. More directly related to crime and in contrast, Torrecilla and colleagues (2019), however, did not find evidence of a copycat effect for intimate-partner homicides after a Poisson-based analysis of time series data on Spanish intimate partner homicides.

Most of the research on crime-related self-excitation processes looked at events that, unlike copycat crimes, are comparatively common, such as burglaries (Mohler et al. 2012), homicides (Cohen and Tita 1999), terror attacks (Lewis et al. 2012; Porter and White 2012), and gang violence (Egesdal et al. 2010). In this body of research, models with self-excitation factors tend to consistently outperform Poisson-based random models. Varied forms of self-excitation models have been explored, but zero inflation and hurdle models conceptually best fit the possibility of copycat crime. Developed by Porter and White (2012) and apt for copycat crimes, hurdle models are a type of self-excitation model for rare events. Empirically, a hurdle model data series is one in which most of the time the occurrence of a crime of interest is zero, and a "hurdle" must be overcome before the crime will occur. Once the hurdle is reached, the process will self-excite for a time before returning to its resting zero noncrime level.

Another self-excitation model that applies to copycat crime is a zero inflation model in which not only do the zeros, or nonevents, dominate the data series but a number of data zeros (or time points that do not report a copycat crime) observed in the data series are due to masked events (Famoye and Singh 2006; Lambert 1992). This is a plausible reality regarding copycat crimes for offenders who wish to remain hidden. For true, rare surreptitious crime that is not easily observed, zero inflation models are best as they assume some zero time points are due to unobserved masked events. For rare, easily observed copycat crime, which requires a threshold to trigger a contagious cluster, a hurdle model would be better.

Hurdle and zero inflation models present good approximations of a crime process that contains rare but periodic copycat crimes, and they supply an approach to test for the presence of crime outbursts (denoting possible copycat crimes) compared against the probability of a zero-crime count. An alternative to the self-excitation model suggested by Egesdal and colleagues (2010), an "agent-based model," allows including additional factors in the modeling. In their study of gang movement, new gang members, fights, and gang rivalry strength, the agent-based model performed similarly but slightly better than a self-excitation model for modeling gang violence. Agent-based models required more information concerning offenders but might be a possibility in the future as more information about copycat offenders becomes known (Ornstein and Hammond 2017). Unfortunately, crime wave analysis shares the interpretation issues found in the near-repeat research in that nonrandomness does not prove a copycat effect. As with geographic crime clusters, temporal crime waves can be due to both copycat effects and processes unrelated to copycat crime.

Conclusion

The copying of social behavior has been observed across a broad range of situations, and there is ample research evidence of imitation being a common human activity. Copycat crime is not reported to be a common offender experience but has been reported as an experience of a substantial proportion of offenders. Direct evidence of copycat crime is found in self-report offender surveys, but even though there is empirical evidence of crime clusters and crime waves being common, convincing evidence of a common copycat effect operating is not discernable in near-repeat and crime wave research. The possibility of imitation extending to media-linked crimes has not been empirically affirmed or discredited. Copycat crime as a common crime event is not suggested, however. Therefore, research into copycat crime requires a mixed-method approach. Empirical analysis of geographic and time series data can establish crimes that are linked but does not establish that they are linked via copycat effects. Only access to offenders can explore for copycat crime drives and mechanisms.

Claire Ferguson (2018) has argued that three conditions must exist to conclude valid copycat crimes. It must be established that different people are responsible for similar crimes, that an actual increase in crimes, and not simply an increase in reporting, has occurred, and that the copycat offender had knowledge of the original generator crime. The reality is that rigorous recognition and measurement of copycat crimes remains rare and is seldom present in copycat crime research. An additional anchor on copycat crime research is the lack of a theory of copycat crime. While the reviewed and detailed approaches support the plausibility of persistent copycat crimes and their importance, what is additionally needed to forward copycat crime research is to cull the five base theoretical areas for copycat crime insights and develop an inter-disciplinary perspective on the phenomena. Better theory is needed, and without it, copycat crime research will continue to lag. The first steps toward that goal are taken in Chapter 5.

Notes

1. The following discussion of scoring copycat crimes draws from Surette 2016b.

2. For examples of near-repeat research that examines violent crime, see Kissner 2016; Loeffler and Flaxman 2018; Ratcliffe and Rengert 2008; Wells, Wu, and Ye 2012; Youstin et al. 2011; Zhang et al. 2015.

3. "Poisson Distribution," Stat Trek, https://stattrek.com/probability-distributions/poisson.aspx.

5

Imitation, Contagion, Diffusion

HAVING ESTIMATED A PREVALENCE LEVEL FOR COPYCAT crime and reviewed the methodological issues connected to studying it, the five theoretical areas first introduced in Chapter 2 are applied to copycat crime in Chapters 5 and 6. The goal is to establish a theoretical foundation to guide a more rigorous study of copycat crime. Chapter 5 applies ideas from imitation, contagion, and diffusion theory to copycat crime. Chapter 6 applies social learning and media studies to copycat crime and then offers an interdisciplinary perspective that encompasses elements from the five foundational theories.

The Biology and Psychology of Copycat Crime

The mirror neuron system, described in Chapter 2 as a biological basis for the innate copying of behaviors, provides insights into the copying of crime. Mirror neuron dysfunction has been suggested as playing a role in criminal behavior and as an evolutionary foundation for the persistence of dysfunctional imitation, the copying of behaviors that have negative consequences for the imitator (Kasten 2020). As many copycat crimes result in arrest, injury, or social sanctions, why offenders persist in copying crimes that have predictably bad outcomes is an enigma. A biological mirror neuron system offers an explanation for imitation of dysfunctional behaviors that, from a purely Skinnerian view of punishment, should become extinct. The study of mirror neurons indicates that understanding actions and imitating actions are two different neurological tasks that are conducted independently (Carmo, Rumiati, and Vallesi 2012; Kasten 2020). A person can therefore imitate a behavior without understanding the consequences or impulsively imitate even when knowing that negative consequences are likely.

A behavior that is punishing for an individual persists because, for a biological response like imitation to be evolutionarily functional, all that is needed is for the majority of consequences to be positive—for the consequences across the general population to be beneficial compared to the consequences for the general population of not having imitation. For imitation to have an evolutionary advantage, copying by every individual does not have to be rewarded (Dijksterhuis and Bargh 2001). An analogous, purely genetic example would be the advantage for a population of maintaining cystic fibrosis genes, which are thought to provide resistance to cholera and tuberculosis but in a minority of individuals trigger a serious genetic illness (Bosch et al. 2017; Withrock et al. 2015). Thus, copying a crime may be dysfunctional for the individual offender, but the imitation of crime can persist because the benefit of imitation for the social functioning of the overall group remains strong. The broad benefits to a species from the ability to imitate outweigh the occasional negative consequences to individuals from copying crime.

Adding to a biological imitation drive, a psychological drive from priming appears to operate regarding copycat crime. For example, Allan Mazur (1982) reported that bomb threats directed at nuclear energy facilities increased significantly following increases in news coverage of nuclear power issues. Mazur's study is important in that it indicates that media content can generate crime even when the content does not provide explicit crime models to copy. In Mazur's study, the bomb threats to nuclear facilities increased following news stories that were not bomb related. Establishing that generator and copycat crimes need not closely resemble each other, Mazur (1982) concluded that the news media coverage primed some people to make bomb threats even though the coverage did not provide bomb-threat models. More recently, Kostinsky, Bixler, and Kettl (2001) and Simon (2007) reported analogous results for threats of school violence following the Columbine high school killings that were dominated by bomb threats, not acts of violence.

Other research suggests similar crime-priming dynamics are operating so that individuals with prior exposure to offenders, the criminal justice system, and crime-related media can be primed toward commit-

ting copycat but not identical crimes (Dijksterhuis et al. 2000; Dijksterhuis and Bargh 2001; Dijksterhuis et al. 2000). Also relevant for generating criminal behavior, Carlson, Marcus-Newhall, and Miller (1998),
in an early meta-analysis of the available research on priming, offered
empirical support for the priming of aggression via media cues. In their
review, the presence of a weapon in media content was identified as a
particularly powerful aggression prime and, akin to Mazur's 1982 finding, was connected with crime attitudes and behaviors not directly tied
to weapon possession (Carlson, Marcus-Newhall, and Miller 1998). In
this literature the media are seen as enablers of crime without explicitly modeling it. A crime is not necessarily directly copied, but the idea
of committing a crime is.

Similarly, imitation research is relevant for hypotheses concerning
both generating and preventing copycat crime by the media. Research on
role play by children indicates that the media immersion and copying of
criminal personae reported in several anecdotal copycat crime case studies appear to be an adult return to the childhood role-play state.[1] John
Hinckley Jr.'s assassination attempt on President Ronald Reagan and the
associated film *Taxi Driver* would be an example. In these cases, the
media provide the criminal roles the copiers assume (Wilson and Hunter
1983). Less engaging and having less immersion capability, anticrime
media efforts will unfortunately be less effective in preventing criminal
behavior than criminogenic content will be in stimulating it.

Research on imitation also established that copying behavior is
innate but is often inhibited in humans, so copycat crime needs explanations for both the copying of crime by a few and the lack of criminal
copying by most (Decety and Chaminade 2005; Kinsbourne 2005). The
biology and psychology of imitation indicate that exposure to crime
models will cause people to often physically and mentally set up to
copy a crime, but the suppression of automatic imitation means that
commission of a copycat crime will be rare and exhibited by only a
small number of uniquely situated, at-risk persons, a supposition supported by the copycat prevalence estimate of a self-reported copycat
crime history for about one in four inmates (Surette 2014).

Furthermore, by increasing the complexity and diversity of copycat
crimes, selective imitation impacts the reality of copycat crime. To utilize
selective imitation requires that copiers understand the causal relationships between behavioral steps, that they understand what each step
accomplishes, and that they see what steps can be omitted (Harris and
Want 2005). The less understanding there is about the causal connections

between the modeled behavior steps, the less selective imitation can be invoked, and the more rote the imitation process becomes. The more causal understanding is present, the more effective selective imitation can be for attaining the goal of the model without rote mimicking of the model's behavior (Whiten, Horner, and Marshall-Pescini 2005). Both rote and selective imitation apply to copycat crime, where one can find crimes that are rote copies, such as suicide bombings, or selective copies, like varied Ponzi schemes. Lastly, imitation research indicates that crimino-genic media that show errors and copying failures but include content on how to avoid them will induce strong imitation effects. If potential copy-cat offenders derive lessons from generator crimes on how to eliminate the errors they observe, the likely copying of media-modeled crimes should be significantly enhanced (Ramsland 2013).

Together, mirror neurons provide a biological mechanism for the imitation of media-portrayed crime, with role play, selective imitation, and a theory of mind providing psychological processes to cognitively incorporate, refine, and sometimes attempt the crime. Basic research on imitation provides biological and psychological concepts and processes for understanding how copycat crime might originate. Understanding copycat crime and the broad social processes involved, however, requires a more pointed focus on criminal imitation, the roots of which originated in the work of Gabriel Tarde in the late nineteenth century (Tosti 1897). A narrow, more specific, and more directly applicable copycat crime research question asks how the imitation of criminal behavior arises.

Gabriel Tarde—the Father of Copycat Crime

Study of the imitation of crime begins in the late 1800s with the writ-ings of Gabriel Tarde, who summarized his thoughts on crime imitation with the statement "Infectious epidemics spread with the air or the wind; epidemics of crime follow the line of the telegraph" (Tarde [1912] 1968, 340).[2] A number of copycat crime waves, such as dual gar-roting panics in London and Boston in the 1860s (Adler 1996; Davis 1980; Sindall 1987), established the phenomena and preceded Tarde's writings. With a preexisting accommodating cultural setting, Gabriel Tarde coined the term *suggesto-imitative assaults* and was the first criminologist to offer an explanation of crime in terms of normal learn-ing, employing imitation as his main crime engine. Tarde perceived two types of imitation, each associated with characteristics of their home cultures (Curtis 1953). The first type, custom imitation, is found in societies where older established ways of doing things reign. In a custom-dominated culture, people imitate the past. The second type, fashion imitation, emphasizes copying new, exotic behaviors, and past behaviors are easily abandoned. Both cultures change via imitation, slowly in a custom-dominated culture, quickly in a fashion-driven one. What they shared in Tarde's view was that, in both, individuals had to decide whether to imitate new behaviors. When adopted imitated behaviors are socially beneficial, society advances; when the imitated behaviors are negative, such as when crime is copied, society degrades. For Tarde, the aggregation of society's individual imitation decisions determines whether crime waves develop.

In his writings, Gabriel Tarde provided a number of specific examples of eighteenth-century imitative crime. In addition to the infamous set of murders by Jack the Ripper, which he linked as copycat-generator crimes to homicides in England, Europe, and America (see Chapter 1), among the crimes and vices he cited as imitative were drunkenness, smoking, poaching, poisoning, vagabondage, irreligiousness, and arson. Tarde ([1912] 1968, 278) clearly felt that copycat crime was a common criminal mechanism and phenomenon: "The criminal always imitates somebody, even when he originates; that is to say, when he uses in combination imitations obtained from various sources. He always needs to be encouraged by the example and approval of a group of men." Tarde ([1912] 1968, 340) also saw females as prone to copying violent crimes:

> In 1881, a young actress, Clotilde J____, threw vitriol over her lover, at Nice. When she was asked at what time she first thought of avenging herself, "since the day," she replied, "when I read in a Paris newspaper an article dealing with the revenge of women[."] . . . Another instrument of feminine hatred is the revolver; its use in a much talked of case in Paris was very soon followed by a similar shot at Auxerre. In 1825, in Paris, Henriette Cornier cruelly put to death a child of which she had the care; not long afterwards, other children's nurses yielded, for no other reason than this, to an irresistible desire to cut the throats of their employers' children.

In Gabriel Tarde's worldview, copycat crime made up the bulk of crime; noncopycat, newly invented crimes were rare.

In addition to making imitation the central dynamic in the generation of crime, Gabriel Tarde was also the first criminologist to see the media as a significant source of crime ideas. In Tarde's writings, the media came into play through the concept of publics, which he opposed to crowds (Turner 1964). Tarde argued that crowds, which he perceived negatively, were an ancient form of human association, but a public, which had positive social potential, was a product of modern media. As a public's members are geographically dispersed and connected only through shared ideas, public awareness could only be achieved after the emergence of new nineteenth-century media and transportation technology. For Tarde ([1901] 1969, 278), publics were the result of the printing press, the railroad, and the telegraph:

> The strange thing about it is that these men who are swept along in this way, who persuade each other, or rather who transmit to one another suggestions from above—these men do not come in contact, do not meet or hear each other; they are all sitting in their own homes scattered over a vast territory, reading the same newspaper. What is the bond between them? This bond lies in their simultaneous conviction or passions and in their awareness of sharing at the same time an idea or a wish with a great number of other men.

When he applied his ideas about media and publics to crime, Tarde saw copycat crime as spreading downward and outward. Describing societies as undergoing waves of imitations, continually launched and spreading out through the population, Tarde saw the waves interfere with, merge into, and cancel one another as they propagated.

Tarde thus described crime as originating from a generator crime, which was encouraged in the media and spread through imitation. According to Tarde, imitation followed three social laws, two of which are relevant for copycat crime.[3] His first law of imitation is similar to Edwin Sutherland's later concept of differential association: people imitate one another in proportion to how much close contact they have with one another. Cities increase imitation by crowding people together, whereas in rural areas, contact is less common, imitation of new behaviors is less frequent, and established customs dominate (Vine 1973). Tarde's second law of imitation is that inferiors imitate superiors. Tarde argued that the propagation of behaviors from the higher to the lower classes in society is found in every cultural area: language, philosophy, fashion, ideas, values, and desires. Tarde ([1912] 1968, 331) states, "Strange as it may seem, there are serious reasons for maintaining that the vices and the crimes of today, which are to be found in the lowest orders of the people, descended to them from above." Tarde believed that crime waves originate in urban upper classes and migrate via imitation downward to the lower classes and outward to rural areas. Regarding an upper- to lower-class imitation flow, in Tarde's words ([1912] 1968, 338), "While crime formerly spread, like every industrial product, like every good or bad idea, from the nobility to the people . . . today we can see crime spreading from the great cities to the country, from the capitals to the provinces." In sum, Tarde saw new crimes as beginning as urban fashions and, as societies evolved, eventually becoming rural customs (Vine 1973).

Tarde recognized the dilemma of applying the same dynamics to both positive and negative social behaviors. Although he argued that both are acquired via imitation because crime is antisocial behavior, he reasoned that copying crime was different from imitating law-abiding behaviors. Demonstrating a modern insight for a nineteenth-century theorist, while he saw crime, like other social behavior, as learned, Tarde believed crime was learned through interaction with deviant friends and required a criminogenic social environment to flourish.

> The majority of murderers and notorious thieves began as children who have been abandoned, and the true seminary of crime must be sought for upon each public square or each crossroad of our towns, whether they be small or large, in those flocks of pillaging street urchins, who, like bands of sparrows, associate together, at first for marauding, and then for theft, because of a lack of education and food in their home. . . . [A] child who was the most normally constituted . . . [is more] influenced by half a score of perverse friends by whom he is surrounded than by millions of unknown fellow citizens. (Tarde [1912] 1968, 252–253)

In answer to the question of why some commit crime and others do not, despite similar exposures to criminogenic models and environments, Tarde advanced, but did not define, psychological predispositions as accounting for differences. For example, he described those with "vicious dispositions" as more likely to become violent, and he employed other vague terms, like "a special kind of fever," "a fermentation," "an agitation," and "a disturbance," to describe these predispositions (Tarde [1912] 1968, 261).[4]

In the end, Gabriel Tarde's most important contribution was the introduction of the idea of copycat crime to criminology; he described the phenomenon and set the stage for the later serious study of media and crime—which did not happen for more than half a century. Part of the reason for the delay was that, while descriptive and compelling, his writings did not develop a testable theoretical model and instead forwarded a simplistic social system built on his ambiguous definition of imitation (Curtis 1953; Vine 1973). He also wrote in a time when media were solely print based, barely qualified as mass media, and were limited to the literate.

Criminology, media, and imitation therefore went in different directions in the early twentieth century and did not reunite until the 1950s. While imitative crime was widely accepted by the public in the nineteenth and twentieth centuries, the media as an imitation source for crime was not seriously considered in criminology until the emergence of commercial television networks in the 1950s. The work of Gabriel Tarde provided the foundation for the contemporary study of media-sourced copycat crime, but in criminology the study of crime imitation looked at direct interpersonal contacts and focused on peer-to-peer imitation in delinquency. The early impacts of Tarde's nineteenth-century ideas about copycat crime were connected to the publicly accepted views that imitation was a widespread social process applicable to a broad range of social behaviors, that imitation of crime was common, and that the media play important roles. However, in criminology the role of media-based crime models was seen as minor, and Tarde's nineteenth-century considerations of copycat crime were abandoned. The study of imitation was instead taken up in psychology in the early twentieth century (Surette 2015b). During this period of criminological disinterest, the study of copycat crime was kept alive in research on social contagion.

The Social Contagion of Crime

The early interest in imitation and the spread of crime led to the question of whether crime is as contagious as law-abiding behaviors. As nineteenth-century sociologist James Baldwin (1899, 537–538) stated, the social contagion of crime has been long argued: "Discrepancy between the social 'ought' and the social 'is' is found in the phenomenon of contagion of crime [and] . . . there are epidemics of crime of this sort or that. A suggestion of a criminal sort will spread through a community; and a sensational story will excite the readers, both young and old, to perform the crimes with which the narrative concerns itself." As discussed in Chapter 2, there was much interest in contagious behavior in the late 1800s by the public and academics.

Research on contagion in the first half of the twentieth century focused both on large, violent crowd actions and on small-group dynamics. Allport (1924), Blumer (1939), and Park (1904) focused on large, violent crowds; Miller and Dollard (1941) and Sherif (1936) researched contagion in small groups.

Research on the underlying mechanisms that drive criminal contagion, however, did not begin until Fritz Redl (1949) applied a Freudian-based "latent tendencies" perspective to conduct a study on the processes of criminal contagion. Redl examined spontaneous deviant imitation among small groups of juveniles. His study came to be criticized along methodological lines, however, and little empirical support for the widespread contagion of crime followed. Research on the contagion of crime continued to focus on volatile crowds and terrorism (Holden 1986; Loftin 1986; Poland 1988; Tuman 2010; Turner 1964). Two separate contagion mechanisms applicable to crime have been subsequently studied but have received limited empirical support.

The first contagion mechanism, approach/restraint conflict, states that for social contagion to occur, tension between copying (or approaching) the modeled behavior and restraining (not copying) it must be resolved by each individual (Freedman 1982). The desire to copy behavior, driven by material benefits, peer status, or psychological rewards, must outweigh the avoidance forces that hold one back from committing the behavior—potential punishment or public shame, for example (Diener et al. 1976). Thus, looting an electronics store would be desirable (approached) due to the tangible products gained or avoided (restrained) due to the potential for arrest. For individual copycat offenders, the contagious crime model can both demonstrate the reward of performing a behavior, thereby making approaching and committing a crime greater ("he's running away with a new smart phone"), and reduce copier responsibility, guilt, or expectation of harm from copying a crime, thereby weakening the strength of prior restraints against the crime ("and no one is stopping him") (Levy and Nail 1993). The lowering of restraining forces and attitudes is seen as essential for the contagion of illegal behavior, as their removal will allow the immediate tangible rewards from copying a crime to ascend.

The second contagion mechanism applicable to copycat crime, deindividuation, operates as an additional contagion driver that weakens restraints on copying crime. Deindividuation occurs when an individual is able to hide within a crowd where the accompanying anonymity lowers normal restraints against criminal behaviors and reduces concern over arrest (Wheeler 1966; see also Festinger, Pepitone, and Newcomb 1952). Research support for the significance of deindividuation for criminal behavior contagion is provided by Edward Diener and colleagues (1976), who reported the results of a unique field experiment. The Diener research group found evidence that deindividuation supported increased contagious copycat stealing of Halloween candy by juveniles. In the small groups studied, the contagion of stealing increased in a group where individual identities of the group members were unknown. In their field research setting, the direct observation of a modeled successful crime (the first child in the group steals candy) was noted by other juveniles. Youth in each group were then given an unmonitored opportunity to steal candy in a setting where a smallest and youngest child had been purposely chosen and assigned responsibility for the behavior of the entire group. Examination of group dynamics in this scenario led the researchers to the conclusion that criminal contagion was the result of not just a single factor but the interaction of multiple ones. According to Diener and colleagues, anonymity was important (the names of the group members were unknown to one another), as was membership in a group where others first modeled theft and the placement of a young, uninfluential child in charge of the group reduced authority control. Deindividuation remained crucial for individual deviant acts though, as copycat theft fell significantly when individual names were known but the other crime-encouraging factors remained.

Unfortunately, despite this early interesting research, there were no subsequent studies with a media element included in the deindividuation research, and until recently little research has incorporated the media in a study of criminal contagion (Levy and Nail 1993). Instead, the nonmedia focus on face-to-face interactions remained the primary contagion force researched. Interpersonal contact was seen to help contagiously distribute information on how to behave as well as to lower uncertainty about the consequences of copying a new behavior. A media role was not needed and subsequently not studied.

In contrast, the current omnipresence of social media is thought to eliminate the need for face-to-face contact with criminogenic models while simultaneously maximizing deindividuation (Surette 2017). One can google how to make a bomb and download detailed directions, and both the source models and copycat criminals can retain their anonymity. Social media has supplanted the need for face-to-face model-to-copier communication and undercuts much of the direct social interactions forwarded as necessary for copycat crime in the contagion research. Despite this shift in media capabilities, the contagion of crime has continued to be largely studied without the media included as a factor. Instead the research has focused on peer-to-peer co-offending under the approach/restraint conflict perspective.

In a review of the literature on co-offending, Albert Reiss (1988), for example, did not directly examine copycat crime or include the media but did find support for crime modeling and contagion at the individual peer-to-peer level. A twenty-first-century example of this type of contagion research is provided by Jens Ludwig and Jeffrey Kling (2007), who employed crime mapping in a "dose exposure" medical model conceptualization, where exposure to more doses of a disease heightens the infection rate. In their contagion-of-crime study, crimes are seen as resulting from contact between infected offenders and uninfected individuals. Invoking the approach/restraint concept, they argue that local crime prevalence may change an individual's propensity to engage in crime behavior by reducing the social stigma associated with crime, increasing expectations about the rewards from crime, and reducing constraints against crime by lowering the perceived probability of arrest. While well conceptualized, the Ludwig and Kling (2007) study was unable to detect empirical evidence in support of the contagion of crime. Despite this and other failures to empirically establish significant crime contagion effects, belief in the contagion of crime remains strong. For example, in the 1980s a well-known, frequently cited essay, "Broken Windows," by James Q. Wilson and George Kelling (1982), inferred a contagion process in neighborhood deterioration, vandalism, and rising crime rates. The crux of their argument was that visible signs of a lack of informal neighborhood surveillance and collective ownership of public spaces signaled the absence of restraints against crime. A disheveled neighborhood was a neighborhood open to criminal contagion.

Faced with weak empirical support, contagion-of-crime researchers only recently expanded the view of crime contagion to include a media role while continuing to perceive contagion through a medical transmission lens (Ugander et al. 2012). The contemporary perception is that criminal violence is contagious and spreads in a disease-like dose-level exposure process in which the media can be contagion vectors that distribute infectious doses of crime. In this perspective the time between exposure and outbreaks of infections can be years (Patel, Simon, and Taylor 2013). Violent crime is currently thought to be contagious through either direct victimization or through the witnessing of violence in the media or in real life. Media have come to be seen as significant sources of crime contagion "doses," setting the level of exposure to contagious criminal behavior in a society in interaction with other social and individual factors. In the crime contagion perspective, crime became one more contagious behavioral disease that can be caught directly from an individual carrier or indirectly from infectious media models (Jones 1998).

Specific examples of copycat crime contagion research in this media-inclusive tradition include Berkowitz and Macaulay (1971), who cite the 1966 mass homicides by Richard Speck and the 1963 John F. Kennedy assassination as generator crimes. Berkowitz and Macaulay concluded that coverage of both crimes was followed by unusual increases in the number of robberies and assaults, which they interpreted as a contagion-of-criminal-violence effect. They speculated that perception of a crime's "wrongness" suppressed or insulated against copycats for a brief period immediately following the generator crimes, but eventually contagion effects rose to the level that the sensational crimes elicited aggressive social reactions by reducing social restraints against violence (Berkowitz and Macaulay 1971). Berkowitz and Macaulay (1971, 259–260) conclude, "Our thesis does not maintain that most violent crimes are instigated by news reports in the mass media. Other determinants are more important. Contagious influences operate on top of these other determinants, and probably in conjunction with several of them." This media-based contagion of crime was seen as an exacerbating factor that came into play after other more basic social forces had created a pool of potential copiers. The perception of the media as an impetus added after other causes remains the consensus view (Surette 2015a).

More recently, analysis of time series crime data has reported empirical evidence of contagion within studies of gun violence.[5] In an oft-cited 2015 study, Sherry Towers and colleagues report empirical support for the contagion of mass and school shootings. Applying a self-excitation contagion model, Towers and colleagues report that mass killings involving firearms are encouraged by the presence of similar events in the immediate past. Their analysis found that each prior mass shooting incited .3 additional mass shootings, and each school shooting incited .22 new school shootings. Both effects were statistically significant and were active for an average of thirteen days. Along the same lines, Kissner (2016) explored the contagion of active shooter events and concluded that a significant factor driving copying was offender competition with earlier events (who had killed the most people, for example). Kissner found the presence of an active shooter within the prior two weeks to be a significant predictor of a subsequent shooting. He concluded that mass shootings arrive in contagious micro-bursts.

In contrast, Torrecilla and colleagues (2019) did not find evidence of a copycat crime effect concerning intimate partner homicides in an analysis of recent Spanish data. In their study, the occurrence of an intimate partner homicide did not predict the occurrence of a subsequent homicide. Additional research by Fox and colleagues (2021), King and Jacobson (2017), and Lankford and Tomek (2018) did not report a contagion effect for gun violence. Surprisingly, one study suggests that it may be less crime that is contagious. Wyant and colleagues (2012) reported a contagious deterrent effect following the arrest of a shooter.

The contagion of homicides has been researched from a near-repeat perspective by Jacqueline Cohen and George Tita (1999). In their study, contagion is seen as one aspect of a more general diffusion process. Cohen and Tita saw two types of diffusion: contagious diffusion and hierarchical diffusion. Contagious diffusion reflects the physical proximity between adjoining geographic areas, while hierarchical diffusion spreads broadly through commonly shared influences (shared social conditions that independently arise in different locales or cultural mechanisms such as media influences). Cohen and Tita (1999) also saw two subtypes of contagious diffusion. One is "relocation diffusion," where a phenomenon spreads outward from a point (a forest fire or crime displaced by surveillance cameras, for example), thereafter declining at the original point of origin (the forest fire goes out after burning up its initial fuel, and crime falls in front of the surveillance cameras as offenders move to new areas). In their second type of contagion diffusion, expansion diffusion, after a phenomenon diffuses, the central origin point continues to experience high incidence rates (crime continues in the original location; gang turf battles and open-air drug markets are examples).

For Cohen and Tita, contagious diffusion depends on direct contact in the manner of the classic medical model of disease contagion. In contrast, they also explore hierarchical diffusion, which reflects Tarde's laws of imitation from higher to lower social groups or larger to smaller communities; this form of diffusion does not require direct physical contact but occurs through adoption of similar criminal behaviors in reaction to similar environments or through the imitation of media crime models. Cohen and Tita cite urban youth gangs adopting lifestyles portrayed in the media and the spread of gang fashions as support for a media role. In this conceptualization, hierarchical diffusion is analogous to media copycat-generator crimes. Cohen and Tita interpreted changes in crime in geographic areas that physically abut as due to traditional, direct peer-to-peer contagious diffusion. In areas that do not touch, they credited crime change to hierarchical diffusion operating through media channels. Relevant for copycat crime and social media, Cohen and Tita report an important role for hierarchical contagion in homicide and thereby in media-linked copycat crime. Reflecting the limitations of near-repeat crime research, their findings do not provide direct evidence of copycat crime but only suggest the existence of media-linked crime without establishing the linking mechanism. Nevertheless, their results led them to the hypothesis that as media increases in social significance and pervasiveness, physical contact between individuals will become less important.

Another crime-related research area where the idea of contagion has been commonly applied is terrorism (Fagan, Wilkinson, and Davies 2006; Jeter 2014). Brigitte Nacos (2009), for example, discussed the contagion of terrorism and offers as evidence of contagion the clustering of terrorist attacks, reporting that it is more common for terrorism contagion to involve spread of a specific technique or strategy rather than a motivation for terrorism. Tactical terrorist crime waves are seen as developing when one terrorist group has success with a new tactic, and the contagion of this tactical behavior spreads with the expectation that other targets will be equally vulnerable (Nacos 2009). Copycat suicide bombing campaigns provide ongoing real-world examples.

A parallel set of research on contagion of collective behavior examined deviant fads (Miller 2000). Unlike short-term collective acts like crowd actions, fads involve sequential behavior over significant time periods. Crime fads are, in essence, copycat crime waves and share with noncrime fads a similar natural history of emergence, growth, peak, and decline (Surette 2020a). Studied crime waves include outbreaks of vandalism (Caplovitz and Rogers 1961; Ehrlich 1962), recreational cocaine use (Brownstein, Fatton, and Fox 1996), terrorist beheadings (Friis 2015; Lentini and Bakashmar 2007), and suicide bombings (Asad 2007). Reflecting a historical focus on rare crimes, violent crime fads have usually been the subject of study (Davis 1980; Sindall 1987). A well-researched example of crime contagion involving vandalism through the graffitiing of swastikas is provided in Box 5.1.

Box 5.1   Swastika USA

On Christmas Eve 1959, a swastika was painted on a synagogue in Cologne, Germany (Caplovitz and Rogers 1961). Following reports in the US news, over the following nine weeks, swastikas were painted on properties across the nation; 643 incidents were reported to the police. As graphed below, the crimes were distributed in a typical contagion cycle, rapidly increasing to a peak followed by a slow decline and final dissipation.

Figure 5.1   US Swastika Vandalism Incidents per Week

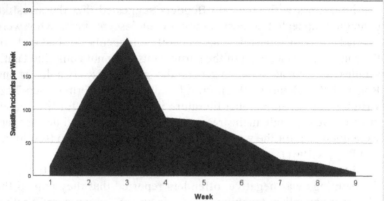

Figure 5.2   US Swastika Incidents Cumulative Weekly Total

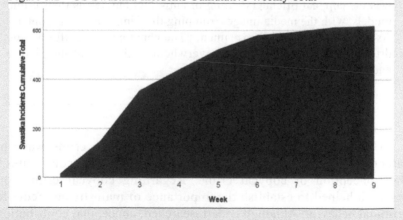

continues

Box 5.1   Continued

Examination of the individual crimes revealed that they were evenly divided between Jewish (320) and non-Jewish (323) targets and that two-thirds consisted of only painting a swastika (Caplovitz and Rogers 1961). Reflecting the importance of a preexisting pool of potential copycats, community crime rates were predictive of the number of swastikas that appeared (Ehrlich 1962). The swastika contagion also followed Tarde's urban-to-rural imitation law, with the copycat swastika wave appearing first and strongest in larger cities, followed by smaller communities (Ehrlich 1962, 266).

Interviews with copycat offenders suggested that the swastika contagion appealed almost solely to adolescent boys who were divided between antisemitic and general delinquents. At the height of the contagion cycle, most of the participants were not committed antisemites but were acting upon general deviant impulses (Caplovitz and Rogers 1961; Deutsch 1962). Print literature in the form of neo-Nazi writings and organizational literature was influential for the antisemitic copycats, while mainstream television, movies, and newspapers were important for the weakly motivated delinquent group (Caplovitz and Rogers 1961).

Even though much of the news coverage about the swastika graffiti paintings was negative, offenders reported that they copied the idea as a vandalism technique ("here is an act we can copy") rather than as a source of motivation ("we should be antisemitic"). Of note was the copycat offenders' citing of anti-Nazi movies as their crime models, with the media images trumping the films' anti-Nazi content. As Deutsch (1962, 115) explained, "The chanting, the uniforms, the drums, and unity of movement overwhelmed the rest of the picture and its message."

Despite a focus on crowds and on what sets a crime wave off rather than how it spreads, contagion-of-crime research contributes to the conception of copycat crime. Regarding copycat crime, this research helped to establish the importance of mainstream media for criminal behavior. Although underresearched, conceptual contributions include two individual-level mechanisms for the emergence of copycat crime: an approach/restraint conflict resolution and the presence of deindividuation within a crowd. It also established crime contagion as nonlinear and inherently unpredictable. Although inferred in some of the results, the inability to clearly distinguish copycat effects from other non-copycat cluster mechanisms remains buried in this research. In much of this research, the research subjects may be committing similar crimes but not because they are copying prior crimes. To obtain a better handle on copycat crime, we must ask a question originally raised but not addressed by Tarde: How do new criminal behaviors diffuse through society?

Diffusion of Innovations and Copycat Crime

Although not particularly interested in crime, diffusion theorists provide many insights regarding the likely characteristics of generator crimes, the adoption process that copycat crime offenders undergo, the social settings that encourage copycat crime, and, along with contagion theory, the dynamics of copycat crime waves. Diffusion theory is most useful when applied to innovative copycat crimes, as diffusion research focuses on the spread of innovations. Diffusion best explains copycat crimes where the generator crimes model new ways for committing crime rather than the sudden clustering of known crime techniques like mass school shootings. The spread and adoption of innovative copycat crimes align well with the concepts found in diffusion theory.

Regarding the qualities of a successfully copied generator crime, a beginning but questionable premise is that generator crimes will mirror the characteristics of other types of successful innovations. If strictly applied, diffusion theory says that generator crimes that possess the characteristics of increased relative advantage and compatibility, observability, trialability, and reduced complexity should be copied more often than crimes that do not (see Chapter 2). Of these characteristics, relative advantage is the most pertinent for copycat crime. Generator crimes that look to be improvements over prior crime techniques should logically be copied more than ones that do not.

It is important to note that the perception of the value of an innovative crime's characteristics may differ from its actual value, so an ineffective generator crime might be copied due to the mistaken assignment of positive attributes by copycat offenders. Offenders may therefore adopt a media-portrayed crime believing that it gives them an advantage against arrest when it does not. In the diffusion literature, this is described as overadoption, where an innovation is adopted to the

detriment of its adopters (Rogers 2003). Overadoption of a crime innovation likely occurs because a crime's relative advantage is commonly
assessed as a reduction in the risk of arrest, but a generator crime's perceived relative advantage can also be a gain in social status or visibility.
Therefore, less effective but more spectacular means of committing a
crime would translate into a relative advantage for some copycat
offenders. An innovative crime technique can also deliver other benefits
such as money, goods, and excitement. Some crimes are copied not
because they lessen the likelihood of arrest and capture but because they
raise the likelihood of fame, social impact, or excitement. This appears
to be particularly true for terrorist media-oriented crimes and mass
shootings (Langman 2018; Lankford 2016, 2021; Lankford and Tomek
2018; Surette, Hansen, and Noble 2009; Surette 2015a).

Along these lines, Everett Rogers (2003) identified a unique group of
innovations, termed *preventive innovations*, aimed at lowering the probability of some unwanted future event, such as changing one's diet to prevent a future heart attack. In the criminal justice field, innovative law
enforcement policies can be perceived as deterrent-aimed preventive
innovations aimed at reducing crime. For copycat crime and offenders,
preventive innovations to avoid detection and arrest are expected to have
slower rates of adoption than innovative crimes because the negative
effects being prevented tend to be distant in time, and the rewards from
avoiding those negative effects are often delayed. In other words, the benefits of not committing a crime can be uncertain and distant, while punishment for committing a crime is often mitigated or evaded. The reality
is that crime often does pay in the short term, so for career offenders, not
copying a crime weakly competes with the not-guaranteed distant benefits of obeying the law.

Concerning the applicability of the other characteristics of successful diffused social innovations to crime, compatibility is expected to play
conflicting roles. Encouraging copycat crime, increased compatibility
with preexisting social norms can increase copying. Media content can
simultaneously provide how-to instructions and forward new social values, which increase tolerance for criminality. Conversely, sometimes
crime innovations are desirable because they are incompatible with the
past. Where crime is motivated in part by a desire to bring about social
change, a crime innovation may become popular because it directly challenges existing norms. In these circumstances, crime innovations are
copied due to their low compatibility with past practices (Rogers 2003).

Flexible and more widely applicable generator crimes should diffuse
faster than narrow crime types requiring rigid crime techniques. A tech-

nique for hacking a specific computer model based on a unique design vulnerability, for example, will generate fewer copycat crimes than a general hacking technique that can be utilized to compromise multiple machines. The characteristic of trialability of a new crime technique that can be practiced beforehand, such as a technique for identifying and getting potential victims into position to be victimized prior to robbing, raping, kidnapping, or assaulting them, would increase the copying of innovative generator crimes. Media renditions of successful crimes may also function for copycat crime as the equivalent of trialability. Media attention can raise an innovative crime's observability and increase copycat crime by publicizing successful generator crimes and functioning as a high-visibility cue to action (Rogers 2003). For copycat crime, a cue to action would be an event that generates favorable attitudes toward a type of crime and can be as simple as a news report of a successful crime that encourages potential but undecided copiers to act. When potential copycat offenders can see criminal success by others who have copied an innovative generator crime (noting that success in some cases can simply be the media attention), diffusion-based copying of crime will be enhanced.

A significant caveat for the direct application of diffusion research findings to crime exists though. While the above conclusions appear reasonable based on research on the diffusion of legal behaviors, diffusion research on copycat crime is sparse, and the results may not translate unaltered to copycat crime. For example, the existence of passive copycat rejecters (those who have absorbed criminogenic knowledge but never consider copying), active copycat rejecters (those who seriously consider copying but do not attempt it), and copycat adopters (those who become copycat offenders) can be inferred from the diffusion research, but comparative research on differences between the three groups has not been pursued.

As described in detail in Chapter 2, the five types of adopters, categorized according to when they adopt an innovation, reflect how quickly different individuals commit to attempting a copycat crime. Adopters with high levels of criminal innovativeness copy crime early; those with low levels adopt late or never. Cautiously extrapolating the diffusion research findings to copycat crime leads to the expectation that first-wave copycats (innovators and early adopters in diffusion terminology) will significantly differ from second- and subsequent-wave copycats (diffusion's early majority, late majority, and laggards). Rogers (2003) saw those who decide to copy early as dealing better with uncertainty, a trait obviously useful when committing crime. Also pertinent for the diffusion of negative innovations like crime, the additional characteristics of gullibility for early adopters and astuteness for early rejectors has been forwarded (Bandura 2001).

As the launchers of a copycat crime wave, criminal innovators and early adopters appear most relevant for understanding copycat crime, as they theoretically would be most attuned to generator crimes and pay closer attention to innovative crime techniques. Concerning media effects, Rogers (2003) argued that the media are more important for earlier adopters (first wave copycats) than for later adopters (second and ensuing copycat waves) because at the time the early adopters copied a crime, there would be few peers available for comparison, and observable consequences from copying would not be widely known. These would be the first individuals to copy a crime and hence provide examples of how wise that decision was.

From a copycat crime perspective, an innovation equals a generator crime, and first-wave copycat offenders would be Rogers's innovator adopters. The early adopters through laggards would be new imitators. Applying Rogers's adopter groups, the total of first-wave copycat crimes would be committed by both innovators and imitators. The difference between innovators and imitators would be their source of copycat influence: innovators would be responding to innovative generator crimes; imitators would be responding to observing the innovators. Adam Lankford (2021) notes an analogous innovator and imitator distinction in his case study of two killers of police officers. Generally, innovators are media-driven copycat offenders who are strongly influenced by exposure to prior crimes. Imitators are copycat offenders who are responding to a mix of the actions of the copycat innovators and the media-distributed generator crime. With innovators and imitators in mind, two critical time stages in diffusion life cycles are found. One is the time between the beginning of the copycat crime adoption process, which is set by the number of innovative copycat-generator crime models available, and the diffusion takeoff point when copycat imitator copiers begin to rapidly increase. The second critical stage is when the previously innovative generator crime begins to lose its relative advantage (Peres, Muller, and Mahajan 2010).

For copycat crime, the first stage refers to when the potential criminal innovators initially available in a society begin to copy the generator crime and ends at the point when imitation of the new innovative crime begins to grow quickly. In the second stage, the point when the innovative crime begins to be replaced by newer crime types or techniques marks the beginning of the end of a copycat adoption cycle. For copycat crime, innovators would start with the crime models in the media-portrayed generator crimes and include those who copy those crime innovation models, while the crime imitators would be the offenders who copied only after seeing the consequences for the innovators. In the copycat crime diffusion process, therefore, the importance of innovators will be greater at the beginning of the diffusion time span but will diminish over time as more observable results from copying accrue. Both are strongly influenced by cultural factors (Bass 1969). In the diffusion research, mass media's influence concentrates early in the cycle when there are few who have direct experience with the innovation or the consequences of copying. When extended to crime, the Bass model literature predicts that potential copiers who prefer crime media will be more likely to be copycat crime adopters and will do so earlier in the crime diffusion process (Bass, Krishnan, and Jain 1994; Mahajan, Muller, and Bass 1995).

Beyond an innovative crime's characteristics, when the decision to copy occurs, for a diffusion of crime to take hold, communication channels must distribute information on how to commit the crime, morally justify committing it, and influence a potential copycat offender's calculation of the odds of detection and arrest (Baker and Faulkner 2003). The diffusion literature says little about the media and has traditionally researched interpersonal communication networks while acknowledging but minimizing media's role. Rogers (2003), for example, suggests that a media-based communication campaign might increase knowledge in a third of an audience while influencing only 3 percent to adopt. If these percentages are correct and hold for copycat crime, the one-third of the audience showing an increase in knowledge will include both active and passive copycat rejecters (potential copycat offenders who do not seriously consider copying a crime and those who actively weigh but reject copying the generator crime), as well as a small number of actual copycat offenders. In line with the other theoretical perspectives, diffusion research suggests that many learn how to commit a crime but few go on to actually do so. Thus, many video game players can play violent video games while few emulate the criminal acts they repeatedly commit virtually (Ferguson 2015).

Research on the diffusion of positive innovations also indicates that media channels will usually be more rapid and efficient for distribution of crime knowledge, but interpersonal channels will be more effective in persuading copying decisions. If copycat crime diffusion follows a similar pattern, the media would increase knowledge of a criminal innovation, while peers and local face-to-face networks would persuade copycat adoptions. Due to pervasive crime content, however, exposure to media is hypothesized to more often encourage crime adoptions than interpersonal face-to-face networks (Surette 2015a). For positive social innovations, peers are important for later adopters by providing a two-way exchange of information; social media, though, may be decreasing the impact of face-to-face communications (Rogers 2003, citing Valente and Saba 1998). Such a shift has implications for copycat crime. Terrorist recruitment of juveniles via social media, for example, provides an example of social media functioning as an alternative to face-to-face persuasion. Cross-culturally, this suggests that in developing countries, interpersonal networks should dominate the copycat crime process; in developed countries, social media networks should be more important.

Timing is central to diffusion theory, and success is often determined by how quickly they diffuse. Regarding copycat crime, the first time-based diffusion decision translates into how quickly a potential copycat offender reaches a decision to copy or not. The steps laid out for reaching a decision in the diffusion literature transpose well to copycat crime. The five diffusion steps become gaining knowledge of the generator crime, being persuaded that copying the crime is a good idea, deciding to copy the crime at some future point, attempting to copy the crime, and assessing the results from copying the crime. How quickly these steps are traversed and the decision to copy or not copy a crime is reached determines the copycat crime time span for individuals. All five steps can occur quickly (a viewer watching the news sees someone in another city ignite a car, decides this is a good idea, and within minutes ignites a nearby car) or over an extended period (an offender spends years culling the media for information on Ponzi schemes before attempting one).

Another diffusion time question looks not at individual decisions but at the aggregate rate of copying over time. Crime innovations need not necessarily follow the S-shaped adoption rate typically found for socially positive behaviors in the diffusion and contagion literature. Taboo innovations are thought to diffuse differently because individuals cannot discuss them freely, decreasing the influence of face-to-face networks. Here again, social media communication platforms may be upending this barrier. Except for crimes committed with an audience in mind, observability is also restricted because committing crime is usually a surreptitious activity. As media portrayals can substitute for interpersonal networks and simultaneously increase observability, it is logical that crimes that do receive media attention will diffuse significantly more rapidly than those that don't and will follow the standard S-curve diffusion pattern. Without media attention, the diffusion of an innovation would likely assume a slow linear growth rate driven by haphazard interpersonal criminal social networks.

Due to their unique networking characteristics, contemporary social media are hypothesized to be more significant copycat crime diffusion engines than traditional media (Surette 2016c; Surette et al. 2021). Crime diffusion may be similarly influenced so that copycat crime will have two diffusion rates: high media attention will produce the S-curve diffusion found with positive innovation diffusion; low media attention will display a slow linear diffusion pattern. Cultural settings are important though, as the less a type of crime is seen negatively and as taboo, the more the diffusion of crime can be expected to follow the common S-curve diffusion pattern.

The last diffusion area, a crime's social system, involves the cultural setting that an innovative crime is diffusing within. The role of change agents who champion the adoption of innovations comes into play within social settings. For crime, the change agent process usually would be through a potential copycat offender looking to the media to help solve a risk-of-arrest concern and obtaining innovative risk-reduction crime techniques. In that case, the level of media exposure would be analogous to the number of contacts with change agents, which the diffusion research has shown to be positively related to innovation adoption (Rogers 2003). The more change agents are available and the more contacts with them, the more potential copycats become actual copycats.

A second social role in diffusion theory is opinion leader. Delinquent gang leaders would be examples for criminogenic opinion leaders, while internet bloggers would exemplify social-media-based ones. A contemporary concern regarding copycat crime is how effectively media-provided models can serve as change agents and opinion leaders, especially for socially isolated individuals. Additional social system factors important for the diffusion of copycat crime would be preexisting supportive social norms about crime, the availability and quantity of criminal models circulating in a culture, and the level of opportunities to apply acquired innovative copycat crime skills. The presence of delinquent gangs, high crime rates, and crime-ridden neighborhoods would indicate a social setting conducive to heightened attention to media generator crime and the creation of subsequent copycat crimes.

The recurring existence of periodic crime waves signifies the applicability of diffusion theory to crime (Sacco 2005). In many respects, copycat crime qualifies as an example of overadoption of an innovation that to external observers should have been rejected. The key diffusion research question regarding copycat crime is whether the diffusion of negative social behaviors like crime mirrors the diffusion of the more commonly studied socially positive behaviors, like getting a new medical treatment. While the moral problem cited in positive innovation diffusion literature is the lack of equitable access to positive innovations for society's lower classes, for copycat crime the opposite is the issue—the socially down are more likely to be exposed to criminogenic media and to imitatively react to the content. For example, in that copycat criminals are people on the lower end of the social structure (the "downs" in diffusion terminology), media criminogenic content aimed at low achievers, the poor, and the illiterate should be more criminogenic—the opposite of what the diffusion research reports for positive innovations (Rogers 2003). Therefore, in a reversal of the diffusion literature, crime media is hypothesized to be a powerful source of behavior models for socially isolated individuals and expected to be particularly impactful on criminally inclined loners (Bandura 2001). It is speculated that individuals who copy crimes will differ significantly from those who copy law-abiding behaviors in their social standing and access to social resources.

To the extent that most diffusion research sees innovations as positive, it is useful to conceive of copycat crime as reverse social marketing campaigns and the opposite of the voluntary adoption of good behavior. Copycat crime can be perceived as the involuntary unplanned diffusion of negative behaviors. A prosocial media-based campaign is purposive; it intends to generate specific effects on many individuals, usually within a specified period and through a purposely designed set of communication activities. In contrast, most media copycat crime effects are nonspecific influences on a small number of individuals disseminated over an open-ended time frame through an unorganized communication mass media effort (Surette 2015a, 2020b). It is expected that haphazard criminogenic communication campaigns will diffuse less effectively, but as successful purposive campaigns often rely on delivering their messages in entertainment formats, the potential diffusion and impact of nonpurposive, haphazard criminogenic content remains substantial. The research on diffusion provides a conceptual framework for understanding how crime innovations propagate. For copycat crime, diffusion can be both planned (terrorist calls to action) and spontaneous (video game imitations). The diffusion research further provides a list of reasonable hypothesized characteristics for both crime innovations and crime copiers that combine with the other four theoretical pillars to produce the set of testable copycat crime propositions found in Chapter 7.

Conclusion

Imitation, contagion, and diffusion each contribute to understanding copycat crime in different ways. Imitation established copying as common, widespread, and applicable to a broad range of crimes and first gave the media important roles. The contagion research suggests that through mechanisms such as deindividuation and restraint reduction, criminal behavior is as likely a contagion candidate as law-abiding behavior. Social settings where the restraints on committing crime are removed through anonymity are especially prone to crime contagion. The contagion research also indicates that the spread of social behavior is nonlinear and that social conditions like poverty will be poor predictors of when a crime wave might materialize, that modest law enforcement or social efforts to reduce contagion-linked behavior may have little effect, and that in a fertile environment, once a threshold level of exposure to contagious criminogenic content is met, a small initial push from a crime model can result in a large unpredictable burst in crime (Cook and Goss 1996). In terms of copycat crime this means that a general theory of copycat crime that focuses on individual-level characteristics will not be particularly useful for predicting crime waves or the effectiveness of anti–copycat crime policies.

The diffusion of innovations research contributes to understanding copycat crime by laying out hypothesized generator crime characteristics and the plausibility that copycat offenders will share some traits with innovators and early adopters. These common traits will be more prevalent in first-wave copycat offenders as those copiers have to deal with the large levels of uncertainty regarding the consequences of first copying crime. Second and subsequent copycat waves should match the characteristics of early and late majority adopters as observable copycat crime trials become available. The diffusion literature also provides expectations about media roles and social media in crime waves and the rates of expected diffusion for innovative crimes. Last, diffusion theory emphasizes social systems and the key roles of opinion leaders and change agents within them as crucial for the diffusion of crime.

The main concern when applying diffusion theory to copycat crime is perceiving generator crimes as equivalent to socially supported innovations. The diffusion of innovative generator crimes should not be expected to mirror the diffusion of law-abiding social innovations, and generator crimes are more likely to be copied for different reasons and in different patterns by established offenders than is found for law-abiding adopters of noncriminal innovations. Diffusion research does well at describing the expected characteristics of successful innovations and the likely adopters of socially encouraged innovations. However, adopting an innovative crime is not the same as adopting an innovative approach to farming, and some of diffusion's postulates must be reversed to logically apply to copycat crime.

While imitation, contagion, and diffusion provide a foundation for studying copycat crime waves, they do not explore how behavior is socially learned within the waves. Social learning theorists addressed that gap and looked at what was required for individuals to learn new criminal behaviors in social settings. Tied to classical and operant conditioning theory, social learning theory promotes observational learning as vital for understanding copycat criminality and, with media studies research, emerges as a valuable source of copycat crime concepts. Copycat crime within social learning theory is the initial focus of Chapter 6, followed by an application of media studies research to copycat crime. Chapter 6 concludes by forwarding an interdisciplinary perspective for understanding copycat crime and the development of testable copycat crime research propositions, which are contained in Chapter 7.

Notes

1. For discussions of media immersion, see Fisch 2002; Green et al. 2006; Polichak and Gerrig 2002; Singhal and Rogers 2012; Slater and Rouner 2002.

2. The discussion of Gabriel Tarde and copycat crime draws upon Surette 2015b.

3. Tarde's third law, termed "insertion," states that newer fashions will displace older customs so that when two mutually exclusive imitations collide, one will be substituted for the other (Tarde [1912] 1968; Vine 1973). Over time, the newer method becomes a custom. His three laws describe a continuous social imitation engine that drives societies forward via repeating waves of imitation (Tarde [1912] 1968).

4. Despite a belief in predispositions, Tarde was not a determinist and acknowledged the importance of individual choice, chance, and social conditions in the generation of crime (Tarde [1912] 1968, 252).

5. For example studies of the contagion of gun violence, see Fagan, Wilkinson, and Davies 2006; Kissner 2016; Kostinsky, Bixler, and Kettl 2001; Larkin 2009; Loeffler and Flaxman 2018; Papachristos et al. 2015. Gould and Olivares 2017 provides a literature overview.

6

An Interdisciplinary
Perspective

CONTINUING THE APPLICATION OF EACH THEORY TO COPY-
cat crime, this chapter's two opening sections discuss the areas most
directly related to copycat crime: social learning and media studies.
Contemporary social learning theory combines early ideas from Albert
Bandura's observational learning theory (copying a new behavior from
watching a model) and Edwin Sutherland's differential association theory (learning crime from closely interacting with an offender). The second section on media studies provides copycat crime concepts and pathways to comprehend how interacting with media generated crimes can
lead to copycat ones. The chapter's third section discusses how the five
theories translate into an interdisciplinary perspective for the study of
copycat crime.

Social Learning and Copycat Crime

Social learning looks at criminality as acquired in the same manner as
other social behaviors. Delinquent peers and criminal family members
have been noted as strong predictors of juvenile delinquency, and social
learning theory based on real-world crime models has done well in
empirical tests.[1] Criminological social learning theory begins with Edwin
Sutherland's concept of differential association, which he employed to
argue that whether people commit crimes is determined by the meanings
people give to their social experiences and conditions. The meanings, in

turn, are acquired by individuals interacting with their associates. In Sutherland's initial conceptualization the socially acquired meanings were more important than real-world social conditions for determining criminal behaviors; the subjective view of the world was seen as more influential than the objective reality of the world. Sutherland soon amended this rejection of social conditions as significant for crime and offered an additional societal-level concept, differential social organization, or where in society individuals are located and to whom they are differentially exposed, to account for culture conflict and the influence of factors such as poverty and racism as crime generators. While offering a general theory of crime acquisition, Sutherland and his criminology descendants did not consider media as important and actively disparaged media effects (Surette 2015b).

The blending of social learning and differential association with media influence followed the creation of the United States' national television networks in the 1950s. Criminological interest in the media had been fallow since the 1800s, but in 1956 criminologist Daniel Glaser introduced the media into the differential association perspective as a powerful learning source for crime. Reacting to the influence of television, Glaser raised the central criminological question of whether media in the form of movies and television could substitute for Sutherland's face-to-face, real-world associations. Glaser argued that Sutherland's ideas did not require direct interpersonal contact to generate criminogenic effects. For Glaser, Sutherland's idea of differential association became the new concept of differential identification. In Glaser's words (1956, 444), "People pursue criminal behavior to the extent that they identify with real or imaginary persons for whom criminal behavior is acceptable or required." Glaser incorporated economic conditions, prior subject frustrations, learned moral codes, group participation, and other features of an individual's life to the extent that they could be shown to affect the role models individual offenders chose to copy. At its root, criminal identification operated as a psychological process in which, akin to role play by children, an individual imagines how the crime model they identify with would behave in the world and act accordingly. For criminals, the response to a behavior choice would be driven by a "What would Jessie James do?" style of consideration. The offender would think, "I'm that type of criminal, so I must imitate that type of criminality and try to act as that type of criminal even in new situations where I have to guess how my criminal model would behave." In this social-psychological process, criminal behavior would not have to be exactly imitated but could be freshly created in role-playing extrapolations. Criminal identification would occur naturally during direct real-world social interactions, such as membership in a delinquent gang, but the process could also occur through identification with criminal models portrayed in mass media (Glaser 1956). With Glaser's publication, the possibility of media-generated copycat crime gained academic credibility.

Shortly following Glaser, in the 1960s Albert Bandura developed his influential theory of social learning and how new behaviors are acquired in social settings. Bandura (1973) specifically noted two areas where media-generated social learning of crime is significant. On the media side, he noted the impact of crime news; on the crime side, he specified bizarre violence. Regarding crime news, Bandura (1973, 283) stated,

> Observers can learn from newscasts how to firebomb with Molotov cocktails, how to conduct a sniper siege, and the steps required to hijack airliners. In the news media, rewards are more frequently shown, punishments less so. Showing people running off with appliances and cases of liquor from looted stores in a jovial atmosphere is more likely to prompt viewers in similar circumstances than showing the terror and suffering caused by massive destruction of one's neighborhood.

The second area, bizarre violence, involves rare violent acts by an offender with no clear violent history. Bandura (1979) discussed mass murders and spree murders in which offenders display a history of intense, repeated exposure to violent media and commit violence prompted by bizarre beliefs (see Box 6.1).

Box 6.1   Albert Bandura's Copycat Crimes

Like Gabriel Tarde in the 1880s, Albert Bandura (1973) cited a set of crimes pulled from the news as copycat examples.

From 1961: "Members of an assaultive gang styled themselves after the gangsters on The Untouchables" ("Untouchable Gang," *Cleveland Press,* May 19, 1961, 1).

From 1963: "Brooded over for two years. Shortly after seeing Oswald shot on television, the brooding husband sought and shot his former friend. It looked easy on TV, says the man held in killing" ("Husband Slayed Friend Who Kissed His Wife," *Portland Press Herald,* November 28, 1963, 1).

continues

Box 6.1 Continued

From 1971: "Another employed burglary tactics from the television show, 'It Takes a Thief'" ("Youth Theft Ring Cracked," *Washington Post,* January 30, 1971, B1).

Bandura also lists as examples a shooting that copied the Manson Family murders ("Youth, 18, Slays 4 Women and Child in Beauty School," *New York Times,* November 13, 1966, 1) and airline bomb threats following *The Doomsday Flight* movie ("TVs Show Blamed by F.A.A. for Rise in Bomb Hoax Calls," *New York Times,* December 21, 1966, 79). As with other listings of copycat crimes, Bandura's are offered based on the impressions of journalists.

Bandura's most important social learning characteristic is self-efficacy, or an individual's belief in his or her ability to learn a new behavior and accomplish a task (Bandura 1995). In terms of copycat crime, high criminal self-efficacy is hypothesized to lead to an increased motivation to copy a crime in various ways. As conceived by Bandura and Walters (1963), in terms of copycat crime, high criminal self-efficacy will raise an individual's criminal goals and cause offenders to try to commit more difficult crimes and to seek out instructional crime models. High self-efficacy should also increase the effort offenders are willing to expend on crime attempts; expecting success, they become more willing to work harder and longer to learn a new crime. Furthermore, their expectation of eventual success should augment their perseverance in the face of obstacles and their resilience to failures. In the social learning perspective, prior arrests that did not deter would add to offenders' perception of criminal self-efficacy and their ability and desire to copy and commit crimes they see modeled.

A long criminal career comes into play for Bandura as in a Skinnerian fashion, a history of rewards and punishments for past crimes determines individuals' current assessments of their criminal self-efficacy and their future expectations of success from copying modeled crimes (Bandura 1995). And while high criminal self-efficacy is thought to influence confident innovative offenders, low self-efficacy regarding law-abiding tasks such as the ability to hold a job translates into a propensity to commit simple copycat crimes. The combination of high criminal self-efficacy and low law-abiding self-efficacy (belief that one cannot succeed at work or school but can get away with crime), combined with other factors, would put individuals at high risk for copying media generator crimes.

Bandura, like Sutherland, stressed the importance of the reinforcement of crime, seeing it as intertwined with self-efficacy. As well as providing instructional models, the media can create a permissive social environment and increase the anticipation of rewards for criminal behavior. Rewards can be tangible, in a direct "crime pays" reinforcement process, or intangible, like social praise for being the most fearless gang member or social status gains such as increased prestige in a neighborhood (Bandura 1973; Rosekrans and Hartup 1967). Delayed vicarious reinforcement, where an individual is not immediately rewarded for a criminal act but expects to be rewarded after observing a model benefiting from a crime, has also been established as a copier motivator (Bandura 1973; Bandura and Walters 1963). Vicarious reinforcement can serve as a copycat crime motivator by raising expectations of similar rewards for copying and arousing emotions that encourage copying and diminish crime-suppressing fears and inhibitions (Bandura 1973).

A third type of reinforcement, psychological self-reinforcement, is also possible. Self-reinforcement can have either enhancing or suppressing effects on copycat crime, depending upon whether the psychological impact from committing a crime is negative (feeling guilty) or positive (feeling powerful). In addition to the role of reinforcement for copycat crime, Gresham Sykes and David Matza (1957) forwarded a set of eight cognitive neutralizations offenders use to reduce negative psychological effects from committing crime:

1. Slighting of crime impact by advantageous comparison (others commit worse crimes). Media content focuses on violent predatory criminals whose crimes are more harmful than those of most real-world copycat offenders.
2. Justification of crime in terms of higher principles (crime as righteous). Media content provides many justifications for crime, and the "criminal hero" is a popular trope.
3. Displacement of responsibility (just following orders). Portrayal of criminal minions following the directions of crime overlords is common in the media.
4. Diffusion of responsibility (the individual plays a minor part in a large group action). Media content frequently shows crime as a large organizational operation.

5. Dehumanization of victims (media use of derogatory labels and slang, especially toward women). The promotion of group identity—an "us versus them" mentality in media portrayals of crime—justifies victimization of perceived outsiders.
6. Attribution of blame to victims (they deserved it). With dehumanization, media content often shows victims as contributing to their victimization through bad decisions, companions, and lifestyles.
7. Graduated desensitization. Repeated exposure to the frequent portrayals of crime content over time satiates and eliminates normal negative reactions. Social and personal restraints on criminal behavior are weakened.
8. Minimization and selective forgetting of harmful effects. The action and adventure of media crime tend to be remembered, while negative effects of crime are downplayed and forgotten.

These eight neutralizations are pervasive in media crime-related content (Surette 2015a), and crime and justice media content can generally be expected to neutralize feelings of criminal responsibility and to increase the palatability of crime for copycat criminals. Using these neutralizations, Bandura (1973, 2001) argued that crime can be justified, advantageously compared, or euphemistically labeled; personal responsibility can be displaced and diffused; and harms can be minimized, negative consequences ignored or misconstrued, and victims dehumanized and blamed for their victimization. Akin to the approach/restraint process described in the contagion literature, exposure to pervasive media crime content can disable the normal negative psychological and moral impacts from committing a crime, easing the learning of crime techniques.

In addition to how media content can encourage the learning of criminality, an important conclusion reached by Bandura is that social setting is more important than individual traits in determining the performance of socially learned behavior. Bandura (1973) argued specifically that social conditions that increase the acceptance and value of a behavior outweigh personal predispositions. For copycat crime, the supposition is that a criminogenic social environment will be more impactful than criminal predispositions on copycat crime attempts. At-risk copycat offenders will be distinguished through their criminal environments rather than through criminal personalities. The copycat crime cycle inferred from Bandura's ideas would be as follows: Crime-laden media increase the social learning and acquisition of crime knowledge and the growth of criminogenic cultures, social structures, and local environments and reduce the psychological pain of committing crime. These criminogenic social environments, in turn, increase the capability of media to distribute generator crime models for copycat offenders to observe, learn from, and employ. In this social learning cycle, the punishment and rewarding of crime emerge as key elements. How punishment is portrayed in the media at the cycle's beginning and experienced at the cycle's end is crucial for the social reality of copycat crime.

Social Learning, Copycat Crime, and Punishment

John Conklin (1998) listed the most common rewards for crime as money and goods, enhanced reputation, excitement, domination, and satisfaction in a successful crime. He describes the "sneaky thrills" youth report from shoplifting and the perception of crime as play for middle-class delinquents. Unfortunately, media crime content emphasizes these material and emotional rewards that accrue to a successful criminal. The risks of crime—arrest, fines, incarceration, injury or death, fear, shame, anxiety, and social stigma—are less emphasized (Surette 2015a). In effect, a media consumer is given only a partial image of the possible consequences of crime, weighted toward rewards. In reality, committing a copycat crime can be simultaneously rewarding and punishing, and individuals' perception of the likelihood of rewards or punishments will be idiosyncratically determined by their social setting and personal predispositions. The variations in how likely they think the differing outcomes are and whether they view those outcomes as rewards or punishments explains how the same crime content can have widely divergent effects on different individuals.

What is learned from media-portrayed punishment? In the social learning perspective, whether a criminal history increases or decreases the likelihood of copycat crime is determined by the roles that punishment plays in the life of a potential copier's real and media worlds of crime (Fisch 2002; Surette 2017). Punishment is related to the social learning of copycat crime in three ways. First, the punishment observed in the media content and levied on the media criminal model is important. Second, the estimation of the likelihood of punishment that a potential copycat copier extracts from the media and expects to experience in the real world is more important. Third, the punishment that is administered to and experienced by the copycat offender is most important. The cumulation of these three punishment effects determines the ability of punishment to deter copycat crime. In the generation of copycat crime, punishment in the first sense, the media-portrayed punishment, may not reduce the copying of a crime because the estimation of punishment in the second sense, the expected punishment, may not be reduced. This can be true even when substantial punishment in the third sense, the received punishment, ultimately occurs.

Media-portrayed punishment, hence, can be an ineffective deterrent, even a counterproductive one (Bandura 1973). For example, a media message common to some music video narratives portrays the police as oppressors, and audiences may side with negatively portrayed characters and emulate punished criminal models, particularly when they are portrayed heroically (Vidmar and Rokeach 1974). The second consideration of media-portrayed punishment is its effect on a copier's expectation of punishment from copying a modeled crime. When a criminal model reflects past rewards more than punishments for crime, copying increases (Bandura 1973). Even if crime in media content is not directly portrayed as rewarded, criminal models that "look" like they have been rewarded for past crime, for instance, in their lavish lifestyles, will encourage imitation of their crimes (Bandura and Walters 1963). As it is the expectation of results that most strongly determines initial copying, the effect of the observation of media-portrayed punishment on the expectation of real-world punishment is more important than the level of punishment observed in the media. Seeing a criminal repeatedly rewarded over the course of a media-portrayed crime story and punished at the end does not automatically increase for the copycat offender the perceived likelihood of being punished in the real world for copying the same actions.

Regarding actual experienced punishment, the degree to which copiers have been previously rewarded and punished for their own criminality influences the extent that imitation will occur and persist. After new skills have become entrenched, they can become habitual, even if they are no longer rewarded (Bandura and Walters 1963). Skinnerian conditioning research reports that rewards can be inconsistent, and consequences can be randomly punitive without eliminating a behavior. Applied to copycat crime, Skinnerian tenets mean that random reward patterns for copying crimes will generate copycat crime tendencies that will be difficult to eliminate. As Bandura (1973, 224) stated, "Children who learned that the benefits of crime are obtained at the risk of some negative outcomes are not easily discouraged by non-reward or censure. Sporadic punishment or frequent neutral results for committing crime will not counteract the copy sustaining effects of gaining periodic random but substantial rewards from doing so."

Adding to the problem of relying on media depictions of punishment to deter copycat offenders, even when the media consumer sees the portrayed outcomes to the media crime model as punishments and not as rewards, the media-depicted punishments can be cognitively processed as lessons on how to avoid the modeled criminal's mistakes. Copycat offenders may subsequently act on the belief that with a modification of tactics, they can gain the benefits of the crime in the real world without suffering the punishments portrayed in the media world. An exemplifying copycat offender thought process would be "If I don't leave any witnesses like the criminal in the movie did, I won't get caught." In addition to holding high crime self-efficacy beliefs, offenders often commit the error of overestimating their odds of success and are frequently overly confident that they have reduced their risk of arrest by slightly altering the crime technique they are copying (Bandura 1973, citing Claster 1967). In sum, the common practice of affixing a punishment at the end of a string of successful or nearly successful crimes in a media product should not be expected to erase the crime-encouraging learning effects of crime content and the generation of copycat crimes.

Social learning theory leads to the following conclusions regarding media-portrayed punishment. Beyond its haphazard portrayal in which much crime goes unpunished, when actions are guided by anticipated consequences that are not accurate—for example, when punishment is seen as highly unlikely when it is actually probable—copycat crime will be weakly controlled by its actual consequences for a significant time (Bandura 1973). Until real-world punitive results erase faulty media-generated positive expectations, copying can continue, as the false belief in expected rewards will persist. Along similar lines, the punishment of media-portrayed offenders is not an effective block to copying. The perception of correctable errors committed by media criminals and the accrual of tangible and intangible crime rewards by generator crime models encourage potential copycat offenders to adjust their risk/reward crime calculus toward lower risk and higher reward estimates and to persist in their copycat attempts (Ramsland 2013).

The portrayal of a "crime doesn't pay" message at the end of most media crime products to deter copycat crime has been the default for more than a century (Surette 2015b). Unfortunately, there are no scientific reasons to believe that an end-of-story, closing-scene punishment of a criminal is an effective anti–copycat crime strategy. Faulty extraction of correctable errors by consumers, favorable portraits of criminals, the higher proportion of successful crimes to unsuccessful ones in media content, and offenders' underestimation of real-world crime failure combine to reduce the deterrent effectiveness of media-portrayed punishment.

Socially Learning Copycat Crime

Social learning theory's current relevance to copycat crime has been supported in research reviews and several large-scale studies (Akers 1973; Krohn et al. 1985; Lanier and Henry 2004; Pratt and Cullen 2005; Sellers, Cochran, and Winfree 2003). Counterbalancing the empirical support, one common criticism of social learning theory is the problem of causal order: Which came first, criminal behavior or association with criminals? That those with a greater number of delinquent friends are more likely to be delinquent is a common finding. But someone may become delinquent for reasons other than association with other offenders and only after becoming an offender make friends with other offenders (Barkan 2001). Does exposure contribute to criminality, or do established offenders seek out crime-related media? This which-came-first question has not been fully resolved in the research on either peer-to-peer social learning or exposure to criminogenic media (Megens and Weerman 2012; Young et al. 2013). The study of copycat crime sidesteps this debate by imposing a causal time order on the media-crime sequence. By definition, a generator crime must occur first, and some level of exposure to media must occur beforehand for an offense to be a valid copycat crime.

From its roots in Sutherland, Glaser, and Bandura, and despite the causal-order debate, social learning theory has become a major theme in criminological thought. Ron Akers, the most recent proponent of criminological social learning, includes a significant media role. Grounding his thinking in differential association theory, Akers (2011) argues four major drivers of crime: differential association (exposure to crime models), differential reinforcement (reward and punishment history), imitation (copycat experiences), and definitions (perceptions about crime). The media play a potential role in each.

For Akers, media impact on crime will vary by crime and media type, the media's relevancy to an offender, and whether a crime is a group or solitary effort. For some individuals, the most salient crime models and definitions are found in television, movies, and video games rather than in reality (Akers 2011). Even though the media's effects are seen as less important and less direct than those of primary face-to-face groups, Akers and most current criminologists acknowledge media impact on behavior is greater than it was in the 1930s when Sutherland introduced his theory. For example, the concept of priority, which for Sutherland meant priority in time, for Akers means that first established patterns of behavior persist. For copycat crime that means that early media dependency should later equate to more copycat crime propensity, and the more that media substitutes for family, the more media-related copycat propensity should increase. For Akers, the initial participation of the individual in criminal behavior is therefore explained primarily by the operation of differential association, definitions, imitation, and social reinforcements. After a person has begun to commit crimes, differential reinforcements determine whether the criminal behavior continues. The choice of a behavior such as copycat crime is weighed against all other behaviors in terms of which is more likely to result in a reward. Like most crime, copycat crimes will tend to have quick rewards and delayed, often haphazard punishments, but unlike most other crime, the media component of copycat crime adds rewards not otherwise available, such as notoriety and widespread social status.

Three propositions derived from Akers's work produce the following points regarding media generator crimes, social learning, and copycat crime:

1. Offenders differentially associate with others who commit, model, and support violation of social and legal norms so that high media usage and interest in criminogenic content will correlate with stronger identification with media criminal models.
2. Criminal behavior is differentially reinforced over conforming behavior for offenders so that criminal offending shown in the media will be processed by copiers as successful and rewarding irrespective of end-scene punishment.
3. Offenders' personal crime definitions learned from criminogenic media will be favorable toward committing crime so that copycat criminals will adopt media-supplied criminogenic definitions.

Contemporary social learning theory leads to the conclusion that copycat crimes are plausible outcomes for persons who have perceptions of criminal self-efficacy, criminal life histories, and exposure to real and media rewarded crime models and live in environments that support and reward copying crime. Updating Gabriel Tarde's ideas to the twenty-first century, contemporary social learning theory establishes that crime is learned and copied in ongoing lifelong interactions. The individual instructional setting, societal conditions, and media characteristics determine whether potential copycat offenders learn to be actual copycat offenders. While social learning theorists currently give the media important roles in this process, they do not address the characteristics of the media that are crucial. That information and the final source for pertinent copycat crime research is found under the umbrella of media studies.

Media Studies

As the sole area that puts the media central in its research, media studies is unquestionably useful for understanding copycat crime. Media studies does not offer a single theoretical perspective and is better thought of as covering different approaches and concepts that share an emphasis on media impact. The media studies research that is most useful for comprehending copycat crime has looked at how media persuade and influence people and how people learn from the media. In this area, information applicable to the generation of copycat crime is accompanied by information about how the media might deter copycat crime. Media persuasion research contributes concepts and theoretical models for understanding how media content influences media consumers to change attitudes and behaviors and leads to the consideration of the copycat criminal as a media audience member. From that orientation, it follows that research is needed to understand the audience, to identify subaudiences, and to direct efforts to audience groups receptive to media campaigns (Rice and Atkin 2002). The three keys for media-generated copycat crime as extracted from media persuasion research are (1) identifying target audiences (for copycat crime, youth who aspire to criminal careers); (2) specifying the target behavior (what crimes are most likely to be copied); and (3) elaborating the intervening variables between exposure to media and behavior changes (detailing the steps for individuals going from being exposed to a generator crime to attempting a copycat crime).

Many of the media studies ideas that apply to copycat crime are focused on the individual, and when applied to copycat crime, they invoke a search for differences between offenders and nonoffenders. In relevant media studies research, a copycat criminal is differentiated from noncopycat criminals by how he or she interacts with the media. However, in terms of their media exposure, there is reason to believe that copycat offenders and noncopycat offenders are fundamentally similar (Newburn 1994; Surette and Maze 2015). Regardless of the questionable historically held view of offenders as being different regarding the media, which steered much of the research (Rennie 1978), a set of theoretical concepts applicable to copycat crime have emerged from media studies research.

The first concept associated with media and copycat crime is the idea of criminogenic media, or media content that results in crime. The presence of enormous amounts of crime-related media has been established in a large number of studies covering centuries of media content. Crime has been a prominent component of news, entertainment, and infotainment media since at least the 1600s, has seldom waned, and has changed mostly by becoming more graphic (Surette 2015a). While violent media content delivered in radio, film, and television programming and novels, comic books, and newspapers has attracted the most attention, violent media is not the only, or even the most likely, crime-generating content. Other types of media content have been suggested to have criminogenic effects, such as hate speech and violent political rhetoric (Alkiviadou 2019; Mathew et al. 2019). Criminogenic content can also be content that does not directly involve committing crime but changes attitudes toward law breaking by others, so that most media consumers do not commit crimes but become less disapproving of others who do (Surette 2015a).

In addition, the tenets of instruction are found in media crime content. As delivered, media crime content can encourage the transfer of generator crime knowledge to first-time copycat crime offenders while influencing the social environment to be more tolerant of crime. Media studies generally supports a "criminogenic media content → criminal behavior → more crime-tolerant environment" loop in which the transmission of crime ideas through the media encourages imitative criminal behavior, which alters a culture to be a more fertile crime environment (Surette 2017). Specific media studies concepts that support the content-behavior-environment loop include media uses and gratifications, priming and scripts, and exemplars.

The "uses and gratifications" perspective lends support for the commonsense prediction that offenders already committed to a crime will be more attuned to media generator crimes. In media studies terminology, criminogenic media should gratify such consumers and be used by them to fill a crime information need (Rubin 2002). As the crime goals of offenders differ (some will want to reduce risk of arrest, others to maximize attention and fame), different types of criminogenic content will be sought out, and the size of the potential copycat offender population and the susceptibility of this population to media-generated copycat effects will vary. The copycat effect of a particular piece of media content will therefore differ by the manner in which a consumer is using the media and how well that content gratifies the consumer. Thus, the same movie content may be equally gratifying to two different viewers but strongly criminogenic for one who is using the media to actively learn how to commit a type of crime and not for another who is using it as an escape from boredom.

The concept of script acquisition in media studies also applies to copycat crime (Bushman et al. 2013; Phillips 2017). Scripts apply to both the acquisition of new criminal behavior and the media-primed performance of older stored criminal behaviors. L. Rowell Huesmann (1986) suggested a reciprocal script acquisition process that when applied to copycat crime suggests that viewing crime media can lead to a subsequent crime cycle in self-perpetuating loops. In his explanation, criminogenic media will lead to the creation of new crime scripts, stimulating crime fantasies and the mental rehearsal of crimes, which in turn increases the retrieval of past, already-acquired crime scripts. If a retrieved crime script is performed and reinforced, it will become habitual and more likely to be retrieved in various future situations, which in turn will encourage both more crime and more criminogenic media use (Huesmann 1986). Applying Huesmann's (1998, 102) idea of scripts to copycat crime generates the following reasoning:

> Not every [copycat crime] they observe is encoded or stimulates the encoding of a [copycat crime] script. Not every [copycat crime] script is retained or remains accessible for long. The more salient an observed [crime] scene is to the [copycat offender] initially, and the more the [offender] ruminates upon, fantasizes about, and rehearses the observed [crime] scene, the more likely it is that a [crime] script based on that scene is recalled and followed. The more the [crime] is consistent with the scripts that the [offender] has already acquired the more easily it is integrated into memory. The more the [crime] is perceived as consistent with the [offender's] beliefs about the appropriateness of [crime], the more likely it is to be integrated into memory.

If such an application is correct, it follows that a substantial portion of copycat crime is a spontaneous short-term retrieval process carried out by established offenders presented with a crime opportunity. The acquisition process for crime scripts combines the consumption of crime media with exposure to real-world crime models and involves the social learning subprocesses of modeling, skills acquisition, rehearsal, and performance (Bandura 1973). Once a crime script is created, the match between preexisting scripts, recent exposure to crime models, and the social norms regarding crime held by an individual significantly increases the performance of a copycat crime.

Dolf Zillmann's media studies concept of exemplars is a starting point for exploring the characteristics of copycat-generator crimes. Zillmann's (2002) idea of exemplars suggests that generator crimes that evoke strong emotions will more easily generate copycat crimes. Recasting Zillmann's exemplars as generator crimes results in a set of exemplar-linked copycat crime propositions. First, a series of exemplars of iconic, emotion-laden crimes (such as a string of heinous child murders) will have stronger copycat effects on attuned potential copycats than a set of placid exemplars of abstract crimes such as economic frauds. Second, exemplars based on real-world crimes will be more influential than fictional ones, and images of crime will be more influential than facts or statistics about crime. Visuals and passions will outweigh texts and data. Lastly, emotional exemplar generator crimes will cause potential copycats to estimate that such crimes are common and, if portrayed as successful, will increase their expectation of success when copying them.

Applying the media studies research on media-linked primes and exemplars to copycat crime, we expect constant exposure to crime and criminal justice media content in general to engender more consideration to commit copycat crimes by individuals. As sources of ideas and beliefs that construct a particular social reality, crime-related primes will foster the perception that the nature of the world is such that a particular crime is appropriate and likely successful. The most powerful exemplar generator crimes would be recent, emotional, visual crimes whose impact was unchallenged by other contradictory exemplars. Thus, showing successful offenders without showing arrested ones should increase the number of copiers. Once primed, an individual is more likely to copy a media-modeled crime, particularly if the prime cues up preestablished criminal scripts. At the individual copycat offender level, priming works as a short time frame mechanism that encourages the acting out of preexisting criminal behaviors, while social learning processes work as long-term behavior-modifying procedures that result in acquiring new criminal scripts.

Cognitive Pathways and Media Persuasion

A significant contribution to copycat crime study from media studies involves detailing how media content persuades individual decisionmaking and behavior.[2] As discussed in Chapter 2, the media's role in decisionmaking leads to the two individual-level decision routes of systematic and heuristic reasoning (Kahneman 2011). Copycat crimes in the systematic path are thoughtful, planned, and instrumental ("Here are detailed instructions on how to successfully commit this crime; evaluate, learn, and follow"). When making the decision to commit a crime, a systematic path copycat offender assesses the realistic chances of successfully committing the crime under consideration and conducts an extensive search for relevant information, evaluates that information, and weighs counterarguments that question the accuracy of the information.

The mimicked bank robbery in the film *Set It Off* is an example of copycat offenders following a systematic route.[3] The film's plot was used to plan and execute a real-world crime: a 1998 bank robbery. The bank robbery was committed by four young females and one older female who had watched the film numerous times in the two weeks prior. Their bank robbery closely mirrored the conduct of the movie's bank robberies and the robbers' actions prominently portrayed in the movie. The four younger females took on the roles of the film characters and acted like them during the bank robbery. The copycat bank robbers used disguises, jumped on the bank counter, counted down the time spent inside the bank, discarded their outer clothing, and fled the bank with a plan to escape to Mexico by bus—all actions portrayed in the movie's fictional, partially successful bank robberies. Following their arrest in the real world, police retrieved a copy of the film in a home shared by the copycat robbers.

In contrast to systematic path crimes, heuristic path crimes are emotional, less rational, and more spontaneous ("People are rioting on television, and no one's getting arrested! It looks exciting! Let's do the same here!"). Stealing on finding an open, unguarded pocketbook is one example, as are spontaneous assaults, rapes, and hate crimes. A heuristic copycat crime example is found in the swastika graffiti wave in the 1960s in the United States, which reflects a heuristic, shallowly considered set of copycat crimes (see Box 5.1). Interviews with apprehended offenders compiled by Martin Deutsch (1962) indicated that a substantial number of the vandalism incidents were unplanned acts. Regarding the precrime thought processes of the swastika copycats, simple boredom was reported in nearly all interviews. Copycat offenders who did not express antisemitic values were more likely to have spontaneously copied the vandalism. For example, one copycat vandal claimed no animosity towards Jews, expressed sorrow for painting a swastika on a synagogue, and said that he did it for the thrill; he'd thought of it because he and his friends had seen it on television, and it seemed to be the thing to do (Deutsch 1962). Further reflecting heuristic reasoning, even the strongly antisemitic copycats often picked their vandalism targets randomly. For example, a copycat offender who was a member of a Nazi gang did not know that there was a synagogue in his town and said that he had to look in the telephone book to locate one on which to paint swastikas.

While both cognitive decision paths have relevance for copycat crimes, they require a conscious decision to commit or not commit a copycat crime on the part of the media consumer. A less conscious media-influence route, narrative persuasion, is felt to be the most strongly related to copycat crime. A narrative persuasion copycat crime is exemplified by John Hinckley Jr.'s attempted assassination of President Ronald Reagan in 1981. After becoming psychologically immersed in the fictional story of Travis Bickle in the 1976 film *Taxi Driver*, Hinckley took on the narrative of the film character. In the film, Bickle saves a young prostitute, played by Jodie Foster, from a life of prostitution. He does so by graphically killing her pimp and two other movie characters. At the movie's end, Bickle becomes an applauded hero; his violent acts result in positive social acclaim and rewards.

Hinckley extended the film's narrative to the real world, where he pursued the actress Jodi Foster at her university, vowing to save her in a manner analogous to how Travis Bickle saved her character in the movie, at times quoting similar lines from the movie in communications with the actress. Hinckley watched the film more than a dozen times prior to his assassination attempt and referenced the movie in postarrest interviews. Hinckley was emotionally and psychologically persuaded by the film's narrative to act out its storyline. Although he knew he was following a movie storyline, Hinckley felt that following the narrative would have positive real-world consequences. While Bickle approaches but fails to assassinate a politician and is scared off by secret service agents in the movie, Hinckley managed to shoot and wound the president and others in the real world.

When the narrative persuasion process is strong, psychological engagement with criminogenic content will be high, transformation or absorption of knowledge deep, and the copier transported to a world where crime is justified, rewarded, and unlikely to be punished (Green and Brock 2000). Even when the narrative is clearly labeled as fiction, real-world beliefs can be affected so that once a potential copycat offender is carried along inside a compelling media narrative, the beliefs implied in the story can be adopted regardless of whether they make sense in the offender's actual world. Narrative persuasion further offers an explanation of criminogenic media content's ability to influence initially unsympathetic, resistant noncopycat offenders through empathetic transitional models (Green 2004; Slater and Rouner 2002). By portraying characters in the narrative who are initially opposed to committing a crime, the process of attitude and behavior change, common in media Robin Hood crime tropes, is modeled for the media consumer. Individuals initially unlikely to copy a crime may be persuaded to do so by observing an initially unwilling model undergo a transformation where the crime comes to be seen in a positive light (Polichak and Gerrig 2002).

Due to the large quantity of crime-related narratives in the media, media content can be conceived as a haphazard entertainment-education effort in which narrative persuasion is a prevalent mechanism (Fisch 2002). Reported content characteristics that enhance learning include clarity of presentation and explicitness of content, both of which are present in much crime-related media (Surette 2015a, 2017). Michael Slater and Donner Rouner (2002) relate that copycat crime viewer characteristics that enhance entertainment-education effects are prior knowledge of content (for copycat crime, a preexisting criminal history) and consumer interest in content (a decision already in place to commit a crime). Research on media-based entertainment-education concludes that successful instruction in media entertainment narratives requires a rich understanding of the subject matter, content that is presented as useful in multiple situations, and a match between the content and a real-world situation where it can be applied (Fisch 2002). For copycat crime narratives, these elements are found in the presence of varied, exciting, and innovative crime content, where crimes are portrayed as ubiquitous and useful, are realistic, and are portrayed in familiar environments.

Finally, it is important that the possible copycat crime impact of the narrative persuasion path is bolstered by characteristics of new media. Interactivity, media immersion, and consumer transportation are strong points of the new-media consumer experience (Grodal 2003a, 2003b; Surette 2017). Interactivity—the ability of media consumers to affect the content as they simultaneously consume it—is most apparent in video games. The interactivity found in many games involves violent and criminal acts that are felt to prime aggressive scripts, suggest a violent world, and promote violent criminal problem-solving strategies (Mundorf and Laird 2002). Interactivity is also thought to increase the likelihood of media immersion, where the consumer becomes fixated on media content, and consumer transportation, where the media consumer is distanced from his or her prior beliefs and experiences a disconnection from reality. Social media and online gaming, in addition, can reach and link large audiences so that when live peers are not available, social media relationships can substitute, magnifying the effects of exposure to media content.

Copycat Crime—an Interdisciplinary Perspective

Why should one expect crime that is seen, heard, or read about to be copied in today's world? Crime has always been a rewarding experience, delivering money, goods, challenge, excitement, personal satisfaction, and reputation enhancement, all strong motivations for copying a crime successfully. In addition, the media have substantively changed in the twenty-first century in ways that boost the dynamics that encourage copycat crime. Why is the twenty-first century a particularly apt time for copycat crime to occur? First, in an analogous fashion to how the first television-raised generation spiked delinquency rates in the 1960s, the current generation of youth is the first to mature under the influence of interactive, immersive, transportive social media. Second, for the first time in history, most of a child's exposure to the world outside his or her family can occur without parental supervision or mainstream media interpretation. Today's youth can consume media physically alone and in the privacy of their rooms while psychologically globally connected to external virtual social groups (Brown, Fuller, and Vician 2004). One result is less opportunity for adult intervention in or conversation about what children see, hear, and read or for mainstream gatekeepers to contextualize media content. Third, crime-related and instructional crime content in the media is more pervasive, and more of the world's youth are exposed to it. For many, global media experiences like YouTube, Twitter, and TikTok are everyday realities, and the dark web offers additional content to the criminally inclined (Chertoff 2017; Finklea 2017). In this social environment, what do the five theoretical perspectives offer to an interdisciplinary view of copycat crime?

Despite substantial amounts of suggestive parallel research, copycat crime remains a phenomenon where public embrace of and belief in the idea far outruns scientific knowledge. Much is believed about copycat crime based upon little direct evidence. Part of this separation is due to the multiple levels of analysis that come into play when studying copycat crime. An explanation of *analysis level* is helpful to categorize and understand what the foundational theories collectively contribute to copycat crime and where the study of copycat crime currently stands. Human behavior, including copycat crime, can be studied and explained in different ways depending upon the level of analysis utilized (see Table 6.1).

At the lowest level of analysis reside biological and genetic explanations. Concepts and explanations at this level apply to all organisms that share the same biochemical systems. For copycat crime, mirror neurons best exemplify conceptualization at this level, having both a biological base in brain cells and a genetic base in behavioral evolution. For copycat crime, imitation is the lowest foundational-level concept in the sense of being multispecies and the most basic, but it is not the least important. No higher-level theory or explanation can contradict accepted findings from the biological level of analysis. At the next highest level are individual human-level concepts such as predispositions and environmental experiences. This level of analysis looks at the behavior of individual copycat offenders. As an explanation of behavior, Skinnerian conditioning theory, with its concepts of rewards and punishments and

Table 6.1   Analysis of Behavior by Levels

Level of Analysis	General Behavior Concepts	Core Copycat Concepts
Biological	Genes, biochemicals	Mirror neurons, imitation
Individual	Personality and conditioning histories, punishments, scripts	Priming, rewards, selective imitation
Small group	Group dynamics, social roles, social networks	Social learning, role play, environments
Large group	Crowds, communities, societies, cultures	Crime waves, crime clusters, collective behaviors

an individual's predisposition to exhibit certain reactions to specific stimuli (innate irritability or anxiety, for example), fits into this level of analysis. Biology merges with environmental conditions, and for copycat crime research, selective imitation and composite models are a focus. The third level encompasses the analysis of small social groups. Social interactions between individuals and their effect on concepts such as personality, group cohesion, norms, and values come into play. Family, peers, delinquent gangs, and significant others are central in the research on small groups. For copycat crime, the dynamics of diffusion and contagion are the pertinent elements for research at the small-group level of analysis (Green, Horel, and Papachristos 2017; Papachristos et al. 2015). At the fourth analysis level, community, national, and cultural phenomena enter, and the concepts of society, culture, and societal histories become central for explaining aggregate copycat crime levels and copycat crime waves and clusters.

No analysis level is inherently more important than another; instead they exist in an interlocking structural scaffold. The higher levels combine more individuals into larger groups for analysis (comparing the residents of one country with another, for example) but cannot forward theories or explanations that contradict established findings from lower levels. For example, a theory of copycat crime at the small-group level of analysis cannot rest upon concepts or explanations that prove to be biologically impossible (telepathy as a copycat crime contagion mechanism, for example). And causal processes and explanations forwarded at a higher analysis level must eventually be translated or linked to process from lower analysis levels. Thus, the psychological concept of priming must eventually be connected to biological processes for final validation.

With a hierarchical perspective in mind, an examination of the theories that are relevant for comprehending copycat crime reveals that they sit at different analysis levels and explore different associated research questions. Copycat crime is explored at the biological level using mirror neurons, at the individual psychological level through script acquisition and priming, at the small-group level using role models, role play, and social learning, and at the large-group level using crime waves and crime clusters. Copycat crime is simultaneously an individual-level biological and psychological phenomenon, an act performed by an individual within a group, and an aggregate society-wide multicultural phenomenon. A copycat crime will be related to biological and psychological effects on individual potential copycat offenders, small-group influences on those significantly immersed in a real or media social network, and downstream effects on the larger social collection, societies, and cultures where a generator crime and its copycats reside. At the most basic level, an individual must decide to copy a media-modeled generator crime; this decision to copycat is often made within a social group but can be an isolated act. However, how often copycat crime occurs will differ across societies, as will the types of crimes that are copied.

What generates media-connected copycat crime? Each level of analysis will have its own answer, but attempts to link levels have been made, most notably for the biological and social learning theories (Proctor and Niemeyer 2020). Box 6.2 summarizes the most basic copycat

---

Box 6.2   Research Findings and Questions by Hierarchichal Level

Copycat Crime by Imitation Biology and Psychology
Findings: Copycat crime waves go downward and outward.
            Many are instructed in crime techniques; few copy.
Research questions:
            Why isn't there more copycat crime?
            How does an individual become primed for copycat crime?
            What is the biological basis for observing crime to become copying crime?

continues

Box 6.2   Continued

Are there biological or psychological differences between copycat and noncopycat offenders?

Copycat Crime by Contagion and Diffusion

Findings: Copycat crime waves follow S-curve growth patterns. Crowd behavior is complex, and individuals within crowds behave similarly for different reasons.

Research questions:

How does criminal behavior spread in a group and in society?

Do copycat crime waves follow the lifecycles of noncrime behaviors?

How does the media contribute to approach/restraint conflict resolution and deindividuation?

Are copycat crime waves inherently unpredictable?

Are the diffusion dynamics of copycat crimes opposite to those of socially supported behaviors?

Copycat Crime by Social Learning

Findings: Copycat crime is learned in a similar fashion to noncrime behavior.

Research questions:

What are the roles of selective copying and composite modeling in copycat crime?

How important is criminal innovativeness and criminal self-efficacy for copycat crime?

How effective is media-portrayed punishment for deterring copycat crime?

Copycat Crime by Media Studies

Findings: The media play significant but varied roles in the generation of copycat crime.

Research questions:

What is the impact of crime media on copycat crime?

How do interactivity, immersion, and transportation relate to copycat crime?

crime research findings and unaddressed research questions associated within each hierarchical level.

Collectively, the five theoretical perspectives lead to one unresolved overarching research question: What are the characteristics of generator crimes, individual copycat offenders, and copycat-prone groups, societies, and cultures? Until the basic descriptions of copycat crimes, copycat offenders, and copycat settings are compiled, the research questions listed in Box 6.2 cannot be addressed. The population of copycat crimes and criminals must be defined and settled before research on the phenomena can proceed.

An interdisciplinary perspective suggests that copycat crime will trace a reiterative cycle. The initial social and cultural conditions will result in a number of generator crimes produced in the media that will be exposed to potential copycat offenders. A small number of the potential copycat criminals will attempt a copycat crime and will either be rewarded or punished. Whether their post–copycat crime environment is generally rewarding or punishing will determine the continuation of copying by other individual copycat offenders, the level of social tolerance for such crimes, and the number of available opportunities to apply the copied crimes. The cumulative impact of copycat crime will affect the social and cultural conditions and the available media content regarding similar crimes. A feedback loop to the number of generator crimes that exist will be produced, and the copycat crime cycle will begin again.

Conclusion

The requirements set out in the research for behavioral instruction are met by the media's crime-related content, and the transfer of generator crime knowledge to potential copycat crime offenders should be common. The imitative impact of media depends upon the nature of the content, the way that individuals' process the media-supplied information, and the social context in which potential copycat offenders find themselves. Copycat crime is forwarded as not simply a subset of general crime but as occupying a realm that involves concepts ranging from individual-level bioneurology to broad-scale cultural factors. As such, copycat crime should be considered as a unique crime process with a set of unique research questions. Copycat crime is not a type of crime in the usual sense but a class of widely different events that share a unique dynamic interaction between media, individuals, and societies. As any type of crime can be a copycat crime, understanding copycat crime will not come from studying a specific crime, like school shootings. Instead, it will require a broad-based eclectic approach that is sensitive to multilevel processes and variations tied to different copycat crimes, copycat offenders, and copycat environments.

While media play a significant role in some of the contemporary theoretical areas, they are not central in imitation, contagion, and diffusion and are historically absent in early social learning theory. Only for recent contagion and social learning theorists and for media studies researchers do the media occupy central roles in the generation of crime. Collectively, the most apparent benefit to copycat crime from these theories is that they provide a strong plausibility for media-generated criminogenic effects and an initial but not validated explanation for copycat crime. The plausibility of copycat crime is bolstered by the meshing of the theories' assumptions and concepts with deeply held cultural sentiments about the media and crime and the general public's belief in copycat crime. In addition to the support that these theories provide for the existence of a substantial copycat crime phenomenon, a set of testable research propositions about copycat crime can be culled. Despite the sparseness of direct research on copycat crime, much can be stated and tested regarding its hypothesized nature. These propositions are specified and discussed in Chapter 7.

Notes

1. For research and reviews of social learning theory in criminology, see Akers 2011; Akers and Jensen 2003, 2006; Akers and Sellers 2004; Beaver et al. 2009; Bruinsma 1992; Conklin 1998; Ferguson, San Miguel, and Hartley 2009; Megens and Weerman 2012; Park et al. 2005; Pratt et al. 2010; Rowe and Farrington 1997; Warr 1993, 2002; Young et al. 2013.

2. The discussion of cognitive pathways draws upon Surette 2013b.

3. A clip from the movie *Set It Off* can be found at "Set It Off (1996)—Last Bank Robbery Scene," video posted to YouTube by Koron Bracey, July 28, 2019, https://www.youtube.com/watch?v=VpcTXqj45l0.

7

Crimes, Criminals, and Environments

USING RESEARCH FINDINGS FROM THE FIVE FOUNDATIONAL research areas, this chapter develops and discusses hypotheses about copycat crime.[1] The reader should note that the propositions listed are hypotheses, not declarative statements about copycat crime. Some are based on crime-related research, some on media research. Most do not have direct research support regarding copycat crime but rely on indirect evidence to draft working hypotheses. These hypotheses therefore represent the current best ideas concerning copycat crime and its dynamics, not definitive findings. They have been largely extracted from non–copycat crime research efforts and applied with a caveat to copycat crime.

Reasonable speculations regarding the descriptions and relationships associated with copycat crime, criminogenic media content, copycat offenders, and types of copycat crime are presented. Given that a copycat crime at a minimum requires a "media generator crime model → exposure to media generator crime content → subsequent copycat crime" sequence, copycat crime hypotheses related to multiple points in the required sequence were culled. Specifically, the characteristics of crime media and generator crime content are specified and the probable traits of copycat offenders described. The settings where copycat crime media are consumed, the communities where copycat crime opportunities are common, and the broad social norms and cultures that support copycat crime also are specified. Sets of research-testable copycat crime hypotheses are offered, with the dual goals of clearly stating what can be theorized about copycat crime and encouraging more rigorous copycat crime research.

Media Content and Copycat Crime

The first set of copycat crime propositions deals with the characteristics of media content hypothesized to contribute to copycat crime. The content is examined along four dimensions. First, what is the broad portrait of crime associated with copycat crime? Second, what is the portrayal of specific generator crimes found in the media that encourage copycats? Third, what portrayal of crime models in generator crimes raises the probability of the models being copied? Fourth, what characteristics of media increase the number of generator crimes?

General Media Content That Supports Copycat Crime

General media content that encourages copycat crimes need not portray a criminal event, and most media content that does contain a portrayal of crime does not generate a copycat crime. Nevertheless, media content can enhance media copycat effects, and a set of media content characteristics beyond those associated with specific generator crimes is hypothesized to contribute to the generation of copycat crime. For example, general crime content that suggests that crime is appropriate and likely to be successful is expected to encourage the copying of media-portrayed generator crimes (Akers 2011; Doley, Ferguson, and Surette 2013; Wilson, Colvin, and Smith 2002). Also, general content that improves the mood of media consumers and increases their belief that positive consequences will follow from generally committing crime will also increase copycat crime (Bryant and Miron 2002; Petty, Priester, and Brinol 2002).

Additional noncrime media content that encourages copycat crime is that which lessens individual responsibility, changes moral values, devalues crime victims, reduces shame, decreases the perception of harm, and condones deviant acts as righteous (Akers 2011; Bandura 1973; De Graaf et al. 2012; Rosekrans and Hartup 1967). Such content will encourage crime in general and is hypothesized to encourage copycat crime in particular. Other general media crime content thought to increase copycat effects includes explicit, engaging, exciting, realistic, and action-laden crime narratives (Bandura 1973; Fisch 2002; Haridakis 2002; Shrum 2002; Slater and Rouner 2002). Related to criminal self-efficacy, content that persuades individuals that they possess the ability to successfully commit crime and provides instructional techniques is hypothesized to be particularly impactful on copycat crime (Akers 2011; Bandura 1995). Lastly, the overall quantity of media crime content is a hypothesized copycat crime enhancer. Copycat crimes are felt to increase with increased news coverage of crime and with entertainment media that is crime saturated (Akers 2011). Although this general media content is not directly linked to copycat crime, through these multiple avenues the media are felt to create a cultural environment that fosters copycat crime. The hypothesized general media content that encourages copycat crime is summarized as follows:

1. Content contains stories that are more engaging and heavily involve the consumer in their narratives; it is more realistic, has more action, and is more exciting.
2. Content neutralizes the negative effects of crime by reducing individual responsibility for and distress from crime, reduces the perception of crime harm, condones crime, or shows crime as righteous.
3. Content portrays crime as appropriate and likely to be successful in multiple ways and circumstances.
4. Content persuades individuals that they possess the ability to commit crime.
5. Content contains more characters committing crimes.

Looking at the overall research on general media content, these five summary points describe the expected impact of general media content on copycat crime. The first content attribute hypothesized as important is how transportive it is. The more media content can criminogenically engage an individual, the more successful generator crimes can be. Additionally, psychologically educational media research on narrative persuasion provides insights regarding general instructional media content and copycat crime. Associated research on the factors related to the transfer of learning from visual content, for example, emphasizes the impact of two characteristics: clarity of presentation and explicitness of content (Fisch 2002). Both characteristics are common elements of crime media (Surette 2015a). The second general content characteristic is the presence of crime-neutralizing content (Bandura 1973). Portrayals of crime that model defensible righteous crime are speculated as adding legitimacy to and weakening restraints on criminality (Akers 2011; Bandura 1973). Related to neutralizing content, portraits that suggest that crime is usually successful and socially approved should further encourage copycat crime. Third, crime shown as frequently rewarded will undercut the crime-deterrent effect of media portrayals of the punishment of crime (Bandura 1973; Rosekrans and Hartup 1967). Fourth, content that persuades individuals that they possess criminal self-efficacy (Bandura 1995) or contains crime techniques (Akers 2011) will increase copycat crime even when the content is not crime specific. Finally, the sheer quantity of crime models circulating within media content, regardless of how portrayed, is hypothesized to heighten the probability of exposure to copycat-generator crimes in a society.

In contrast to the five copycat-crime-enhancing characteristics in media content, copycat-crime-reducing factors can also be derived from the foundational research. For example, media criminogenic models decrease in impact with increased availability of noncriminal models. Media crimes that are unsuccessful and punished, if not competing with successful crime portraits, will decrease copycats (Wilson, Colvin, and Smith 2002). Media crime content that does not include neutralization techniques or detailed instructions and dissuades individuals from a belief that they possess the capabilities to commit crime will decrease copycats (Akers 2011; Bandura 1973), as will content that is less realistic, engaging, and transportive (Bandura 1995).

The main research point regarding general media content and copycat crime is that while the examination of specific copycat-generator crimes is crucial, the inclusion of the broader crime-related media content that the specific portraits of generator crime exist within is necessary to fully understand the generation of copycat crime.

Copycat Generator Crimes

Looking next at the specific crimes that become copycat-generator crimes, the copycat foundation theories suggest some specific characteristics. Foremost, the portrayed success of a media-modeled crime is especially important even when followed by an ultimate punishment of a generator crime offender (Bandura 1973). Media portrayals of punishment of crime, when they enhance a crime model's status and simultaneously lower the status of law enforcement officers, are hypothesized to increase the likelihood of copycat crime. For example, media content that contains the administration of inequitable punishment by the criminal justice system may free copycat offenders to guiltlessly copy a crime and justify retaliative aggression (Bandura 1973). This remains more likely even if mistakes by the media model are portrayed. Accompanying detailed instructions are hypothesized to significantly increase a generator crime's adoption.

It is additionally speculated that media-portrayed crimes shown as innovative and low skill will be more successful as copycat-generator crimes (Akers 2011; Bandura 1973; Rogers 2003). According to media studies research, media-portrayed crimes shown with emotional, clear, explicit visual content are also hypothesized to generate more copycat crime (Fisch 2002; Zillmann 2002). Exemplification theory further predicts that emotion-laden generator crimes will cause potential copycat criminals to overestimate the number of people committing similar crimes, thereby increasing the perception of the generator crime's social acceptability and causing offenders to overestimate the success of copying (Zillmann 2002). Three hypotheses summarize the expected traits of copycat-generator crimes:

1. Crimes portrayed in the media as low skill, innovative, explicit, emotional, and visual will more likely become copycat-generator crimes.
2. Crime portrayals that provide detailed instructions will more likely become copycat-generator crimes.
3. Crimes portrayed as successful will most likely become generator crimes.

In sum, media-portrayed crimes that imply success, provide explicit instructions, and are visually and emotionally engaging are hypothesized to be the most likely to become successful copycat crime generators.

Copycat Generator Crime Models

The characteristics of the crime models associated with generator crimes are important (Lankford 2021).[2] Empirical evidence shows that media models of copycat crimes can serve as crime instructors and as emotional enhancers for potential copycat offenders—both can encourage imitative behaviors (Bandura 1973). The linkages between copycat-generator crime models and copycat offenders are multifaceted, however, and vary widely across copycat offenders. In a recent study of mass killers for example, Peter Langman (2018) lists different ways that mass-killing generator crime models can influence copiers, inspiring everything from simple curiosity about a prior killer to deep psychological connections such as inspiration, idolization, hero worship, and infatuation, to actual imitation of language, appearance, actions, and behavior. Reasons given by the copycat killers for these connections included perceived similarity to a generator crime model, sympathy with a prior modeled motivation (for example, taking revenge or attacking inferiors), and a desire for fame and notoriety, to carry out the will and orders of a generator crime model, or to themselves become a role model for future killers (Langman 2017, 2018).

More generally, generator crime models felt to be most likely to encourage copycat crimes express positive motives for committing crime and are portrayed as heroic, competent, attractive, admired, high status, and instructive (Bandura 1995; Wilson, Colvin, and Smith 2002). The impact of these characteristics increases with a potential copycat offender's identification with a generator crime model and with similarity between model and copier in age, gender, and race (De Graaf et al. 2012; Kambam et al. 2020). Seeing media crime models who are like themselves successfully commit crimes is hypothesized to increase perceptions of self-efficacy and subsequently to increase the copying of crimes by potential copycat offenders (Bandura 1995; Wilson, Colvin, and Smith 2002). The most important model characteristics, above demographics, seem to relate to the portrayed consequences to the crime model of committing the generator crime (Akers 2011; Bandura and Walters 1963). Observed or inferred rewards or punishments that are rendered on the crime model are felt to strongly influence whether a possible copier attempts to imitate criminal behavior. The success of the media crime model is seen as more important than whether the criminal behavior is portrayed as good or bad or there is a demographic match between the media crime model and observers considering copying them (Bandura 1973).

In sum, media crime models shown as having positive motives (breaking the law to protect the weak for example), as heroic, competent, and instructive, and as similar in age, gender, and race to potential copycats are hypothesized to generally increase the copycat effect (Bandura 1995; Bandura and Walters 1963; Wilson, Colvin, and Smith 2002). An important source of influence is speculated to be the rise in the perception of criminal self-efficacy in offenders due to portrayal of successful media crime models (Bandura 1995; Wilson, Colvin, and

Smith 2002). It also follows that media crime model portrayals that foster an illusionary pseudosocial relationship with media consumers are expected to result in more individuals acquiring crime instructions from their criminogenic media friends (Rubin 2002, citing Horton and Wohl 1956). In the diffusion of innovations perspective, this enhancing effect would be heightened for crime models who are additionally perceived by candidate copycat criminals as trusted change agents and social opinion leaders (Rogers 2003). Together, these expectations lead to five characteristics of generator crime models. The hypothesized content that encourages copycat crime includes the following:

1. Successful and unpunished crime models
2. Generator crime models portrayed as heroic, competent, attractive, admired, high status, and instructive, with positive motives for committing crime
3. Generator crime models who are identified with and demographically similar to potential copycat offenders
4. Generator crime models who foster a media-based social relationship with potential copycat offenders
5. Generator crime models who serve as change agents, opinion leaders, or observable examples of successful criminals

In sum, regarding the portrayals of generator crimes and copycat crime models, the current position regarding copycat-generator crime and media crime model content is that the most imitated crime content will be that which reinforces criminality, contains numerous criminal role models, and teaches that crime is successful, permissible, justified, rewarded, and unpunished. The most important crime model characteristics relate to portrayed consequences of crime that lead to positive expectations about copycat crime and raise criminal self-efficacy on the part of copiers (Bandura and Walters 1963). Having considered the media content most likely to create a successful copycat-generator crime, we next discuss the traits expected to be common among those who copy those generator crimes.

Copycat Criminal Characteristics

What are the expected characteristics of copycat offenders? An empirically supported supposition is that a media copycat effect is concentrated in existing criminal populations (Surette 2016a, 2017; Surette and Chadee 2020). For example, in the reported anecdotal cases, most of the individuals who mimic media crimes had prior criminal records or histories of violence (Bailey 1993; Coleman 2004; Helfgott 2015; Myers 2000; Wilson 1987). In the available survey data, incarceration strongly correlated with self-reported copycat crime histories and likely with criminal self-efficacy (Surette 2002, 2013a, 2020b; Surette and Chadee 2020; Surette and Maze 2015).

Additionally, the foundational theories indicated, and surveys of self-reported copycat criminals empirically supported, the two demographic factors of gender and age as traits that consistently distinguish copycat from noncopycat offenders. In one survey of 1,420 inmates, older inmates were significantly less likely to report past copycat crime involvement, and the mean age reported for committing a copycat crime was eighteen (Surette 2020b). Multivariate analysis of data from another survey suggested that younger, socially isolated juveniles were more at risk for copying crime (Surette 2013a). Similarly, gender was reliably associated with self-reported copycat crime, with males substantially more likely to report copycat histories than females. Race is not a factor, with copycat crime being equally likely for US whites and African Americans (Surette 2002, 2013a, 2020b; Surette and Maze 2015). Gould and Shaffer (1986), Hassan (1995), O'Carroll and Potter (1994), Pirkis and Blood (2001), and Stack (2000) have found that additional matches between media crime models and real-world copiers on age, race, and gender enhance imitation. Gender appears to interact with age and exposure to real-world crime models and criminal innovativeness, indicating a different copycat crime dynamic for males and females (Surette 2013a 2020b). And while increased age was associated with decreased copycat histories overall, the decrease was significantly greater for females than for males (Surette 2020b).

Personality Traits

In addition to the demographics of being young, male, and already involved with crime, additional psychological and social factors further describe a typical copycat offender. For example, it is hypothesized that copycat criminals will significantly differ from those who copy law-abiding behaviors in their social standing and access to social resources. The personality trait, however, that is hypothesized as most important for a copycat offender is high criminal self-efficacy (Bandura 1995), which is expected to lead to increased motivation to copy a crime via expanded crime goal setting, a willingness to expend more effort in copycat crime attempts, increased perseverance in the face of difficulties, and resilience to copycat crime failures (Bandura 1995). Copycat offenders with high criminal self-efficacy are expected to copy more difficult crimes and see such crimes as posing challenges rather than threats. Two indirect surrogate indicators of criminal self-efficacy measured by number of prior arrests and prior and current incarcerations were reported in multiple studies as significantly correlated with copycat crime, particularly for juveniles (Surette 2002, 2013a; Surette and Chadee 2020; Surette and Maze 2015). The cumulative expectation is that established, confident offenders who see copying media-modeled crimes as good means for attaining material or social goals will copy a crime when presented with the opportunity (Rogers 2003).

The copycat crime offender characteristic seen as second in importance is criminal innovativeness. From social diffusion research, covariates of innovativeness for socially endorsed behaviors were found to be higher education, literacy, social status, and upward social mobility. Innovative people additionally were found to be more empathic, favorably view change, cope better with uncertainty and risk, and think of themselves as in control (Rogers 2003). The relevant question is whether being criminally innovative is similarly situated. Some personality traits related to criminal innovativeness are very likely to be reversed from general noncriminal innovativeness. For example, those with lower social status may be more criminally innovative, and it is logical that criminal innovativeness might be higher in those who are less educated and literate and have lower social status, social mobility, aspirations, and empathy. Based on the nature and social approbation associated with most crime, the expectation is that copier characteristics associated with criminal innovativeness will be substantially different from those associated with socially positive innovativeness. In addition to criminal self-efficacy and innovation, other individual-level characteristics have been hypothesized to increase copycat crime effects, some empirically supported in the copycat offender surveys. These include low self-esteem, low self-control, disinhibition, fame and sensation seeking, a history of reward for imitation, weak social bonding, and high dependency (Akers 2011; Bandura and Walters 1963; Gottfredson and Hirschi 1990; Haridakis 2002; Pratt and Cullen 2005; Surette and Maze 2015).

The perceptions of copycat offenders concerning personal and institutional relationships are also important (Langman 2018; Lankford 2021).

First, do they feel a strong personal connection with the copycat generator crime model to the point of mentally assuming the model's role? Do they role-play the generator crime offender? Second, is their relationship to the criminal justice system and punishment for past crime one that increases copycat effects? Enjoyment in seeing laws broken, a high interest in crime-related media content, and a haphazard history of punishment for past crimes have been linked to copycat effects (Bryant and Miron 2002). Specific to the rare violent copycat offender, the linked characteristics for males with bizarre copycat violence include delusional personalities, histories of high interest in guns and law enforcement, and personal psychotic deterioration (Bandura 1973; Haridakis 2002; Lankford 2021; Sparks and Sparks 2002, citing Zillmann and Weaver 1997).

Lastly, research related to the role of copier intelligence produces mixed hypotheses (Surette 2016a). Elaboration likelihood theory posits that high intelligence helps reception of new information, thereby making following crime steps easier, but that low intelligence helps the yielding processes, so that a low-intelligence person will more easily agree that copying a generator crime is a good idea (Petty, Priester, and Brinol 2002). Therefore, both high and low intelligence are speculated to increase copying crime but by different routes. Higher intelligence is speculated to increase the acquisition of criminogenic knowledge; lower intelligence is hypothesized to ease the decision to copy the criminal behavior.

In total, seven resulting hypotheses summarize the expected characteristics of copycat offenders:

1. The most important copycat crime personality trait is high criminal self-efficacy.
2. The second most important copycat crime personality trait is high criminal innovativeness.
3. Individuals with low self-esteem, social status, self-control, inhibition, education and literacy, social mobility, empathy, and dogmatism, who are sensation seeking, enjoy seeing laws broken, and have a history of being rewarded for imitation, will more likely be copycats.
4. High intelligence increases the acquisition of criminogenic knowledge and the learning of crime steps, and low intelligence increases the tendency to decide to copy criminal behavior.
5. Delusional individuals with high interest in guns and law enforcement, intense exposure to violent media generator crimes, and

social situations of idleness, seclusion, resentment, and perceived persecution are more likely to copycat criminal violence.

6. Individuals who mentally substitute themselves for a media crime model are more likely to copycat.
7. Individuals with a criminal history of inconsistent punishment for crime are more likely to copycat.

Among the hypothesized significant characteristics of copycat offenders, the most important personality trait is thought to be high criminal self-efficacy, followed by high criminal innovativeness. After those two characteristics, a large set of possible traits have been suggested, and individuals with more of them are hypothesized to be more at risk for committing copycat crimes. Violent copycat criminals are thought to have a unique set of characteristics and represent a distinct subgroup of copycat offenders (Lankford 2021). With competing hypotheses, the role of intelligence level in copycat crime remains ambiguous. Importantly, the characteristics associated with copycat crime offenders are expected to significantly differ from those found for the copiers of socially positive innovations. Belying and confounding a search for characteristics that differentiate copycat offenders from noncopycat offenders, many pro-copycat crime traits also correlate with general-community criminality. An individual sharing these traits is more at-risk to commit crime but not necessarily copycat crime. As indicators rather than determinants, these traits help with recognizing copycat offenders, but the more important key differentiating factors are hypothesized to pertain to copycat crime offenders' relationship to media and media crime content, not their personality traits.

Copycat Offender Relationship with Media

First, as noted earlier, the quantity of media consumed is not a reliable factor for distinguishing between copycat criminals and noncopycat criminals. Prior studies by Bandura (1973) and Newburn (1994) found few differences between juvenile offenders and nonoffenders in media consumption and use. Both copycat and noncopycat offenders interact most often on a daily basis with the medium of popular music. Although interaction with television and film is reported as less frequent than that with music in terms of hours, both copycat and noncopycat inmates rate visual media as more popular than music (Surette 2013a, 2020b). Notably, and in contrast to the level of public concern they generate, video games are reported as the favorite medium by only about one in ten copycat crime offenders.

Hence, for copycat crime it appears that the quantity of media is not as important as the quality of the interaction. When quality of interaction is examined, media immersion and fixation on criminogenic content have been argued as copying precedents (Mundorf and Laird 2002; Rogers 2003) and found to be significantly correlated with a history of copycat crimes (Surette 2013a). An immersive state is thought to be linked to a narrative persuasion effect.[3] The more transported, absorbed, or engaged consumers become with criminogenic content, the more likely they are felt to become immersed in and fixate on generator crime content. In addition, the more individual offenders fixate on a single media source, the more they are expected to copy embedded generator crimes. Along the same lines, media dependence at an early age should increase copycat likelihood by narrowing the knowledge sources about the world used by copycat criminals. Finally, a person's level of interest in media crime content has also been forwarded as an indicator of copycat tendencies.

The level of interactivity and perception of usefulness afforded the media are additional hypothetical media interaction factors thought to increase the likelihood of copycat crime. Increased interactivity boosts children's liking of characters, and video games that employ vicarious aggressive action and prime aggressive scripts have been cited as sources of violent problem-solving strategies (Mundorf and Laird 2002). Concerning the perceived usefulness of media criminogenic information, uses and gratifications theory predicts that offenders and persons dedicated to committing a crime will see generator crimes as more useful and will be more at-risk for copycat effects (Fisch 2002; Rubin 2002; Surette 2002, 2013a). Empirical support for this connection is provided by Surette (2013a), who found that copycat offenders who saw the media as a helpful source of crime knowledge and simultaneously were immersed and engaged in media content were more likely to report personal copycat crime histories.

An emerging copycat crime research question concerns new media's ability to move consumer interaction with media crime content from passive to active coproduction and distribution of content (Surette 2017). One expected result is that the narrative persuasion impact of criminogenic media will increase when delivered via new media as narrative media products and new-media technologies share the goal of enhanced, more engaging, and more lifelike media experiences (Biocca

2013). Increased media interactivity and higher virtual reality capabilities should also lead to higher levels of user immersion in media and subsequently higher copycat crime levels (Mundorf and Laird 2002; Surette 2017). Thus, new-media generator copycat crimes can be coauthored by potential copycat crime consumers and tailored to meet specific idiosyncratic user crime needs, easing the acquisition of crime scripts and heightening the likelihood of crime implementation.

To date, the bulk of the research in the copycat foundational theory perspectives has been based on conceptualizing human interactions through face-to-face primary group encounters with family and friends. New media, however, have created a new category of primary groups that eliminate the need for face-to-face encounters and provide a copycat pathway that combines the power of face-to-face encouragement while maintaining anonymity when seeking out crime instructions (Etzioni and Etzioni 1997; Porter 2004). It is expected that the combination of the two will substantially increase new-media-based copycat effects. In sum, individuals who prefer crime content, see that content as instructional, and immerse themselves in criminogenic media content are predicted to be more likely to be copycat offenders (Akers 2011; Haridakis 2002). These effects are heightened for isolated consumers of new media. There are seven associated hypothesized links between the media and copycat offenders:

1. The quantity of media consumed will not significantly differentiate copycat from noncopycat offenders.
2. Visual media will be the most criminogenically helpful to copycat criminals.
3. Lower amounts of reading will be linked to higher copycat likelihood.
4. Immersion, fixation, isolation, and a preference for crime content will increase copycat effects.
5. Individuals who prefer media crime content that is more transporting, absorbing, and engaging are more likely to copy an associated generator crime.
6. Interactivity and virtual reality capabilities of new media will increase the copycat crime rate and the strength of a copycat crime effect.
7. Preestablished offenders with risk-of-arrest concerns will cull the media for innovative risk-reduction crime techniques and new criminal behaviors.

To close this discussion of media content, copycat crime, and the expected characteristics of copycat offenders, a set of hypothesized copycat crime characteristics that distinguish copycat from noncopycat offenders is suggested. In surveys of incarcerated juvenile and adult males and females (Surette 2002, 2013a, 2020b; Surette and Chadee 2020; Surette and Maze 2015), the respondents who described a past copycat crime provide a basis for constructing a profile of a typical copycat crime and copycat offender. In addition to being committed most often by young males, most copycat crimes are perpetrated by lone offenders as opposed to offender groups. More than half of the reported copycat crimes are spontaneous, and the large majority involve property rather than violent crimes. More than half are successful in terms of going unpunished and undiscovered. Contrary to its media portrait, the typical self-reported copycat crime is neither homicidal nor violent but is instead a crime involving property and committed by a young male acting alone on the spur of the moment.

Copycat Crime Setting and Culture

The setting where potential copycat offenders sit has been long forwarded as more important for copycat crime than their individual characteristics or the characteristics of their media content. The media are not the dominant cause of crime in society, but media-supplied criminal models and crime techniques can create a conducive social atmosphere for the criminally predisposed to emulate crimes. It has been felt for a half century that culture, local environment, access to weapons, existing crime levels, and other social-setting characteristics determine the copying of crimes (Bandura 1973). The presumption is that the prevalence of copycat crime is determined at the social-structural level, and some cultures, social structures, and community environments increase the capability of media to generate copycat crime independent of audience traits or media content (Akers 2011). From this premise, it is hypothesized that the most impactful copycat crime settings will be found at the family and neighborhood levels.

Parents, Family, and Neighborhood Crime Models

Family context and parental actions are seen as keys to copycat crime in offenders. The interaction of real-world and media crime models has been found to be significantly related to self-reported copycat crime (Surette

2013a). In addition, the most important media-consumption settings are the family and neighborhood as they determine what a potential copycat offender expects the social reaction to a copycat crime to be and their estimation of the likelihood of reward versus punishment for copying a crime (Akers 2011; Bandura 1973). It follows that the single most important setting characteristic for copycat crime is the availability of real-world crime models in the home and community. Exposure to multiple crime models significantly interacts with criminal innovativeness, increasing the crime model's importance for copycat crime (Surette 2013a).

While both family and neighborhood are hypothesized to play significant roles in copycat crime, those roles are not yet specified. At the family-setting level, criminal parents should produce more copycat criminal offspring, while early exposure to law-abiding family models will be a copycat crime insulator (Mazur 2002; Bandura and Walters 1963). Individuals less involved with family are hypothesized to be more likely to be media dependent and hence more likely to be copycat offenders (Akers 2011). Additionally, criminal parents, even when they preach law abiding and punish law breaking, model and thereby encourage criminal behavior. By observing criminal successes in both media content and real-world settings, at-risk copycat offenders will also have reduced the deterrent power of media-portrayed punishment (Bandura 1973; Surette 2013b). Similarly, an enhanced copying effect is expected for offenders weakly networked into neighborhood law-abiding groups and strongly networked into criminal groups (Akers 2011; Rogers 2003).

At the neighborhood level, exposure to real-world crime has been indicated as one of the more predictive factors of copycat crime (Heller and Polsky 1976a, 1976b; Pease and Love 1984b). Exposure to real-world crime can come from criminal friends and other neighborhood residents, in addition to parents and family members (Bandura and Walters 1963; Loeffler and Flaxman 2018; Mazur 2002). Social disorganization at the neighborhood level is additionally expected to increase the copycat effect of media generator crimes by providing more opportunities to implement a copycat crime. Similarly, a school milieu that is crowded, tense, and violent encourages general criminality and is speculated to be an important social-context factor related to juvenile copycat crime (Pepler and Slaby 1994). Thus, in high-crime, low-punishment communities, the estimation of the probability of being caught and the perception of comparatively low severity of likely punishment should result in copycat criminals having increased confidence that they can reduce their risk of punishment and overestimating their chances of criminal success (Bandura 1973).

Culture and Copycat Crime

Beyond the family and neighborhood, the larger social culture is an important copycat crime factor (Niederkrotenthaler and Stack 2017). For example, the questionable but depended-upon deterrent of media content showing punishment of crime is expected to be substantially derailed in cultures where punishment is haphazard and intermittent (Bandura 1973). Copycat crime in these cultures will be the hardest to eliminate as the copiers will not expect a reward for each crime but will anticipate that the next crime might be rewarded. Criminal justice systems that are viewed as oppressive or illegitimate should exacerbate the ineffectiveness of punishment and increase the acceptability of copycat crime in their respective societies. Where a crime-saturated culture has substituted for a law-abiding one, the additional cultural traits of crime tolerance, high societal crime levels, and a crime-soaked media will collectively increase copycat crime levels and the diffusion of copycat crime (Akers 2011).

In sum, cultures with inconsistent patterns of punishment and rewards are hypothesized to generate copycat offenders who will be the hardest to dissuade. Along similar lines, Ruth Penfold-Mounce (2010) and Majid Yar (2012) describe the intersection of crime, celebrity, and media so that societies with real and media crime models and with values, structures, and histories that support and encourage crime can be expected to generate the highest aggregate copycat crime rates. The following seven characteristics increase the likelihood of copycat crime and are associated with family, community, and culture characteristics:

1. Criminally involved parents
2. Availability of observable real-world crime models
3. Neighborhood social disorganization, racial strife, income disparities, and deteriorating social conditions
4. Weak neighborhood law-abiding group networks and strong deviant group networks
5. Combined crime culture, crime-saturated media, and coexposure to real-world and media crime models
6. Social conditions and cultural beliefs that increase the permissibility and functional value of crime
7. Family, neighborhood, and cultural histories of crime rewarded, justified, and unchallenged

A Copycat Crime Offender Profile

Based upon the hypotheses to this point and the research from the five reviewed research traditions, what does a profile of a copycat offender look like? At-risk copycat offenders are hypothesized as best flagged by the presence of four factors: media immersion, criminal self-efficacy, a haphazard punishment history for committing crimes, and a crime-supporting cultural, neighborhood, and family setting (Surette 2016a).

Concerning media immersion, copycat offenders are hypothesized to be individuals who prefer media crime content, see that content as instructional, and submerge themselves in the criminogenic content. Second, individuals with high criminal self-efficacy beliefs are felt to be significantly more at-risk for copycat effects. Although the rank order of the personality traits is not yet known, criminal self-efficacy belief is thought to relate to the highest copycat risk. Third, a personal criminal history that reflects more reward than punishment for prior criminal behavior will increase individuals' belief in their criminal self-efficacy and their expectation of success from copying a media-rendered crime. Last, living in a larger culture and in immediate family and neighborhood environments that encourage and justify crime is hypothesized to be a strong flag for copycat crime risk. The highest copycat crime rates should be generated in countries where criminogenic media models abound and where crime has cultural and local social value (Penfold-Mounce 2010; Yar 2012). Prevalent media messages that portray crime as rewarding, justified, and unchallenged provide aggregate-level copycat crime flags; personal offense histories, pro-crime attitudes, and family and neighborhood criminal environments provide individual-level flags.

A copycat crime at-risk profile built around an individual's media immersion, criminal self-efficacy belief, criminal punishment history, and family, neighborhood, and societal environments emerges. Matching the profile at a number of points, many present-day young-adult offenders globally are theorized to be vulnerable to copycat crime influences. Note that the copycat offender profile does not imply that all matching offenders will commit a copycat crime. The profile encompasses the factors that most raise the probability of an offender committing a copycat crime. While most at-risk for committing a copycat crime, profile-matching individuals may be protected by other anti–copycat crime insulators or simply lack opportunities to act on their acquired copycat crime knowledge.

Therefore, regarding the dynamics of copycat crimes, whether copycat crime effects emerge in any specific instance depends on the interaction of the content of a media generator crime and the characteristics of offenders and their environments. First, detailed instruction in a successful unpunished crime, combined with demonstrations and guided practice for potential copycat offenders, is hypothesized as the most powerful media-based engine for copycat crimes. These copycat engines are predicted to influence young males more than other demographic groups. The fact of youth being a significant copycat offender characteristic suggests two explanations. Either maturation reduces copycat behavior or interactive new media have increasingly criminogenically influenced younger people. Some combination of these two dynamics is likely, as the association between crime histories, criminal relatives and neighbors, and copycat crime has been consistently reported (Surette 2013a; Surette and Maze 2015). The existence of low-crime societies with high levels of media crime content (Japan, for example) indicates the importance of culture and its ability to trump media content and individual characteristics.

Combining research results from the foundational theories and the copycat crime self-report surveys, the hypothesized most likely copycat criminals are socially isolated but criminally confident offenders who have immersed themselves in criminogenic media and see themselves as similar to generator crime models. They engage with crime-saturated media, live in crime-saturated cultures, are surrounded by crime models, and are presented with ample opportunities to commit crimes. Collectively, the speculations drawn from the five foundational theoretical areas and relevant research lead to three general copycat crime hypotheses:

1. Copycat effects are relatively rare and most likely to appear in at-risk individuals predisposed to crime in preexisting criminal populations.
2. The effect of the media is more qualitative, affecting criminal behavior, than quantitative, affecting the number of criminals.
3. New media's ability to generate at-risk individuals predisposed to copycat crime will enhance copycat effects.

Rare and concentrated in at-risk, established offenders, copycat effects are not expected to have a strong criminalization impact on individuals, affecting the precommitted and predisposed by shaping crime more than triggering it. However, characteristics of new social media and how the young interact with them are predicted to increase copycat crime effects in the future. Taken together, the above three hypotheses suggest that in the near term, copycat crime will remain a mostly youthful act and not a common aggregate-level crime phenomenon. Copycat crime is expected to increase among youth as the impact of social media spreads but not in amounts that will quickly become apparent in overall crime rates.

A Copycat Crime–Copycat Offender Typology

The copycat crime hypotheses imply that copycat crime is not monolithic and that many varieties of copycat crime exist. A copycat crime can be a minor, trivial offense, a horrendous mass-fatality event, a property crime, a felony, a misdemeanor, or another type of crime. What makes a crime a copycat are not the elements of the crime but the dynamics of its birth. Given the wide range of copycat possibilities, how to categorize copycat crime for study is an issue. Varieties of copycat crime can be differentiated along various dimensions and combined into different subsets depending upon what features are used.

Nearly forty years ago, Susan Pease and Craig Love (1984a) presented the first attempt at a copycat crime typology based on the two dimensions of time and motive, using a mix of personal characteristics, offense features, and motive-related variables, for four types of copycat crime: instrumental spontaneous crimes (opportunity theft), instrumental planned crimes (planned robbery), emotive spontaneous crimes (bar fight assault), and emotive planned crimes (plotted revenge). Other possible dimensions for a copycat crime typology could take into account whether the copycat crime is simple or complex, as the copycat process will differ for complex crimes and the precrime requirements for simple and complex copycat crimes will contrast substantially. Copycat crimes could also be typed based on Rogers's (2003) diffusion of innovations ideas, applying his adopter groups of innovators, early adopters, and so on, or a typology based on differentiating loner from group copycats could be pursued.

In this work, a copycat typology developed for copycat arsonists by Doley, Ferguson, and Surette (2013) is adapted to categorize copycat crime. The copycat crime typology offered in Table 7.1 is based upon three dimensions felt to be the most important for distinguishing copycat crimes from one another. One dimension takes into account a characteristic of the crime, a second looks at the role of the media, and a third looks at the motivation of the copycat criminal. While not exhaustive, the resulting typology factors in the crime, the media, and the offender and provides an initial map for conducting research on copycat crime. In this typology, copycat crimes can be either planned or spontaneous crimes;

Table 7.1 A Copycat Crime Typology

	Crime Type		Media Role		Crime Motivation	
	Planned	Spontaneous	Genesis	Metamorphic	Risk Reduction	Media Attention
Copycat crime characteristics	Goal directed Profit or prestige Common	Reactive Emotion driven Rare	Media as trigger, creating a crime that would not have occurred otherwise Rare	Media as rudder, shaping the form of a crime that would have occurred anyway Common	Purposely hidden to hide crime or offender connection to crime Common	Purposely open to attract attention or show connection to crime Rare
Copycat offender characteristics	Males Juveniles Career offenders	Males Juveniles Career offenders History of violence	Trouble discerning reality from fiction Identification with media crime models	Males Juveniles Career offenders	Males Juveniles Career offenders	High need for fame Socialization into deviant group
High risk factor	Career property offender	Career violent offender	Inappropriate interest in crime scripts	Criminal history	Attitudes and values that support criminality	High need for fame
Other risk factors	Gang membership Self-regulation issues	Self-regulation issues Violent family and community environment	Attitudes that support crime Disorganized personal history	Gang membership	Self-regulation issues Inappropriate interest in crime scripts Exposure to criminal models and recidivists	Attitudes and values that support crime Radicalization Inappropriate interest in crime scripts
Features	Attitudes and values that support criminality	Impulsivity Antisocial values and attitudes that support criminality	Immersion in crime media Fascination with violent media Impulsivity	Immersion in crime media Poor communication skills Impulsivity Isolation	View of media as credible High criminal self-efficacy Chronic criminal behavior	High need for recognition Antisocial personality disorder Chronic violent behavior
Motivators	Material gain or increase in peer group social status	Revenge Anger Thrill seeking Boredom	Boredom Need for recognition or attention	Varied Spanning all copycat crime types	Sanction avoidance	Publicity

Source: Adapted from Doley, Ferguson, and Surette 2013, 1482.

media-triggered genesis crimes in which the media causes a new crime to occur or media-molded metamorphic crimes in which the media shape how a crime unfolds; or a copycat crime committed with the goal of reducing the risk of apprehension or conversely to gain media attention.

Planned copycat crimes are normally those that have an instrumental goal such as money and will be distinguished by their precrime rehearsals, acquisition of supplies, and postcrime steps. In contrast, spontaneous copycat crimes will be spur-of-the-moment opportunity crimes usually without a clear material goal but frequently committed simply for excitement. Precrime thought is minimal, and postcrime plans are largely absent. Both planned and spontaneous copycat crimes are likely to be committed by juvenile male career offenders with antisocial attitudes. The two types differ in that spontaneous copycat crime offenders are thought more likely to have violent histories and to commit violent copycat crimes, whereas planned copycat crime offenders are thought more likely to be career property offenders or delinquent gang members. An example of a planned copycat crime is the bank robbery attempted by a group of offenders modeled on the movie *Set It Off* (see Chapter 6). Examples of spontaneous copycat crimes would be the swastika vandalism wave described in Box 5.1.

Regarding the two roles that media can play, genesis copycat crimes would not have occurred without the media and are likely rare. Media metamorphic copycat crimes, on the other hand, in which offenders look to the media for crime models and crime instructions, would have been committed in some fashion without the media's input but are substantially shaped by the media. Thus, if a crime would not have been committed without the media's influence, it qualifies as a genesis copycat; if it would have been committed but differently, it is a metamorphic copycat. Metamorphic copycat crimes are more likely to be planned and committed by career offenders. Genesis copycat crimes are hypothesized to be committed by persons who are deeply immersed in media crime content and identify more strongly with media characters. Examples of genesis copycat crimes include some of the *Grand Theft Auto*–related crimes where the copycat offenders stated that they simply wanted to see how it felt to commit a crime similar to ones in the game (see Box 8.8). Metamorphic copycat crimes are exemplified by homicides committed using the killer's mask from the movie *Scream* and John Hinckley Jr.'s assassination attempt based on the film *Taxi Driver* (see Chapter 6).

The typology's third dimension dichotomizes the copycat offender's motivation for copying as either publicity or reduced chance of failure and arrest. The two motivations are best indicated by whether the copycat criminal attempts to hide or openly commits the crime. In the former instance, copiers work to keep their copied crimes unobserved and undiscovered. In the latter, they strive to attract media attention and maximize a crime's news value. The media-attention offenders are high-profile copycats and thought to be rare; the risk-reduction offenders are low-profile copycats and thought to comprise the bulk of copycat offenders as they align closely with traditional criminality. Both types of copycats can be career offenders who see the media in opposite ways. Risk-reduction copycats see the media as confidential sources of knowledge and media information as useful and credible. Media attention copycats see the media as tools to influence others and a way to maximize the social impact of their crimes. Accordingly, the crimes they commit differ. Risk-reduction crimes can be violent, such as homicide, but are thought to more often be property, economic, and white-collar crimes. Media-attention copycat crimes can be low-level crimes like vandalism but are often dramatic, spectacular, visual crimes with multiple causalities, such as suicide bombings and acts of terrorism (Ezeihuoma 2020). The spate of online beheadings beginning in 2014 are examples of media-attention copycat crimes (Koch 2018). Risk-reduction copycats would include the practice of sexual offenders copying *CSI* television program steps to contaminate forensic evidence (Gillis 2005; Surette 2015a). Applying the three dichotomous dimensions, eight copycat crime combinations result:

1. Planned/genesis/risk-reduction copycat crimes: Planned combined with genesis copycat crimes are likely rare as they require foresight combined with media creation of the crime. The logical sequence would be for media genesis to occur first, seeding the idea for the crime, followed by planning to reduce the risk of failure and arrest. The bank robbery copied from the *Set It Off* movie is an example.

2. Planned/genesis/media-attention copycat crimes: A similar logic to planned/generic/risk-reduction copycat crimes applies, except the copycat offender's goal in this copycat set is to garner media attention and maximize publicity. The far-right radicalization of individuals who otherwise would not have committed a crime describes this copycat process. The offender who armed himself and invaded a pizza shop in 2017 looking for a secret pedophile ring linked to Hillary Clinton would be an example.[4]

3. Planned/metamorphic/risk-reduction copycat crimes: Felt to be common, these copycat crimes are thought-out affairs where the media help to mold a crime that would have been committed regardless. The media generator crime is culled for tips and steps

to lessen the copycat offender's odds of failure and arrest. An example would be cases where rapists have attempted to destroy forensic evidence by forcing victims to shower or by dumping ashtrays over crime scenes (Gillis 2005).

4. Planned/metamorphic/media-attention copycat crimes: For pre-planned, media-molded copycat crimes that are aimed at gaining media attention, the copycat offender looks to copy and commit a crime in a way that ensures media coverage. Examples include highly newsworthy suicide terrorist acts where no effort is made to hide identities and intentionally perpetrated in areas saturated with surveillance cameras or tourists (Pape 2006).

5. Spontaneous/genesis/risk-reduction copycat crimes: In these crimes a copycat offender suddenly sees a crime observed in the media as providing a good way to successfully commit a crime of opportunity without suffering negative consequences. An example would be spontaneously shoplifting in a retail store when a clerk is distracted, as seen in a television program (Bai, Wu, and Cheung 2019).

6. Spontaneous/genesis/media-attention copycat crimes: In this set of copycat crimes a copycat offender also suddenly sees the media as providing a good method to successfully commit a crime of opportunity. However, the goal of the crime is to generate publicity and attention. Spontaneous vandalism, such as the spray painting of swastikas, is an example.

7. Spontaneous/metamorphic/risk-reduction copycat crimes: This set includes copycat crimes aimed at reducing the odds of discovery and arrest; the decision to copy a crime is sudden, but the copied crime is not a close replica of the generator crime. A copycat criminal might apply a risk-reduction technique gleaned from one type of crime to another. An example would be political protestors hiding their identities by pulling their shirts over their faces and looters, having seen this on the news, spontaneously doing the same while entering and looting a retail store (Zhu, Skoric, and Shen 2017).

8. Spontaneous/metamorphic/media-attention copycat crimes: In this last set, copycat offenders adapt a previous method to attract media attention to an opportunity crime. The unanticipated decision to burn an unoccupied police vehicle made after seeing arson of buildings in other locations in the news is an example (Hinds-Aldrich 2009).

While sharing some characteristics, each of this octet of copycat crimes is expected to develop and present in different ways. They and the preceding copycat crime hypotheses encourage researchers to move past a narrow, simplistic perception of copycat crimes and to study copycat crime as a multifaceted crime phenomenon. The copycat crime categories may share media roots, but they develop into a broad, diverse set of crimes with unique dynamics requiring distinct explanations. With a conceptual theoretical base for copycat crime and a set of plausible hypotheses to pursue in hand, scholarly research on copycat crime can begin to supplant misleading journalistic descriptions. Characteristics of media content, generator crimes, copycat offenders, social settings, and the interactions between them are all expected to play a significant role in generating copycat crime.

Remaining to be discussed is how media variation associates with copycat crime. Like copycat crime, the media are not monolithic, and copycat crime is not expected to manifest in the same way across different media. With that expectation, Chapter 8 discusses how the dynamics of copycat crime shift across types of media.

Notes

1. Discussions of copycat crime concepts and research questions draws upon Surette 2016a.

2. Unlike the impact of real-world models, the importance of media-provided crime models for violence and criminality has not received consistent empirical research support and remains debated. Initially the research focused on television and violence and more recently on violent video game play and player aggression, the idea that a direct causal connection between media exposure and aggression exists has been heavily criticized (Ferguson and Kilburn 2009; Freedman 1984, 2002; Gauntlett 2005; Grimes, Anderson, and Bergen 2008; Savage 2004, 2008). Those who have looked for a direct criminogenic effect of media exposure have generally reported weak evidence (Ferguson et al. 2008; Ferguson, San Miguel, and Hartley 2009; Ferguson and Dyck 2012; Grimes, Anderson, and Bergen 2008).

3. For examples and discussions of immersive interest in content, see Akers 2011; Bandura 1973; Fisch 2002; Haridakis 2002; Rogers 2003; Rubin 2002.

4. Without a significant criminal history, the "Pizzagate" offender pled guilty and was sentenced to four years in prison for firing three rifle shots inside the Comet Ping Pong restaurant in Washington, DC. He claimed he was attempting to find and rescue child sex slaves that he believed were being held at the restaurant—a belief based on a false story circulating online that connected Hillary Clinton's campaign adviser to the pizzeria through coded messages in leaked emails. Grace Hauck, "'Pizzagate' Shooter Sentenced to 4 Years in Prison," *CNN*, updated June 22, 2017, www.cnn.com/2017/06/22/politics/pizzagate-sentencing/index.html.

8

Copycat Crime
Across the Media

THE MEDIA CAN BE CONCEIVED MOST SIMPLY ALONG TWO dimensions. One dimension follows the different types of media content. The second follows the differing forms of media. The media studies literature has historically described four types of media content: news, entertainment, advertising, and, more recently, infotainment (Surette 2015a). For much of media's history, news and entertainment defined the contours of media content, but infotainment is a recent significant addition and occupies a niche between news and entertainment. Advertising qualifies as another type of content and is extensively embedded within the other three content areas as well as existing within its own products (Surette 2015a).

The forms of media, on the other hand, are not differentiated by their content but defined by their formatting and delivery platforms. Media forms have historically been separated into print, visual, and sound delivery systems collectively known as *legacy media*. A relatively recent addition is media based on digital content and interactive audience involvement known as *new media*. By being fluid and interactive, new media have blurred the media universe by providing simultaneous interactive access via one device to all types of media and all forms of media content. Content in new media often combines print, sound, and visual content and access to news, entertainment, advertising, and infotainment in new ways. Extensive social effects have resulted (Surette 2017). In this volatile media environment, copycat crime is expected to differ both within media content—operating differently across news, entertainment, advertising, and infotainment—and across formatting and forms of delivery in print, sound, visual, and new media. Table 8.1 lists examples of each of the sixteen resulting media content/platform combinations.

Types of Media Content and Copycat Crime

News

The media content marketed as objective and accurate is news content. Mass-media crime news was introduced in the 1840s with the penny press, and by the 1890s crime news was a staple of yellow journalism.[1] As an 1880s editorial by a Reverend Beecher reflects, a belief that crime news is harmful, if not an actual copycat crime generator, has a long history (quoted in Phelps 1911, 267–268):[2]

> Let a man become an atrocious criminal, and, under the pretense of giving news, our daily journals set fourth his life continuously. I do not believe that it is possible for the unshaped young minds of the community to become conversant with the news of crime, in all its forms, and not be injured by it. Familiarity with vice takes away sensibility to vice. And yet gulf streams, vast currents, of criminal news sweep through your houses every day. What would you think if a man were to open a common sewer, and run out of the street through your backyard all the feculent matter of society? Would it conduce to health, comfort, and convenience? And yet to what an extent is the feculent news of the day run through your houses every morning and every evening in the newspapers?

Table 8.1   Media Content and Platforms

	Print	Sound	Visual	New Media
News	Newspapers	Radio news programs	Movie news reels, broadcast news	Twitter, podcasts
Entertainment	Novels	Pop music	Commercial films	TikTok
Infotainment	True crime magazines	Radio dramas	TV news magazines	Podcasts, documentaries
Advertising	Billboards	Product jingles	TV commercials	Social media influencers

The perception of crime news as pernicious continued in the twentieth century and expanded its reach through society. With its delivery via radio in the 1920s and popular visual newsreels shown in movie theaters in the 1930s, the audience no longer needed to be literate (Chibnall 1981; Hughes 1940; Isaacs 1961; Schlesinger, Tumber, and Murdock 1991; Sherizen 1978). In the 1950s television news programs again extended the reach and impact of crime news, providing a home-delivered daily portrait of crime in society. In the late twentieth century, the amount of crime news markedly expanded due to increases in distribution outlets and the emergence of the 24/7 news cycle. As the need for news content expanded, crime news was found to be a cheap, popular filler (Surette 2012, 2015a).

As it developed, contemporary crime news became fundamentally voyeuristic, focusing on rare and distant criminal acts and snapshots of abnormal, usually violent events (Surette 1998). The most dramatic change in crime news occurred with new media, which allow individuals to circumvent the traditional crime news gatekeeping process. News today is rapidly distributed, multidirectional, and fluid. Regarding news of crime, it is common for raw crime portraits to be widely distributed through social media before they appear in legacy media news reports. Thus, contemporary crime news is found either in linear print-based factual renditions (addressing the traditional news coverage questions of who, what, where, when, and how) or in narrative-based visual crime stories where the details of individual crimes are emotionally emphasized (Casey 2010; Drechsel 1983; Freedman 2011; Papke 1987). Both focus on individual crime events more often than on crime as a social issue.

Because crime news focuses on individual criminal events, it emphasizes the reporting of facts and images. One might expect an emphasis on crime facts to result in generator crimes for planned copycat crimes ("Here are news-vetted, fact-based instructions on how to commit a crime; plan accordingly"). However, this is not the case, as news coverage of successful crimes appears to motivate copycat crimes more often than it functions as a source for crime instructions. Paradoxically, copycat offenders report that they look to visual entertainment and infotainment crime media for crime instructions rather than crime news (Surette 2013a; Surette and Maze 2015). Allan Mazur (1982) produced an early research effort on crime news and copycat crime that supports this contention. Showing that crime news content could generate crimes even when not providing crime models, Mazur's study found that bomb threats significantly increased following news coverage of nuclear power issues even though the coverage did not discuss bomb threats.

Additional examples of a copycat effect from crime news content that lacks specific crime instructions included the news coverage of airline hijackings (Holden 1986) and product poisonings (Fletcher 2009; Markel 2014). Neither news coverage of the poisoning of over-the-counter Tylenol pain medicine in the 1980s (see Box 8.2) nor the coverage of a string of airline hijackings in the 1960s provided instructional details, but nevertheless both generated substantial waves of less-than-identical imitations. Support for generator crimes in the news as motivational over instructional is also found in surveys of copycat offenders by Surette (2013a) and Surette and Maze (2015). Incarcerated offenders did not cite news media as a popular source for copycat crime ideas in either of the surveys. Instead, priming and generalized imitation are hypothesized as the main news media mechanisms for a copycat crime effect. Although apparently news coverage rarely serves as a generator of copycat crimes outside terrorist acts and high-profile violent crimes, news of innovative crimes periodically generates copycats. For example, a 2018 news-related copycat crime involved the hiding of needles in strawberries in Australia (Nedim and Holmes 2018). The consensus at this time, though, is that for crime news to generate a copycat effect, the inclusion of do-it-yourself crime instructions is not necessary as the news generator crimes do not have to closely resemble the subsequent copycat crimes.

Box 8.1   Tylenol Copycat Poisonings

The 1982 Tylenol murders were homicidal poisonings via over-the-counter medicines that had been tampered with. The victims had taken Tylenol acetaminophen capsules, purchased in local stores, that had been laced with potassium cyanide and put back on store shelves. Seven people were killed in the original poisonings; several more died in subsequent copycat crimes. The initial deaths were a lead news story nationwide for weeks (Markel 2014).[3] After the massive coverage, illustrating how news can provide motivation without instructions, hundreds of copycat attacks involving Tylenol, other

continues

Box 8.1   Continued

over-the-counter medications, and other types of nonmedicinal products around the United States followed (Fletcher 2009). Two copycat
examples were poisonings resulting from cyanide-laced Excedrin
("Woman Convicted of Killing Two in Excedrin Tampering" 1988).
The copycat criminal had a life insurance policy on her husband that
included a substantial accidental death payment. After he died, doctors
did not detect the cyanide and put the cause of death as due to emphy-
sema. About to lose $100,000 if his death was not ruled an accident, his
widow tampered with five additional bottles of Excedrin and placed
them on local store shelves. Six days later, a second victim died after
ingesting a poisoned capsule. After the second victim's death was
reported in the news, the copycat poisoner called police to state that she
thought her husband had also been poisoned. Investigators became sus-
picious on discovering that she had purchased two of the four known
contaminated bottles at different stores on different days solely by
chance. Eventually, the copycat poisoner's daughter came forward with
an account of her mother's insurance fraud plan. The copycat poisoner
was convicted and given two ninety-year sentences. The original
Tylenol poisoner was never found (Kesling 2013; Pusey 2017).

Concerning copycat crime waves, Vincent Sacco (2005) posited a
sequence for copycat effects to be generated by news coverage. First, a
criminal event with unusual and newsworthy characteristics occurs and is
reported in the news media. Next, some news audience members assess
the crime as helpful in meeting an objective like cash, revenge, or fame.
Some of these audience members subsequently commit similar crimes.
The news media report the copycats as even more newsworthy, which
resets the process as more audience members assess the copycat crimes as
worthy of imitation. Through this process, news media can power substantial crime waves, and when successful and innovative crime models
are provided in the news, the copycat effects can be powerful.

Ironically, while marketed as factual, news content overall appears
to influence copycat crime through delivery not of facts so much as
motivations and generalizable crime models. Traditional news generally
does not provide sufficient instructional details to potential copycats but
instead generates copycat crimes by publicizing successful, simple,

innovative crimes that can be easily modified and copied. Terrorism is one copycat crime area where news coverage appears to provide techniques over motivations and is seen as predictive of copycat events (Jeter 2014, 2017). Brigitte Nacos (2007, 2009) argues that motivated terrorist groups preexist and do not need to be motivated to commit terrorist acts. Terrorists, therefore, take successful innovative terror techniques from news coverage, not encouragement to commit terrorism. Terrorism aside, however, it is the engagement of newsworthy crime that motivates subsequent criminality rather than do-it-yourself instructions (Sacco 2005).

The key difference for copycat crime generation via news is that other types of media content may contain generator crimes, but those crimes do not normally result in the quick creation of more copycat crime–generating media content. While a generator crime in a movie normally takes months or years to produce crime copies, generator crimes that result in news themes operate in compressed time frames (Surette 2016b; Surette et al. 2021). An innovative means to hijack an airline covered in the news can quickly generate a wave of copycat hijackings and second-wave news coverage of them (Holden 1986). Uniquely, the typical news cycle means that copycat crime news can beget more copycat crime news in short order (Chen 2018).

Entertainment

In contrast to crime news, entertainment media involves content that is not forwarded as reflecting reality, its popularity stemming from the pleasurable escape from reality provided through engaging narratives (Surette 2015a). Entertainment content, particularly in commercial movies, is frequently cited as a copycat-generator crime source. Despite entertainment content's not usually reflecting reality, when asked, copycat offenders often mention entertainment products as their source for copycat crime models and crime instructions (Surette 2013a; Surette and Maze 2015). Commercial films like the Batman movies exemplify the entertainment media–copycat crime connection. Dan Frosch and Kirk Johnson (2012, A1) write,

> On July 20, 2012, James Holmes entered the midnight premiere of *The Dark Knight Rises,* the third film in the massively successful Batman trilogy, in a movie theater in Aurora, Colorado. He shot and killed 12 people and wounded 70 others. Witnesses told the police that Mr. Holmes said something to the effect of "I am the Joker,"

according to a federal law enforcement official, and that his hair had been dyed or he was wearing a wig. Then, as people began to rise from their seats in confusion or anxiety, he began to shoot. The gunman paused at least once, several witnesses said, perhaps to reload, and continued firing.

In response to a series of entertainment-content-linked copycat crimes in the late 1990s, John Kunich (2000) contended the entertainment media creators should be held civilly liable for copycat crimes connected to their entertainment media creations. Kunich argued that entertainment content creators are financially successful and frequently admired and reach enormous numbers of paying consumers. In a unique conceptualization to make the generators of copycat crime liable for damages, Kunich described some entertainment media content as "purposely defective" in that its creators and distributors knowingly create dangerously arousing content to attract those most likely to imitate. Kunich (2000, 1225, 1265–1266) argued that mass-entertainment content involving violence appears calculated primarily to appeal to people with an appetite for killing or sociopathic behavior. The preexisting vulnerability of most of the people harmed by ultra-violent entertainment—in a sense, "natural-born copycat killers"—renders them acutely amenable to certain powerful and destructive outside influences. Predisposed to acts of imitative violence, these troubled individuals can be sparked into explosive behavior. The entertainment industry exploits this proclivity by designing and marketing products to appeal to violent urges. These troubled individuals are also predisposed to prefer that type of fringe entertainment. When the entertainment industry designs and markets products to appeal affirmatively to these urges, an entertainment-media shield protecting producers from civil liability becomes difficult to justify. While a unique take, Kunich's argument did not sway the courts, and a copycat crime impact from entertainment remains unfettered.

The irony is that while news media are marketed as realistic and accurate, they are felt to be less instructional (except for terrorists) than entertainment media content. Despite being acknowledged as fictional and frequently portraying physically impossible acts, entertainment media are looked to more often for copycat instructions by copycat offenders. Because crime in entertainment is often detailed and central to the narratives, the speculation is that successful entertainment crimes will increase consumer criminal self-efficacy while providing observable, heavily detailed lessons on how to copy a specific crime. The copycat crime based on *Set It Off* (detailed in Chapter 6) exemplifies how copycat offenders can cull detailed instructions from fictional content. Copycat offenders are more likely to pull crime lessons from entertainment stories about criminals that do not exist than from news reports of real crimes and criminals.

Advertising

Despite the massive amount of advertising that is found across media, copycat crimes linked to specific advertisements have not been reported. This is initially surprising in that advertising content is the only content expressly created to influence behavior. However, while successful with regard to influencing purchasing, social attitudes, fashion, and voting, advertising influence does not extend to copycat crime. This should not be unexpected as inspection of advertising content reveals that advertisements overall portray very little crime, and any violent content is usually shown in humorous contexts (Brown, Bhadury, and Pope 2010). The closest ad-like content comes to generating copycat crime is through media true-crime reenactments, which have been described as crime advertisements (Surette 2015a). In criminology, strain theory sees advertising as an indirect general motivator of property crime. The argument is that the materialistic focus of much advertising causes individuals to desire things they cannot legally afford or socially attain. Karen Hennigan and colleagues speculate that the materialistic messages that dominate advertising generate unmet expectations and frustration (Hennigan et al. 1982), resulting in property crimes in the form of thefts, robberies, and illegal enterprises, albeit not copied from advertising content. Any copycat effect would be a muted one through creation of an ambiguous motivation to steal. To date, product advertising content has not been directly linked to a copycat crime, and ad content has not been forwarded as a significant copycat crime mechanism. Whether the growth of social media will change the current view of a benign relationship between advertising content and copycat crime is a question for future research.

Infotainment

A recent shift in media content is the growth of infotainment. Infotainment content is defined as edited, highly formatted information about the world packaged within ersatz documentary-styled media (Surette 2015a). Infotainment content based on crime and justice has existed for centuries; crime pamphlets and gallows sermons are two early examples. Beginning in the late 1980s, modern crime-related infotainment programs began to appear regularly on television. By the twenty-first century, the line between crime news and crime entertainment content had dissolved (Cavender and Fishman 1998). The feel with infotainment media is that you are learning about reality, when in actuality the consumer receives a highly stylized rendition of a narrow, altered slice of reality (Surette 2015a).

With the development of the internet in the 1990s, infotainment crime content became an immersive copycat-generator crime source, providing instructions, models to emulate, and victim tallies to aim for (Cohen 2015). Because infotainment content is today found in all types of formats and media, its copycat effects are confounded with those related to the other types of media content and technologies but are thought to be extensive. In new-media platforms, the infotainment genre has made celebrities of offenders and popularized iconic generator copycat crimes through easily accessible, extensive online content (Surette et al. 2021). For example, the program *Copycat Killers*, available for viewing on the streaming service ReelZ, offers three years of episodes devoted to murders as copycat crimes.

Today all media forms contain substantial amounts of infotainment content, but it is common in print as true-crime books, like Truman Capote's *In Cold Blood* (see Box 8.2), and in television, films, and podcasts as investigative pseudodocumentary crime stories. Reality-based infotainment crime shows allow contemporary audiences to tag along with police officers, offenders, and victims and learn carefully chosen facts about real crimes. Once digitized, copycat crime messages can be embedded in infotainment products that are felt to attract the full range of copycat offenders described in Chapter 7. Infotainment content provides Albert Bandura's detailed instructions, motivational models, and mental rehearsal necessary for copycat attempts. Marketed as realistic and packaged in narratively persuasive products, generator crimes in visual infotainment formats that are easily and widely accessible in new-media platforms are hypothesized to create the strongest copycat effects. For example, the same generator crime from the print infotainment product *In Cold Blood* (Capote 1966) was not linked to a copycat crime, but the movie based on the book was.[4]

Box 8.2 *In Cold Blood*

Truman Capote's *In Cold Blood* (1966) is an early true-crime book detailing the murders of a Kansas farm family during a 1959 home-invasion robbery planned by a farmhand who had previously worked for the family. The book was a best seller, and a movie based on the book was released in 1967. The murder of a couple on a beach in California twenty years later in 1997 has been labeled a copycat crime linked to the book and to the movie. It was reported that the California killers rented the movie four times and repeatedly watched the step-by-step, documentary-style portrayal of the Kansas killings (O'Kane 2017). Police believed the California murders were random killings inspired by the movie, and prosecutors called them a "thrill killing" influenced by the true-crime story ("Man Convicted in Seaside Slayings" 1999). The California murders matched the Kansas killings in some aspects and differed in others. Both sets of crimes were murder homicides, with the killers setting off for Mexico after the slayings. The crimes differed in that the California murders were not well planned, and there was no prior connection between the killers and victims in California as there was in Kansas.

After making the jump from legacy to new media, media infotainment crime content remains widely popular. Still, the role of infotainment media in copycat crime is not clear, as the content migrates across media content types, formats, and delivery platforms. Due to the amount of such content circulating, infotainment-generated copycat crime has substantial potential. Crime-related infotainment content has the unique ability to combine the motivational potential of news, the instructional detail of entertainment, and the narrative persuasion impact of storytelling, a potential triple copycat crime threat.

Types of Media and Copycat Crime

In addition to different media content, there are different media platforms. The oldest media platforms are the legacy media of print, audio, and video. Each required its own unique technology to create and distribute content. Print required a printer to create the paper page, audio required a radio or phonograph to create a broadcast or record, and video required a camera to create a film and a projector in a theater or a television in a home to distribute images. New media have slowly replaced legacy media by influencing both the creation and the distribution of content and folding the types and forms of media into single devices that deliver digitized content. Contemporary digital media is best known through video games, the internet, and social media.

Print

A link between newspaper reports and public perception of crime waves was reported as early as the 1760s (King 1987). In the 1830s print was the first medium to generate a mass market with the success of penny press daily newspapers and weekly crime magazines. The two most popular print-based entertainment crime genres to emerge in nineteenth-century media were detective and crime thriller magazines and crime dime novels (Casey 2010). In the twentieth century, magazines focusing on crime flourished (Gorn 1992). The comic books of the 1940s are the most recent print-based product to be credited with a serious but questionable copycat crime effect (Nyberg 1998; Phillips and Strobl 2013). Contemporary print media continues to flourish within new-media venues as printed text in digital form in chat rooms, blogs, tweets, and posts (Surette 2017). Much communication today is via the printed word without the printed page.

It is apparently through new media that contemporary print media most strongly generate copycat crime. As the example in Box 8.3 shows, however, from the 1800s into at least the 1970s, print media was a copycat offender's valued source of crime techniques (Hendrick 1977; Surette 2015a). It is thought that engaging, persuasive stories in print were influential copycat crime sources historically. As exemplified by novels such as *The Secret Agent* and *The Sorrows of Young Werther*, print media were regularly accused of generating copycat crime waves. Concerns regarding crime stories published in weekly publications like penny dreadfuls spawned opposition social crusades across the nineteenth century (Dunae 1979; Springhall 1994). For modern legacy media, however, while true-crime books are popular and plentiful, examples of offenders copying a crime based on a true-crime print rendition are rare. Entertainment print media, though, have been more influential on copycat crime, as exemplified by *The Secret Agent*, an early-twentieth-century novel discussed in Box 8.3.

Box 8.3   *The Secret Agent*

First published in 1907, *The Secret Agent* is set in London in 1886 and follows the activities of a spy working for a foreign country. The secret agent in the novel keeps a shop in London, where he lives with his wife, her infirm mother, and her learning-disabled brother. The agent becomes reluctantly involved in an anarchist plot to blow up the Greenwich Observatory. The novel uses characters and events drawn from real life, including the attempted bombing of the Greenwich Observatory in 1894 (Conrad 2009). Conrad's unwitting learning-disabled bomber character shares a fate in the novel with a real-world nineteenth-century French anarchist who died when explosives he was transporting prematurely detonated (Mulry 2000). Since publication, Conrad's novel has been adapted multiple times for film, television, radio, and opera, and it was heavily cited in coverage following the 9/11 terrorist attacks in the United States (Reilly 2018; Shulevitz 2001).

The copycat crimes frequently linked to Conrad's novel are the bombings of Unabomber Ted Kaczynski. Kaczynski had a lifelong connection to the novel prior to his bombing spree, having read it multiple times and modeled himself on the character called the Professor (Conrad 2009; Houen 2002; Woodard 2006). Reflecting a narrative persuasion influence, Kaczynski used the alias "Conrad" during his bombing trips (Conrad 2009; Jackson and Dougall 1998) and advised his family to read *The Secret Agent* to understand him (Oswell 2007). Thus inspired, Kaczynski delivered sixteen bombs around the United States between the late 1970s and the mid-1990s (Lawrence and Jewett 2002). He is serving eight life sentences.

While anecdotal accounts of copycat crimes linked to print media were initially suggestive (Hendrick 1977; National Research Council 2013), as media renditions of the world have evolved to be more realistic, the direct copycat effect of print media has waned (Surette 2017). Recent inmate self-reports do not indicate nondigital, hard-copy print content from books, newspapers, or magazines to be favored sources for copycat offenders (Surette 2013a; Surette and Maze 2015). In combination with visual media, print media is thought to be effective for spreading knowledge about crimes, but today print's copycat impact is thought to arise after it has been digitized and accessibility to its generator crimes freed from a physical paper page (Surette 2020b).

Audio

First delivered and mass-marketed via radio networks, audio media have evolved from vinyl records to their current digital streaming forms. Since the early radio networks, audio media have been able to bypass church, school, family, and community socialization sources and directly influence individuals (Surette 2015a). Audio media are powerful because they deliver information in a linear fashion, like print, while evoking mental images and emotions analogous to visual media. On the entertainment side, radio drama through the 1930s and 1940s broadcast a substantial and popular proportion of crime-fighting, detective, and suspense programming, laying the groundwork for the extensive crime content found in television programming (Cheatwood 2010). For crime news, in the 1920s commercial radio networks established the delivery style of incident-focused descriptive reports of crime.

Audio-linked copycat crime has been most strongly connected to popular music rather than news or drama (Bohm and Surette 2013). Suggesting an audio media–crime link, a set of experiments by Anderson, Carnagey, and Eubanks (2003) report a relationship between violent song lyrics and an increase among listeners in hostile thoughts and aggressive interpretation of social interactions. The extension of such audio-media effects on perceptions and aggression to copycat behaviors has been most strongly argued regarding copycat suicides. Songs like "Suicide Solution" by Ozzy Osbourne, as well as rap, hip-hop, rock, and other types of youth-oriented music, have been forwarded as copycat suicide inducers (Atkin and Abelman 2009). Pop culture songs were also seen as sources for copycat crimes such as homicides, assaults, gang shootings, and rapes (Armstrong 2001; Weitzer and Kubrin 2009). Box 8.4 discusses an example linked to the song "Cop Killer."[5] As with print media, specific how-to instructions for serious crimes are not usually extracted from song lyrics, but motivations and justifications are (Bohm and Surette 2013; Surette 2020a). Accounts of song-driven copycat offenders describe a narrative persuasion process where a copycat listener becomes immersed in the media world created by the music and, often under the influence of drugs, alcohol, or mental illness and faced with a seemingly similar real-world situation, act similarly.

Box 8.4 "Cop Killer"

In 1992, the heavy metal band Body Count released an album containing the song "Cop Killer," a first-person rendition of someone enraged by police brutality who calls for murderous reprisals against police officers. The song contains the following lyrics:

> *Cop killer, it's better you than me*
> *I'm cop killer, fuck police brutality!*
> *Cop killer, I know your family's grievin' (fuck 'em!)*
> *Cop killer, but tonight we get even, hahahaha, yeah!*
> *Cop killer! (What do you want to be when you grow up?)*
> *Cop killer! (Good choice)*
> *Cop killer!*
> *I'm a muthafuckin' cop killer!*

In addition to generating significant social criticism, the song was credited with generating a copycat crime when two Las Vegas police officers were ambushed and fired upon while responding to a domestic call. None were injured, and four juvenile delinquents were subsequently arrested and boasted that the song gave them a duty to get even with a pig (Martin 1993; Watts 2008). Following arrest, one of the juveniles was reported to have recited the song lyrics on the way to jail (Harrington 1992). In this example, the generator crime media did not supply detailed instructions but was able to motivate juveniles to commit a violent criminal act.

Images

Visual media, in the form initially of photographs and then early commercial films, were the first media able to bridge social and linguistic audience differences. Following World War II, television combined the characteristics of both film and radio to become the dominant medium and the primary home entertainment medium (Surette 2015a). With storylines adapted from commercial radio, crime rapidly became a staple of prime-time television entertainment and accounted for around one-third of all prime-time television shows by the 1970s (Dominick 1978).

Visual media appear to be the most powerful copycat crime source and are reported as the most commonly cited influence. Copycat offenders cite films, for example, more than any other medium as their generator crime idea source (Surette 2013a; Surette and Maze 2015).

The movie *The Battle of Algiers*, described in Box 8.5, is an older example, while the television show *Dexter* is a more recent one.[6] The addition of sound to media images has raised copycat crime concerns that became prominent in the 1980s regarding music videos (Atkin and Abelman 2009; Smith and Boyson 2002; Vernallis 2013). Concerns are not surprising as music videos bring engaging storytelling, graphic visuals, and musical elements together in a single immersive media product (Parks and Robers 1998). A contemporary crime-related music video featuring ghost riding of automobiles (see Chapter 1) encouraged copycat crimes across geographically dispersed social groups and resulted in a substantial crime wave in the early twentieth century (Surette 2020a).

Box 8.5   *The Battle of Algiers* and *Dexter*

Visual media are the most commonly cited source of copycat crime ideas, and numerous films and television shows have been connected to copycat waves. Visual media as a copycat crime instruction source are thought popular due to the ease of accessing the content and following clear crime steps embedded within engaging narratives (Surette 2016b). Most movie-linked copycat crimes include a small number of crimes committed by a few offenders. A different sort of example is offered by the movie *The Battle of Algiers,* released in 1965. *The Battle of Algiers* details the creation of a terrorist suicide-bombing cell, its assassination and bombing campaign, and the response by the colonial French authories. Set in 1954–1957 Algiers, it was filmed in an infotainment pseudodocumentary style, unlike the pure media entertainment vehicles that are more often linked to copycat crimes. Following its release, the film was studied by the Irish Republican Army and the Black Panthers in the United States for directions on how to set up and run insurrections, by the US Pentagon after the invasion of Iraq, and likely by al-Qaeda ("From 1966 Comes *The Battle of Algier*s" 2007; Pevere 2004).

The second visual copycat crime example is connected to the television program *Dexter* (Dean 2019). The show's lead character is

continues

Box 8.5   Continued

portrayed as a heroic serial killer who maintains a normal daily life but murders other killers who have avoided justice. The character of Dexter is paradoxically a justice-seeking serial killer hero evoking admiration and, for some, emulation. At least ten real-life murderers have been connected to the show (Green 2017; Ramsland 2014). One of the better known was committed by Mark Twitchell, an aspiring Canadian film maker and fan of the show. Twitchell used the show as a model to create a "kill room" in his garage modeled after Dexter's kill room in the television program and created a fake female online-dating profile to entice potential victims. His first victim managed to escape, but his second victim was killed. Twitchell is currently serving a sentence of twenty-five years to life.

New Media and Copycat Crime

In addition to music videos, new media in the form of interactive video games and internet-based social media platforms have considerable implications for copycat crime. Social media have emerged as copycat crime factors due to having both mass and interpersonal elements and the ability to provide unique one-to-many communication channels (Delwiche and Henderson 2013). New-media users can have multiple online pseudonyms and exchange content in multiple social networks and virtual communities (Rlindlof 1988). Multiplayer internet video games and social media virtual communities with member anonymity are hypothesized as encouraging the diffusion of crime to a greater extent than physically massed crowds (Etzioni and Etzioni 1997; Flichy 2008; McPhail 2017; Porter 2004).

This ability to affect the physically separated arises because new media employ digital content that can take the form of print, sound, and moving or still images, and their combinations are quickly and easily shared among large audiences (Ling and Campbell 2010). Physical separation is no longer a barrier to sharing media content and, regarding copycat crime, can be an inducement (Surette 2020a). In new media, content and consumers are more closely matched than in traditional media, whose generic content targeted broad, diverse audiences (Chae and Flores 1998). In contrast, the content consumed via new media is more often of narrow interest that appeals to a self-selecting audience. Over the last twenty-five years, new media, particularly social media, have changed society so that contemporary media consumption has become an intensive participatory activity (Collins 2011; Grodal 2003a; Kiousis 2002; Persky and Blascovich 2008). Direct effects on criminality have been noted with the new-media-generated phenomenon of criminal flash mobs, for example, and the development of performance crime by people seeking infamy (Chan et al. 2012; Surette 2016c). Box 8.6 offers an early example of copycat crime related to a transitional media form between legacy and new media, the DVD.

At the core, their on-demand nature makes new media more significant than legacy media for copycat crime (Flew 2002; Ling and Campbell 2010; Lister et al. 2003). With new media, the delivery of content is controlled and determined to a much greater degree by the consumer, facilitating repetitive viewing and selective editing. Another difference is interactive content that allows consumers to be active participants in the development of storylines. Interactivity is most

---

Box 8.6   Bum Fights

Originally distributed in a 2001 DVD, videos of homeless people encouraged to fight one another for alcohol, cash, food, clothing, or a hotel room became popular on the internet in the mid-2000s (Montet 2009). DVD and subsequently YouTube videos of bum fights, described as the equivalent of human cockfights, were accused of inspiring joy killings of homeless people (Marlernee and Haas 2006; Schorn 2006). Viewed by millions, the purchased and posted videos were credited with victimizing homeless people in copycat fights and assaults. Homicides of homeless victims, apparently for fun, also followed, with many of the copycat crimes posted on YouTube (Massey n.d.). After their arrests, some bum fight copycat offenders directly cited the bum fight videos as their inspiration (Day 2007).

apparent in video games where game player decisions determine the electronic storylines live (Grodal 2003b). For crime-related games, whether a crime victim is killed or spared, a crime is solved or not, or a criminal is caught or left unpunished is not predetermined by a game programmer but determined by each player after the game has been distributed. Online internet-linked games that combine role playing, competition, interactive story creation, and online live chatrooms provide game players with real-time virtual worlds to interact in and sometimes provide powerful generator crime models (Grochowski 2006).

Relevant for copycat crime, the experience of immersion in new media is significantly different from the legacy media experience. New media's unique characteristics of narrowcasting, on-demand access to content, and interactivity shift the audience members from passive consumers to active content-creating participants. New-media users are often players or surfers, and role playing and content authorship are a common and expected part of the new-media experience (Lee, Peng, and Klein 2010). Combined with high-speed computers that create vivid virtual realities, new-media-based experiences come close to actual experienced reality, and consumer encounters with potential generator crimes can be psychologically deep. For copycat crime, repeatedly playing out a crime sequence in a video game can provide the at-risk player with the guided practice and observable models noted as necessary for imitation by Bandura (1973).

As new-media experiences approach real-world experiences, the question of how this shift has influenced generator crime models' ability to generate copycat crime offenders presents itself. Does the long-standing recognition that delinquent peers heighten delinquent imitation, accepted since development of criminology's social learning theory in the 1930s, transfer to the more realistically presented new-media crime models? Research on narrative persuasion via the media suggests that copying will increase as media renditions of crime stories become more realistic. The more real the world of media-rendered crime looks, the easier it is to psychologically enter that world and to increase hypothesized copycat effects. The expectation is that new media affords potential copycat offenders the ability to seek out like-minded real-world role models and fictional digital ones, interact with them psychologically on an intimate level, maintain their anonymity, and rehearse and learn their crimes. Box 8.7 describes a disturbing copycat crime tied to the internet.

Box 8.7   Slender Man

An example of an internet-linked copycat crime was the homicide attempted by two twelve-year-old girls in 2014, linked to the Slender Man internet meme. Slender Man is a supernatural fictional character that was created by Something Awful forum user Eric Knudsen in 2009 (Dewey 2014). Slender Man is depicted as a thin, unnaturally tall humanoid with a featureless head and face, wearing a black suit. Posted stories commonly feature him stalking, abducting, or traumatizing people, particularly children (Cohn 2018; De Vos 2012). Following its creation, the Slender Man meme went viral and spawned numerous spin-offs of fan art, cosplay, online fiction known as *creepypasta* (horror stories told in short patches of easy-to-copy text), and eventually a movie based on the meme (Blank and McNeil 2018; Romano 2012).[7] Slender Man became a crowd-sourced monster, interactively created as internet users shared fiction and images (Peck 2015). The media generator crime content did not prominently display crimes or directly instruct consumers to commit a specific crime. In contrast, it was ambiguous enough to be interpreted as requiring a criminal response by a few, motivating crime rather than modeling it.

The twelve-year-old copycats psychologically bought into the Slender Man meme to the extent that they were narratively persuaded to commit a murder to garner, in their minds, Slender Man's attention. Thus motivated, the two girls lured a friend into the woods, stabbed her nineteen times, and left her to die. She survived. Picked up later walking along a highway and stained with the victim's blood, the juvenile offenders explained to police that they had stabbed their friend to appease the Slender Man and were headed to a national forest to join him in Slender Mansion. One told investigators that Slender Man was anywhere from six to fourteen feet tall, could read minds, and had teleportation skills and that they had decided to stab their friend to prove the skeptics wrong about his existence (Chess and Newsom 2015; Greene 2018).

The viral success of the Slender Man meme has been attributed to its participatory, highly collaborative nature, where multiple authors could post about Slender Man, enabling the meme to be socially amplified through multiple evolving portraits (Peck 2015, 2017). In addition to the meme being an example of internet-connected generator

continues

Box 8.7   Continued

---

crime content, the Slender Man saga exemplifies the malleability of new-media crime content and how a derived crime need not mirror specific media instructions; it simply needs to be seen as fitting into a media narrative about the world where an imaginary creature and a violent crime make sense.

New media are expected to have the potential to generate significant numbers of copycat offenses in the combined effects from social media and interactive video games. Periodic reports of crimes linked to the internet and video games like Devin Moore's murder spree related to *Grand Theft Auto* (see Box 8.8) spur public interest in the relationship between new media and copycat crime. Video games have attracted particular attention and have been linked to the media cognitive-processing concept of scripts (Panee and Ballard 2002). It is thought that criminal scripts can be acquired by interacting with criminogenic media during fantasy role playing common to the video game experience (Claxton 2005; Huesmann 1986).

Box 8.8   *Grand Theft Auto*

Life isn't like a video game. Fayette, Alabama, police officer Arnold Strickland found Devin Moore asleep in a stolen car in June 2003 on a day that ended in multiple murders and an infamous copycat crime. For many, Moore's crimes provide clear examples of a copycat link between media consumption and violent crimes (Cavalli 2008; Leung 2005; Markey, Markey, and French 2015). Released in October 2001, *Grand Theft Auto* (*GTA*) opens with the player's avatar being transported to jail. Freed after an attack on the police convoy, the gamer proceeds to advance through *GTA*'s virtual world by committing crimes. The game player undertakes missions including bank robberies, assassinations, stabbings, street racing, carjacking, and soliciting prostitutes (Hourigan 2008).

continues

Box 8.8 *Continued*

A few years after the game's release, Officer Strickland took Devin Moore into the Fayette police station. Moore offered no resistance and had no prior criminal history. During questioning, however, Moore lunged and took the officer's weapon. Armed, Moore shot officer Strickland twice. A second officer, James Crump, heard the shots and rushed into the room; Moore fired and hit Officer Crump multiple times. As he left the police department, Moore shot the police dispatcher, Leslie Mealer, several times. After having shot each officer as least once in the head and killing all three, Moore took the keys to a police cruiser and drove away.

Following his second arrest that day, Devin Moore stated, "Life is like a video game. Everybody's got to die sometime." In addition to this statement, all of Moore's actions after he seized Officer Strickland's weapon closely corresponded with *GTA* scenarios. In one of the game's missions the gamer must escape from a police station, killing police officers, and get away in a stolen police cruiser. Many, including his defense attorneys, concluded that Moore had copied his murders directly from the video game. At his trial, copycat crime induced by immersion in a violent video game became his defense.

At trial it was revealed that Moore had played the game for hours every day over the months before the murders. On the day of the murders, he had played *Grand Theft Auto* for several hours prior to stealing the car he was arrested in. His attorneys argued that immersion in the game's virtual reality had colored Moore's perceptions of the real world and that Moore had behaved exactly as the video game had trained him. Describing Moore as a compulsive, violent video game player, his attorneys argued a "*GTA* defense": that he had lost touch with reality and was acting out the violent scenarios he had repeatedly experienced in the virtual *GTA* game world. Moore had, it was claimed, simply copied the crimes he had committed countless times within the game and acted them out when he found himself in a real-world setting similar to one portrayed within the game (Treshiowski 2005). The jury rejected Moore's *GTA* defense, however, and he is currently on death row in Alabama.[8]

A copycat crime path based on new-media content is also possible through narrative involvement (Green and Brock 2000; Slater and Rouner 2002). This path is speculated to be a possible copycat crime route in both the electronic game-playing experience and internet involvement. It needs to be noted, however, that except in rare cases, neither gaming nor surfing the internet is expected to generate copycat offenders. When potential copycat criminals and the motivation, instructions, and realistic crime models available through social media are combined, though, the blend is thought to be able to create a socially constructed worldview that supports and sometimes results in crime copying. If different media types and content are expected to have different connections to copycat crime, it is important to consider what the specific media preferences of copycat offenders are.

Media Preferences and Copycat Crime

Survey results from self-reported copycat offenders shed light on the relationship between media preferences and consumption and copycat crime. The first examination is of the association between media consumption levels of both legacy and new media and copycat behavior. These associations have been directly examined via surveys of incarcerated and nonincarcerated respondents.

Regarding new versus traditional media and copycat crime, mixed relationships have been reported (Surette 2013a). In a survey of incarcerated offenders, higher consumption of new media in the form of surfing the internet and playing video games was significantly correlated with past self-reported copycat behaviors. Additionally, inmates who cited a new-media product as their favorite medium were also significantly more likely to have committed a copycat crime. New media as the favorite medium and greater amounts of time spent with new media emerged as more consistent predictors of copycat behavior than consumption of traditional media. Reading was the sole legacy media that was statistically significant with copycat crime and appears to be a copycat crime insulator. The more reading inmates reported, the less likely they were to report a past copycat crime.

In addition to the amount of exposure to types of media, becoming more immersed in a favorite medium, as measured by an offender's level of narrative involvement, was an additional significant predictor of prior copycat crime behavior, as reported by Surette and Maze (2015). The more engaged respondents reported becoming with a favorite medium, the more likely they were to report copycat experience. And again, in Surette and Maze's 2015 inmate survey, new-media preferences emerged as consistent correlates of copycat crime. As found in the 2013 inmate survey, spending most of one's free time on the internet or playing video games was associated with a history of copycat crime, and inmates who listed either video games or the internet as their favorite media were more likely to have attempted a copycat crime.

However, while the consumption amounts and preferences for new media were significantly associated with copycat crime, when the copycat offenders were queried about the source of their copycat crime idea, legacy media reigned in both inmate surveys. In the 2015 survey, legacy media made up nearly eight in ten copycat sources cited by inmates (Surette and Maze 2015). Notably, in the 2013 survey Surette (2013a) reported that visual media dominated in the copycat crime sources cited by copycat offenders, with two-thirds citing television and movies as the source of their copycat crime idea. The legacy media of print, video , and audio accounted for eight in ten of the cited copycat crime sources, with new media cited by the remaining fifth. In addition, two-thirds of the new media as source attributions were listed in combination with other media. The internet and internet videos were the sole new-media types mentioned separately from other media, and video games were not cited as a copycat crime idea source by a single copycat offender.

These inmate surveys suggest that although more prevalent and accessible, new media have been slow to supplant legacy media as a copycat source of crime ideas. Whether this remains true today is an open question. The relationship between new media and copycat crime has evolved since 2015, but in what manner is not known. A logical expectation is that as new media have grown in social influence, they have become more popular as idea sources for copycat crimes; however, an unresolved conflict remains between legacy media being the preferred copycat crime idea source while new media reigns as the preferred type of media.

What do these results say about the role new media play in copycat crime? In questions about favorite media, new media emerged as a significant predictor of past copycat behaviors. While other variables are stronger predictors, measures of new-media influence persisted across samples and times. There are substantial discontinuities in the results though. For one, the strongest bivariate media copycat crime predictor was inmates' level of narrative involvement with their favorite media, but narrative involvement was only weakly significant in multivariate models (Surette 2013a; Surette and Maze 2015). In addition, visual media was the most cited copycat crime idea source by these copycat crime offenders, but visual media did not qualify as significant in a multivariate model. On the other hand, comparatively few cited new media as their copycat crime idea source, but usage significantly predicted copycat crime.

These mixed results are speculated to be related to copycat crimes often being teenage acts and occurring therefore in the 1990s in the studied inmates, when new media was not widely available. As the internet and video games became more socially widespread, their connection with copycat crime likely increased, but they remained as infrequent sources of a copycat crime idea. These inconsistent outcomes highlight that copycat crime research currently resides at the beginning, exploratory stage and that copycat crime dynamics will only be clarified through contemporary samples and expanded methodologies. The expectation is that as new media grow in social influence and more recent data becomes available, new media will emerge as a more popular copycat crime idea source.

Conclusion

Contemporary copycat crime offenders appear to prefer images and spend a majority of their free time surfing the internet and on social media. Types of media content—news, entertainment, and infotainment—are expected to interact differently with copycat crime due to their varying characteristics. Both how they deliver content and how consumers perceive the content are important. The same basic crime facts variously delivered in a news story, adapted for a movie or program, or blended into a hybrid infotainment vehicle will have different copycat crime potential.

On its face, access to crime facts in crime news should be more likely to generate planned copycat crimes. However, news of successful crimes appears to be a crime motivator more than a crime instructional source and results in generalizable generator crime models. Regarding entertainment content, despite being acknowledged as fictional, it is more copycat instructional than motivational and thought to increase criminal self-efficacy and thereby copycat crimes. And despite being the sole media created to influence behavior, advertising has not shown a copycat crime effect. The role for infotainment media in copycat crime is not clear but has significant potential by offering seemingly accurate renditions of crime with embedded instructional details in entertainment-formatted content. Although print infotainment media have rarely been linked to copycat crime, infotainment portrayals of crime distributed in visual or digitized formats are hypothesized as a media type with strong copycat effects.

The marriage of different content with different types of media is also important. Contemporary print media are thought to generate copycat crime through new media. For audio media content, copycat crime is connected to popular music rather than to spoken content. As with print media, motivations and justifications sometimes are extracted from song lyrics. Visual media in all formats contain the media content most commonly linked to copycat crime and appear to be the most common contemporary copycat crime idea source.

The combining of the types of media content and formats is maximized in new media, leading to the expectation that future copycat effects from new-media content will be significant. The more realistic new-media-rendered crime looks, the easier it is for copycat offenders to psychologically enter that world. For social media in particular, copycat crime effects are expected to be substantial due to access to real-world crime models and exposure to copycat-generator performance crimes (Chan et al. 2012; Lankford 2021). New media allows potential copycat offenders to maintain their anonymity while interacting with like-minded crime models on a personal level, to observe similar crimes, and to mentally practice and prepare for their copycat crime attempts.

The primary research question left unaddressed is the causal order of new media. Do preestablished copycat offenders gravitate to immersive interactive new media, minimizing their causal role while maintaining their statistical correlation? The converse question is whether inmates gravitate to copycat crime because of their immersion in new media, thereby heightening new media's criminogenic impact. In this view, offenders become copycat criminals first, new-media fans second. There is evidence, such as the citing of traditional visual media as a prime copycat-generator crime source, to support the conclusion that criminalization precedes media exposure. The persistence of new-media indicators across the research supports that possibility. Thus, the correspondence of web surfing and video game playing with copycat crime may relate to their ability to provide immersive platforms more than their specific crime content (Persky and Blascovich 2008).

Depending upon what a potential copycat offender is seeking, all types of media, old and new, have been anecdotally linked to copycat crime. Despite their hypothesized copycat potential, new media have yet to appear significantly in the available copycat offender surveys but are hypothesized to become a major copycat crime engine as the twenty-first century unfolds. At this point, the interpretation of the initial results argues that new media remain a correlate but not a primary cause of criminality. New media appear more to be covariates of preestablished criminal proclivities, which, when exposure to generator crime occurs in the right environment, lead to copycat crime.

Where does the information in this and prior chapters lead regarding a final set of questions concerning copycat crime? What is known about copycat crime versus what is hypothesized? What are the likely dynamics and mechanisms of copycat crime? What research is needed to better understand copycat crime? What legal issues have risen around media-linked copycat crime? And what criminal justice and social policies might address copycat crime? Chapter 9 recaps the current perception of the reality of copycat crime and delves into these six questions.

Notes

1. Discussions of the history of crime news are provided by Casey 2010; Freeman 1912; Papke 1987.

2. Reverend Henry Ward Beecher, "Crime and Its Remedies," published c. 1880 by Howard Association, 5, Bishopsgate Street Without, London, E.C. (c. 1880), quoted in Phelps 1911, 267–268.

3. For a discussion and review of the news coverage and reaction to the Tylenol poisoning, see "A Trusted Pill Turned Deadly. How Tylenol Made a Comeback," *New York Times*, September 16, 2018, https://www.nytimes.com/video/us /100000006106608/tylenol-poison-comeback.html.

4. A clip from the movie based on the book *In Cold Blood* can be viewed at "In Cold Blood (5/8) Movie CLIP—the Last Living Thing You're Ever Gonna See (1967) HD," video posted to YouTube by Movieclips, October 7, 2012, https://www .youtube.com/watch?v=gHAJY34g-LY.

5. The music video for the song "Cop Killer" can be viewed at "Body Count— Cop Killer," video posted to YouTube by thechannelsurfin100, July 23, 2011, https://www.youtube.com/watch?v=LH8gUhDd6WE.

6. The trailer for *The Battle of Algiers* can be viewed at *"The Battle of Algiers*—Trailer," video posted to YouTube by Rialto Pictures, September 16, 2016, https://www.youtube.com/watch?v=vhhoS3zOskE. The trailer for the television show *Dexter* can be found at "Dexter (2006) Official Trailer | Michael C. Hall SHOWTIME Series," video posted to YouTube by Dexter on SHOWTIME, August 24, 2016, https://www.youtube.com/watch?v=YQeUmSD1c3g.

7. The trailer for the movie based on Slender Man can be watched at "SLENDER MAN—Official Trailer 2 (HD)," video posted to YouTube by Sony Pictures Entertainment, July 26, 2018, https://www.youtube.com/watch?v=eRV-c3hs3vw.

8. Devon Moore's (also known as Devin Darnell Thompson) death sentence was upheld by the Alabama Supreme Court during the court's 2018–2019 October term. See *Devin Darnell Thompson v. State of Alabama Appeal* from Fayette Circuit Court (cc-03-62, 60) and *Thompson v. State* 153 So. 3d 141 (Ala. 2014) and Thompson v. Alabama, 574 U.S. _, 135 S. Ct. 233 (2013).

9

What We Know— and Don't Know— About Copycat Crime

WHAT DO WE KNOW ABOUT COPYCAT CRIME? AFTER A FEW centuries of interest, not much. What is known with any confidence about copycat crime is limited to some simple facts, mostly based on atypical cases supplemented by self-report surveys of copycat offenders. The lack of in-depth knowledge means that despite a large amount of interest, only a small number of policies can be recommended. Commercial films are the copycat crime idea source most credited by copycat offenders, but exactly what it is about movies that leads to copycat crime is not yet understood. Deep immersion in media content with repetitive viewing, crime models to identify with, emotional detail, graphic and easily accessed crime portrayals, and the presentation of correctable errors are all strong candidates for a film-based copycat effect, but none have been confirmed through research. The combination of media and real-world crime models has also been reported as significant for copycat criminality.

The limited early research and anecdotal cases indicate a pragmatic use of the media by offenders, with the borrowing of media crime techniques a common practice (Heller and Polsky 1976a, 1976b; Pease and Love 1984a, 1984b). Contemporary media are reported as instructional sources more often than as crime triggers (Helfgott 2022, forthcoming; Marsh and Melville 2014; Surette 2013a). The link between media content and copycat crime has also been associated with exposure to real-world crime models and positive perceptions of media crime content.

183

The media are not felt to be independently causally connected to copied criminality except in rare cases. Instead, a model of media influence in which the media operate as catalytic rudders is supported (Ferguson 2015; Surette 2015a).

In the twenty-first century, copycat crime remains a rare but interesting phenomenon, boosted by the internet, social media, and the growth of performance crime (Surette 2016c, 2017). The information in circulation about copycat crime in popular media suggests a continuation of the backward law of media and crime where the most accessible portrait of copycat crime is the opposite of its reality. It remains, however, that research has not addressed most questions about copycat crime, and the understanding of copycat crime resides at a basic level.

The most crucial research questions involve the role of media generator crimes in the creation of copycat crimes. Are the media triggers and causes of new crimes that otherwise would not have been committed, or are they rudders and molders of criminality that would have occurred in some form independently of media? Initial research results support a media rudder role and indicate that a media copycat crime effect concentrates in preexisting criminal populations (Rios and Ferguson 2020). In the reported anecdotal cases, individuals who imitate media crimes usually have prior criminal records or histories of violence (Helfgott 2015).

Copycat crime prevalence rates among the incarcerated are substantially greater than among the nonincarcerated. The currently accepted assumption is that a media copycat crime effect is more likely qualitative, affecting criminal behavior, rather than quantitative, affecting the number of criminals. Concerning the amount of copycat crime, the research indicates that copycat crimes occur regularly at a significant rate and that copycat crimes are present in a substantial proportion—about one in four—of offender populations (Surette 2014). Two working hypotheses are that copycat criminals are more likely to be career criminals committing property crimes as opposed to violent or first offenders and that when they appear in a criminal career, most of the time copycat crimes occur early.

Regarding the lifespan of copycat crime waves or how long a generator crime's copycat effect persists, copycat suicide research is the most pertinent but has been mixed. Most copycat suicide studies have looked only for short-term effects of a few weeks and cannot offer any insight into how copycat effects operate over long periods. However, anecdotal reports of copycat crime provide examples, such as suicide bombing campaigns linked to the movie *The Battle of Algiers* and crimes linked to the story and movie *The Most Dangerous Game*, where the time between a generator crime and an attributed copycat crime spans many decades (Surette et al. 2021). Irrespective of this long-term potential, most copycat crime cycles appear to have life spans of six months or less. Regarding the end of a copycat crime wave, as with the birth of a copycat crime wave, the media play a role in dissipation of a copycat crime wave, but the dynamics appear to vary substantially across crime waves. Finally, as space- and time-contracting media technologies continue to develop, copycat crime has assumed a new diffusion pattern different from Gabriel Tarde's nineteenth-century urban-to-rural and upper-to-lower-class diffusion (Surette 2020a). The expectation is that as new-media-supplied content supplants real-world experiences, physical proximity will become less important for copycat-generator-crime creation and diffusion, and virtual communities will be more influential regarding what crimes get copied (Porter 2004; Surette et al. 2021).

Lastly, it needs to be emphasized that many of the conclusions about what is known about copycat crime are based upon the extension of research findings about the copying of other behaviors and not directly related to copycat crime. As such, definitive knowledge of the media's role in copycat crime remains, for the most part, just partially confirmed. Related to what the dominant role of the media is for copycat crime, differing models with differing pathways compete. How often the varied paths are followed and how they associate with different types of copycat crimes is not known. With that caveat, from these limited research-supported observations, what models of copycat crime development and pathways to copycat crime can be hypothesized?

Copycat Crime Pathways

Copycat crime needs to be explained at two levels: an aggregate-level model to explain copycat crime waves and societal rates of copycat crime, and an individual-level model to assess individuals' decisions to copy a crime are necessary.[1]

Aggregate-Level Paths

An aggregate-level copycat crime model results from the interactions between the generator crime, media coverage, the social setting, and potential copycat criminals. The aggregate-level model posits a process in which generator crimes emerge from the sea of media crime content, and the generator crimes create a pool of potential copycat criminals. The size of this potential copycat pool is set by the level of attention to media found in a society and by other social factors such as social attitudes regarding crime and the number of real-world opportunities that are available to apply a copycat crime technique. Some societies will generate more criminogenic content, at-risk copycat offenders, and opportunities and cultural support to apply media crime models. Figure 9.1 diagrams this aggregate-level copycat crime model. After an initial potential copycat offender pool is created, the first wave of copycat crimes is thought to result from primed imitation bounded by the number of copycat opportunities in a society. The upper portion involves copycat offenders reacting to the initial generator crime. The lower portion represents second, third, and higher copycat crime waves, where an initial copycat offender gains media attention and births multiple generations of copycats, such as found with the Columbine school shootings.[2]

An aggregate multicycle copycat crime pattern is regarded as more likely to occur with a violent generator crime because of the newsworthiness of violence and the tendency of the media to portray rare crimes the most often (Surette 2015a). The aggregate-level model infers that as media attention decreases over time, copycats will also decrease (Akers 2011). The cumulative effects of the social drives and factors associated with the model generate the aggregate number and lifespan of copycat crimes.

Individual-Level Copycat Crime Paths

The aggregate-level model, of course, depends upon the cumulation of decisions made by individuals, and individual copycat crime offenders can choose from a set of possible pathways to copycat crime. Figure 9.2 offers a theoretical model of the steps individuals can take in reaching a copycat crime attempt. The hypothetical paths copycat offenders travel from exposure to media generator crimes to copycat attempts are diagramed through ten steps.

The individual-level model is based on the premise that the media primarily influence copiers to copy crime first by teaching them how to offend through the acquisition of copycat crime techniques and, second, by positively portraying the functional value of criminal behavior and the likelihood of successfully copying a crime. The model starts at the

Figure 9.1 Aggregate-Level Copycat Crime Model

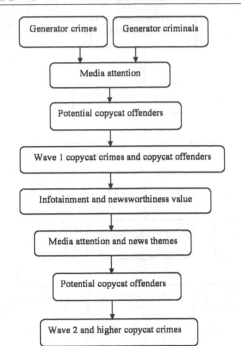

societal level with exposure of individuals through the media to candidate generator crime content within a variety of social settings.

In step 2, "composite crime model," at-risk copycat criminals identify with the generator crime models, often creating a composite model from multiple media and real-world sources (Bandura 1973). Elements from family, community, and legacy and social media can be tapped when forming composite models, and modern social media are felt to function as a primary social group, especially for socially isolated individuals (Lankford 2021). By step 3, a large number of potential copycats have acquired the knowledge necessary to copy and commit a crime.

Step 4 reflects three possible paths to copycat crime: the systematic, heuristic, and narrative persuasion paths (see Chapters 2 and 6). The systematic path is based on the theory of reasoned action and rational choice, which assumes that people consider consequences before acting (Clarke and Felson 1993; Paternoster, Jaynes, and Wilson 2017; Petty, Priester, and Brinol 2002; Pratt 2008). The heuristics

Figure 9.2   Individual-Level Copycat Crime Paths

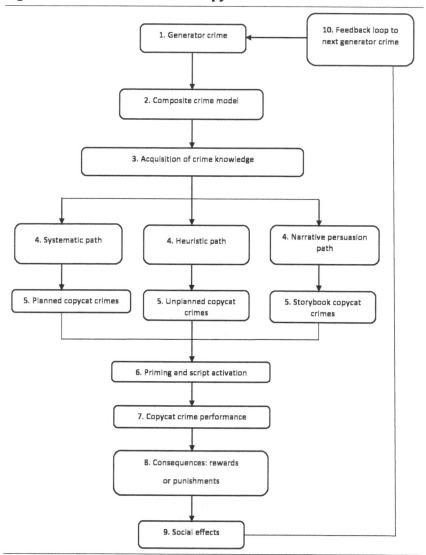

path assumes that behavior is spontaneous and results from relatively automatic mental processes. The narrative persuasion path assumes a deep psychological connection with media content. The three paths function differently regarding copycat crime and lead to different types of copycat crimes.

The first consideration is the perception of likely consequences from committing a copied crime, which determines whether a systematic or a heuristics path is followed. When perceived consequences of a crime are serious, the systematic path applies. When consequences are perceived as low, the heuristic path kicks in (Kahneman 2011). The systematic decision path is tied to thoughtful, instrumental planned crimes, where the media supply do-it-yourself instructions on how to successfully commit a crime. The heuristic copycat decision path links to emotive copycat crimes, where the decision thought process will be quick ("They're burning cars on the news, and no one's getting arrested; let's do the same here"). In addition to the two cognitive paths, narrative persuasion provides a third copycat crime path. This path sidesteps the need for a conscious decision to copy a crime and instead operates when psychological immersion in a generator crime story is present. The narrative persuasion path deals with the impact of engaging storytelling, while the first two paths apply more to factual news and infotainment media content. The narrative persuasion path is hypothesized to be the most frequently traveled copycat crime pathway as it reflects how most people interact with media content as sources of entertainment and escapism. As shown in step 5, different types of copycat crimes are associated with each path: planned copycat crimes for the systematic path, unplanned copycat crimes for the heuristic path, and storybook copycat crimes for the narrative persuasion path.

Planned Copycat Crimes

When consequences and motivations are high, the first path is followed as long as the at-risk copycat criminal also has the ability to cognitively assess the media-supplied information. Systematic processing leads to questioning media-supplied information and seeking additional information beyond the generator crime. An important concept in the individual-level copycat decision process is the level of counterarguing present within each path—the willingness to invest time gathering and evaluating information and the capacity to counterargue with media-provided information (Kahneman 2011; Petty, Priester, and Brinol 2002). When counterarguing with media-supplied content, the potential copycat conducts an extensive search for relevant information, evaluates it, weighs counterarguments, and questions the validity of the crime information received. Due to the extensive search for and evaluation of the information provided, traversing this path takes longer, and permanent changes in attitudes and behaviors can result (Petty, Priester, and Brinol 2002). In instrumental copycat crimes, such as the mimicked bank robbery from the film *Set It Off* (see Chapter 6), copycat offenders follow a systematic decision path to a planned copycat crime.

Unplanned Copycat Crimes

In the heuristic path, a potential copycat offender uses only a subset of the potentially available information that is the most easily accessed from memory, and unplanned copycat crimes result (Kahneman 2011; Petty, Priester, and Brinol 2002; Shrum 2002). This truncated decision process can reflect a lack of cognitive ability to systematically process media information or occur when time pressure derails a systematic review and decision. As most decisions are not deeply considered, the media effects research implies one route for instrumental copycat crimes and another for spontaneous unplanned crimes (Petty, Priester, and Brinol 2002). Expectations of serious consequences encourage thoughtful, planned instrumental crimes and critical review of media information, whereas expectations of trivial consequences encourage irrational, emotional copycat crimes (Bandura 1973). With unplanned copycat crimes, by default media content frequently becomes part of the small subset of information used to reach decisions and direct behavior (Petty, Priester, and Brinol 2002; Shrum 2002). As most people do not exhaustively consider wide-ranging sources of information prior to making decisions, it follows that unplanned copycat crimes are felt to be more common than the more cognitively demanding planned ones.

In sum, when consequences are thought to be serious, a potential copycat criminal considers the accuracy of the media content and makes a systematic decision. In the alternative cognitive route, when consequences are thought not to be serious, decisions result either from shallow cognitive processing or as simple thoughtless reactions (Green and Brock 2000). Due to the speed and shallowness of the cognitive effort involved, the heuristic path is rapidly traversed and logically fits with unplanned copycat crime. Unplanned assaults, the sudden shooting of police officers by a *Grand Theft Auto* video game player (see Box 8.8), and spontaneous sexual assaults, exemplified by the one linked to the made-for-television movie *Born Innocent* (see Box 9.1), provide heuristic copycat crime examples.

Box 9.1 *Born Innocent*

A scene in a 1974 made-for-TV movie, in which a young girl incarcerated in a juvenile reformatory is assaulted in a shower room by four other female inmates, led to an unplanned copycat crime. In the movie, the victim is held down naked and penetrated with a plunger handle. Three days after the movie's broadcast, four minor females came upon a nine-year-old girl, forced her to strip, and, while holding her down, used a discarded bottle to sexually assault the victim. The assailants later admitted to having viewed and discussed the movie and attacked their victim without prior planning (Mintz 1978). The victim's family sued the National Broadcasting Company for damages from physical and emotional injury, alleging that the assailants committed the sexual assault because of the film and spontaneously reenacted the rape scene when they came upon the victim playing at the beach. The family argued that the film was likely to cause imitation and that the National Broadcasting Company should have known that susceptible persons might imitate the crime portrayed in the movie. On appeal, the court dismissed the suit, stating that the plaintiff did not meet the test for incitement or negligence.

Storybook Copycat Crime

The final copycat crime path is driven by narrative persuasion and produces storybook copycat crimes. Consumer interaction with narrative media is qualitatively distinct from interactions in the first two paths and is hypothesized to be the most traveled copycat crime route. Neither the systematic nor the heuristic path captures the phenomenological experience of reading, hearing, or watching contemporary media content. Narrative persuasion describes how people normally interact with media, seeking entertainment and escape rather than instructions. Whereas cognitive-processing theories focus on the amount of thought an individual devotes to a media message, in the narrative persuasion path individuals can be temporarily separated from their personal beliefs (Green and Brock 2000).

Research regarding this path suggests that consumer demographic similarity to characters in a narrative will be less important than how emotionally involved consumers become with those characters. If the media consumer's goal is a vicarious relationship with a media personality or character, increased identification with the criminogenic model will lead to increased engagement. If the goal is arousal and diversion (the consumer likes crime stories) and if the presentation is well crafted and has realistic special effects, increased engagement will also result (Slater and Rouner 2002). As most young people utilize the media as a source of entertainment and much of popular media aims to generate narrative immersion, the majority of copycat offenders, even those who eventually travel paths one or two, are hypothesized to first travel the narrative persuasion path (Surette 2013b). The attempted homicide linked to the Slender Man internet meme presented in Box 8.7 serves as an example, as does the *Taxi Driver*–linked assassination attempt of President Ronald Reagan described in Chapter 6.

The needs of the media consumer therefore determine which of the three paths is followed (Kahneman 2011). Most of the time, the purpose of media consumption is escapism, and copycat offenders can be expected to travel the narrative persuasion path. Narrative persuasion is thought to be capable of directly resulting in a copycat crime as well as routing a copycat offender back through either the systematic or heuristic paths, depending upon the type of copycat crime (planned or unplanned) under consideration.

After the paths are traversed, the individual-level model converges in step 6 in the psychological processes of priming and script activation. For copycat crime, the most important psychological change in an individual is related to efficacy about whether the modeled crime is doable. The first mechanism, priming, occurs when the portrayals of behaviors in the media activate associated ideas that increase the likelihood that a similar crime will be attempted. In that scripts are thought to be first created and later primed by media content (Huesmann 1998), the second copycat mechanism, script acquisition, is conceptually linked to priming. Most commonly acquired via observational learning, scripts serve as behavior guides by laying out the steps necessary to attempt a copycat crime (Bandura 1973). Primes observed in the media and subsequently encountered in the real world increase the probability of activation of previously acquired criminal scripts and, as a result, increase the performance of copycat crimes (Akers 2011; Claxton 2005; Huesmann 1986). For juveniles launching a crime career, the increase in perceived criminal self-efficacy from media-supplied primes and the activation of preexisting crime scripts is felt to be vital.

Once primed at step 6, an individual copycat candidate is finally in the cognitive and knowledge position to attempt a copycat crime. Possession of the requisite precrime information and attitudes leads to the performance of a copycat crime (step 7). As the linchpin between the acquisition of the ability to copy a crime, which many media consumers are hypothesized to reach, and the consequences of attempting a copycat crime, the performance of a copycat crime is obviously the key step in the model. Only with performance is an observable copycat crime produced, and at performance the aggregate-level (Figure 9.1) and individual-level (Figure 9.2) copycat crime models intersect. Performance determines whether an individual attempts a copycat crime and, when aggregated across individuals, determines the spread and prevalence of copycat crime within a society.

Copycat crime attempts are tied to an individual's prediction of consequences. However, mistakes in predicting consequences can result in copycat crime performances that are not in the best interests of the copycat offender. Step 8 in the model addresses what actually happens to the copycat criminal. Social learning and rational choice theory suggest that individual copycat offender characteristics will be less important than setting and environmental factors in determining the rate of copycat crimes (Bandura 1973; Clarke and Felson 1993; Paternoster, Jaynes, and Wilson 2017; Pratt 2008). Hence, the proportion of at-risk copycat offenders in a population may not be significantly different across cultures, but copycat crimes may significantly vary in their social consequences and thereby in prevalence. Media attention is an important consequence of a copycat crime and is important for distributing knowledge of copycat crimes and spurring copycat crime waves (Surette 2020a).

Whereas step 8 involves the effects of committing a copycat crime on the individual copycat offender, step 9, "social effects," involves the impact of a copycat crime on the copier's social environment. If social approbation follows, if media criminogenic content is reduced, and if social norms become less accepting of the crime as a result, the social environment supportive of copycat crime will be attenuated. If the opposite results follow, a more supportive social environment for copycat crime will develop, and a downstream increase in the society's copycat crime rate will eventually follow. Social effects loop back to the size of the potential copycat criminal pool depicted in the Figure 9.1 aggregate-level model and create the feedback loop seen in Figure 9.2 at step 10, which leads back to step 1. Social effects from a copycat crime recycle to influence social settings and the creation of more generator crimes.

The aggregate- and individual-level copycat crime models and their pathways to copycat crime for societies and individuals are research derived but are not research validated. They stand as the best current descriptions of the processes connected to how copycat crimes develop and spread and how individuals go from potential copycat offenders to actual ones. While reasonable and logical, they raise many unanswered research questions.

Research Needs

How to advance the exploration of media's role in copycat crime? Noting that the best predictor of future behavior is past behavior—we become who we were—it is a short jump to the conclusion that those most at-risk for copying media-portrayed crime are those with established criminal histories. Research on comparisons between copycat offenders and noncopycat law-abiding persons has not been pursued, but it is speculated that meaningful distinctions will not emerge (Newburn 1994; Rennie 1978). Of more promise is the comparison between copycat and noncopycat offenders, which has only recently begun to be explored. Here the speculation is that individual situational crime opportunities will better differentiate copycats from noncopycats, with copycat crime opportunities available to criminally predisposed individuals being the crucial factor. Confirmatory research is necessary though.

The aggregate- and individual-level copycat crime models lead to several additional copycat crime areas needing research attention. Whether copycat crime effects emerge depends on the interactions of the media's characterizations of crime and criminals; the media consumer's predispositions toward a modeled crime in terms of that individual's personal criminal history, family, and neighborhood factors; and the media's and the potential copycat offender's broad social context regarding preexisting cultural norms, current crime opportunities, and media pervasiveness. First, criminogenic content must be better specified. Second, where they exist, copycat and noncopycat offender differences need to be detailed. Third, the characteristics of copycat crimes, their distribution, and their wave dynamics need to be analyzed and understood. Fourth, the social-setting factors in which the media are consumed, the social opportunities to commit copycat crimes, and the social norms supportive of copycat crime need to be explored to understand copycat crime rates and their variation across societies.

Copycat Offender Characteristics

Despite growing academic interest, the characteristics of copycat criminals are still in need of empirical confirmation. Pending confirmatory evidence, copycat criminals are hypothesized to more often be career criminals involved in property offenses. The effect of the media on crime is likely qualitative (affecting criminal behavior), not quantitative (affecting the number of criminals), but research is needed to establish the ratio between the two. A second outstanding research question concerns low-risk, nonincarcerated, nonoffender populations. Research on juveniles and young adults and copycat crime is particularly needed. Only one study to date provides a copycat crime estimate of such a population (Chadee 2010).

A related unexplored question involves the hypothesized difference between offenders reporting past copycat criminality and offenders without such activity. What factors, if any, discriminate copycat offenders from noncopycat offenders, and what role do cultural and gender differences play (Surette et al. 2021)? Individual-level copycat offender factors that have been nominated as fostering copycat imitation but are understudied include observers subjected to exciting or angering content, prior offense records, low expectation of real-world punishment, and individuals psychologically neutralizing negative consequences for crime victims. The unexplored relationship between media and copycat offenders generates an additional set of research issues. Media consumer interest in media crime content, video game play, internet use, and seeing the media as criminogenically helpful have been reported as important and as also interacting with exposure to real-world family and community crime models (Surette 2013a).

How copycat offenders perceive the media appears to be particularly significant, but the nuances of the relationship, such as how media encounters are processed and stored in memory, remain blurred (Proctor and Niemeyer 2020). For contemporary copycat crime, an important unresolved issue is whether media crime models can serve as vicarious opinion leaders and speed copycat adoption in Rogers's (2003) diffusion of innovations conception. It would be of interest to know if copycat offenders see media content as accurate for estimating their likelihood of committing a successful copycat crime. Another unresolved research question generated by diffusion theory and related to copycat crime is whether media-provided models serve as electronic change agents similar to the real-world ones. A parallel research issue is whether preestablished offenders with risk-of-arrest concerns cull the media for innovative risk-reduction crime techniques and are encouraged by media-portrayed criminogenic change agents, such as popular song artists or fictional characters, to adopt new criminal behaviors.

Lastly, diffusion research has focused on individuals and their characteristics that predict adoption, but there has been less research on the communication networks that discourage adoption. With its pro-innovation bias, diffusion research has often blamed the individual for not adopting. For copycat crime, however, the interest and research need would focus on what factors help individuals resist copycat crime enticements.

Copycat Crime Characteristics

At the social-setting level, crimes securing material rewards, successful retaliation, social recognition, or self-esteem boosts are hypothesized to be fertile copycat crime generators, but all need research confirmation. Although felt to be the most important factors for copycat crime performance, the specific social conditions and how they interact with media and copycat offenders remain unknown. Additional research on copycat crime at-risk groups and the link between real-world crime and media-modeled crime has also been encouraged (Ferguson, San Miguel, and Hartley 2009; Surette 2013a).

Moreover, research on crime model sources could shed further light on the media-versus-real-world crime model issue. If exposure to media-provided crime models is more predictive than exposure to real-world crime models for crime imitation, then a strong causal role for the media would be indicated. However, if real-world crime models better predict the imitation of crime, the media would be relegated to a catalyst role. The unexplored research question is the comparative role of real-world crime models compared with media-provided crime models (Ferguson, San Miguel, and Hartley 2009). Despite a long-term criminological interest in the impact of real-world crime models, the concurrent examination of real and media crime models has not been pursued. The emergence of interactive media boosts the importance of addressing this research question.

Finally, whether significant differences in copycat crime prevalence exist across cultures deserves examination. The dynamics of copycat crime waves seen in product tampering, airline hijacking, and suicide bombings await further research, and the factors that launch the short-term bursts of high-profile, sometimes extremely violent criminogenic copying are unknown. Two additional empirical questions that have yet to be resolved are whether crime clusters can be reliably forecast and whether the self-reported copycat-crime-prevalence levels are accurate.

Methodologically, all the research questions concerning copycat crime characteristics could benefit from in-depth interviews with a broad group of copycat offenders regarding the specific details of their copycat crimes, their relationship with media, and their social situations. Fleshing out the reality and dynamics of copycat crime for different types of crime, different offender groups, and different societies and cultures would advance understanding of copycat crime enormously.

New Media and Copycat Crime

A final important gap in copycat crime research area is understanding how new media affect copycat crime. This is not a trivial question as past shifts in media forms have harbingered substantial shifts in the impact of media on society, crime, and justice (Meyrowitz 1986; Surette 2015a). How the interaction between new media and the wider distribution of crime instructions to motivated individuals generates copycat crime is a pressing research question. Do interpersonal contacts control the lifespan of a copycat crime, or do social media dominate after a breakout tipping-point level of copycats is reached (Surette 2020a)?

Copycat crimes are presently speculated to be generated more often by social media than by traditional media, but research has not verified this expectation. One flag for an increased impact of new media is the growth of performance crime and new-media-based copycat crime waves (Chan et al. 2012; Surette 2016c, 2020a). It is predicted that the narrative persuasion impact of criminogenic media will increase over time as media technologies lead to more engaging, reality-like media experiences (Biocca 2013; Mundorf and Laird 2002; Surette 2017). Understanding how new media and copycat crime relate and how their dynamics develop will require a substantial research effort.

Concerning performance crimes, as a unique type of copycat crime, performance-crime target audiences were initially small, but social media outlets expanded their audiences from the few to the many, thereby adding an immense copycat crime lure (Surette 2012, 2020a).

How common copycat performance crimes are and what produces them remain unaddressed research questions. Another neglected new-media-related research question concerns whether the periodic reemergence of and long life observed for copycat crime memes are common characteristics of social-media-linked copycat crimes (Surette 2020a). Do the legacy media expectations concerning crime waves apply to social-media-driven copycat crime memes? Associated unaddressed new-media copycat crime research questions include how online copycat crime communities develop and how copycat crimes diffuse in new-media online communities.

In sum, much is not known about which copycat offender traits are most important for moving potential copycat criminals to actual copycat criminals, and except for some broad characteristics like youth and a prior criminal record, the copycat offender remains an ambiguous figure. Similarly, much is unknown about copycat crimes, and research on how they vary and what launches copycat crime waves is a pressing need. Determining which social setting factors are significant is suggested as the most important area needing research. And as the media continue to evolve culturally and technologically, research on the relationship between new media and copycat crime will be needed to specify and then track the impacts of the changes. With substantial areas needing research attention, what, if any, copycat crime policy recommendations can be made is a valid query.

Copycat Crime Policies

The difficulty of recommending informed copycat crime policies is reflected in the case law and court decisions associated with media-linked copycat crimes. A number of attorneys have used varied legal arguments in an attempt to hold the creators of media content liable for harms resulting from copycat imitations (Cooley 2003; Day 2007; Kunich 2000). The precedent history is that the courts have not often rendered decisions related to copycat crime, and when they have, arguments rooted in defective-product, marketing, and other civil tort liabilities have been routinely rejected. A review of these cases reveals the extreme difficulty of using the judiciary to hold producers of media content responsible for copycat crimes. The history of the development of the judicial precedents concerning copycat crime begins with a case concerning liability for a public speech, not media content. The 1969

Brandenburg v. Ohio (395 U.S. 444) US Supreme Court decision established the criteria that came to be used for holding media companies liable for copycat crimes and remains the standard test (Day 2007).

The Courts and Copycat Crime

The Brandenburg liability test came about after Clarence Brandenburg delivered a speech at a Ku Klux Klan rally in Hamilton County, Ohio, in 1964. During the speech, which was recorded by news media, Brandenburg made antisemitic and antiblack assertions and alluded to the possibility of revenge if the federal government and courts continued to suppress the white race. Brandenburg was fined and sentenced to serve one to ten years in prison for violating Ohio's criminal syndicalism law, which made it a crime to advocate the duty to commit or the necessity or propriety of crime, sabotage, or terrorist acts as a means of accomplishing political reform. The appeal to the US Supreme Court created the Brandenburg test, which has come to be applied in cases looking to hold the creators and distributors of media copycat crime content responsible. This test consists of four elements that have to be found for media content to be held accountable: direct advocacy of criminality, intent to incite criminal behavior, likelihood that criminal acts would occur as a result of the media content, and exposure to the content imminently preceding the criminal acts (Kunich 2000). As evidenced by a number of media-content-related cases, the Brandenburg test for finding media content producers legally liable for harm has been nearly impossible to meet.

The first explicit media content case was 1981's *Olivia n., a Minor, etc., Plaintiff and Appellant, v. National Broadcasting Company, Inc., et al.* (126 Cal. App. 3d 488), which involved a televised movie. The 1974 TV movie includes a scene in which a young girl incarcerated in a juvenile reformatory is assaulted in a shower room (see Box 9.1). Plaintiffs sued the National Broadcasting Company for damages from physical and emotional injury, alleging that the movie was likely to engender imitation and that the real-world assailants committed their sexual assault because they viewed the film. On appeal, the court dismissed the suit, stating that the plaintiffs did not meet any elements of the Brandenburg test.

The next case, 1988's *Jack McCollum v. CBS, Inc.* [(202 Cal. App. 3d 994) 1988], pertained to music content. A nineteen-year-old male with a history of alcohol abuse and emotional problems had spent a night listening repeatedly to a heavy metal singer's record albums. Jack

McCollum wore headphones to listen to the final side of a two-record album by Ozzy Ozbourne and, while listening, committed suicide with a .22-caliber handgun. McCollum's parents sued the record company for causing their son's suicide. The courts ruled that culpable incitement was not proven as required by the Brandenburg test, according to which the music must have intended and directed listeners to commit suicide and been likely to produce suicides. The appeals court did not find evidence of intent or foreseeability by the media distributors, noting the number of years between the music's production and release and McCollum's suicide.

In 1989 the content of a commercial movie was central in *Yakubowicz v. Paramount Pictures Corp.* (536 N.E.2d 1067, 1068). The parents of a man killed in gang violence outside a movie theater sued Paramount Pictures, claiming that its film *The Warriors* incited gang members to violence immediately after viewing the movie and as a result caused their son's death. Reaffirming the difficulty of mounting a successful copycat crime case based on media incitement, the court rejected the incitement argument due to the film's not commanding anyone to take any concrete or immediate action.

Unsuccessful attempts to hold media content creators and distributors liable continued through the end of the twentieth century into the twenty-first. In 1997, music was again the focus in *Davidson v. Time Warner, Inc. [S.D. Texas , (No. Civ.A. V-94-006) 1997]*. Rapper Tupac Shakur's *2Pacalypse Now* album included a song, "Soulja's Story," that plaintiffs claimed contained "fighting words" and caused the shooting death of Texas state trooper Bill Davidson during a traffic stop. After his arrest, the vehicle's driver confessed and stated that he was listening to *2Pacalypse Now* as he loaded his weapon and killed the officer. His defense attorneys argued that constant exposure to gangsta rap and its antipolice messages influenced the defendant to kill the trooper. Family members of the trooper used a defective-product argument to sue Time Warner for producing and distributing the album, while Time Warner contended that the music was protected expression under the First Amendment. Reaffirming the Brandenburg test, the court found neither "fighting words" nor incitement to imminent violence, ruling that foreseeability of the crime was not present and there was a low probability of harm from the album, which had sold 400,000 copies with only one case alleging it to be a cause of violence. The court concluded that standards for neither product liability nor incitement to violence were met, and while the song lyrics were objectionable, they were protected.

In 1999 movie content was again reviewed in *Byers v. Edmondson* (712 So.2d 681). In 1995, two teenagers played the Oliver Stone film *Natural Born Killers* repeatedly while consuming LSD throughout a night. The next morning the male spoke about reenacting scenes from the film by killing people at random. The couple drove to a cotton mill near Hernando, Mississippi, where the male walked into the office and shot an elderly man twice in the head. The following night, they drove to a Time Saver store in Ponchatoula, Louisiana. The female entered the store and shot the female store cashier, who was left paralyzed. Both copycat offenders were thereafter caught, convicted, and sentenced to thirty-five years in prison. The victims' families sued the movie director, Oliver Stone, and the film distributor, Time Warner, arguing that the film incited violence and was liable for the deaths and injuries created by the copycat pair. Reaffirming the Brandenburg precedent, the court concluded that the plaintiffs did not prove incitement and dismissed the liability case.

Music lyrics were last revisited in 2001's *Pahler v. Slayer*. Elyse Pahler was a murder victim whose parents sued a thrash metal band, Slayer, as contributing to their daughter's death. The plaintiffs claimed that Slayer songs gave the girl's killers detailed instructions to stalk, rape, torture, murder, and commit acts of necrophilia on their daughter. Their first case was originally thrown out, the judge stating, "There's not a legal position that could be taken that would make Slayer responsible for the girl's death. Where do you draw the line? You might as well start looking through the library at every book on the shelf." Undeterred, the Pahlers sued a second time, claiming that Slayer "knowingly distributed harmful material to minors." This case too was dismissed, with the judge stating, "I do not consider Slayer's music obscene, indecent or harmful to minors." The appeals court again found that a Brandenburg test was not met, that the band's lyrics did not direct or intend to bring about the imminent ritual sacrifice of a young girl, that it is not unlawful to distribute media that is offensive or depicts death, violence, or brutality, that the music did not incite listeners to commit acts of violence, and that murder was not a foreseeable consequence of listening to Slayer music.

In 2002 the content of video games was first examined in *Wilson v. Midway Games, Inc.* (198 F. Supp. 167 [D. Conn. 2002]), and the possibility of holding media legally responsible for copycat crime was further limited. On November 22, 1997, thirteen-year-old Noah Wilson died when his friend stabbed him in the chest with a kitchen knife. Noah's mother filed against the video game company Midway Games, arguing that the friend's addiction to a Midway video game, *Mortal Kombat*, resulted in the fatal stabbing. The suit argued that the friend was so obsessed that he believed he was one of the game characters who kills his game opponents by grabbing them around the neck in a headlock and stabbing them in the chest. The plaintiff stated that the juvenile killer used the same maneuver to stab her son and that Midway's design and marketing of *Mortal Kombat* had caused her son's death. She alleged that she was entitled to damages under the protections of product liability, unfair trade practices, loss of consortium, and negligent and intentional infliction of emotional distress. The plaintiff further argued that Midway Games designed *Mortal Kombat* to addict players to the exhilaration of violence provided by the game and specifically targeted youth.

In its decision, the appeals court concluded that the complaint failed to state a claim upon which relief could be granted: the product liability counts failed because *Mortal Kombat* is not a product within the purview of the consumer protection act; the unfair trade practices claim was time limited and not supported; the loss-of-consortium claim was not recognized in this context under Connecticut law; and the claims of negligence and intentional infliction of emotional distress were precluded by the First Amendment.

Protection of video game content was cemented in a second 2002 case, *James v. Meow Media, Inc.* (90 F. Supp. 2d 798 [W.D. Ky. 2000]), involving a school shooting in Paducah, Kentucky. In 1997, a fourteen-year-old shooter wounded five and killed three at his high school. Investigations revealed that he regularly played *Doom, Quake, Castle Wolfenstein, Redneck Rampage, Nightmare Creatures, Mech Warrior, Resident Evil*, and *Final Fantasy*, which are all interactive first-person computer video games that involve shooting people. The parents of the victims argued that Midway Games produced and distributed defective products that ultimately resulted in the shooting of the Heath High students. As with prior cases, the courts rejected this defective-product argument, and neither the media content creators nor the distributors were held liable.

A last case dealing with media and video game content was heard in 2005. In *Strickland v. Sony (658 So 2nd [Ala 2003])* the copycat effect of the game *Grand Theft Auto* was linked to a triple homicide (see Box 8.8). The focus in this case was on whether a violent video game played a role in the murder of three law enforcement officers in a setting that resembled a scene in the video game. The shooter had played the game for hours prior to the killings and, when presented with a similar real-life setting, had reenacted its shooting sequence. As in other cases, the appeals court rejected any legal liability for the video game producers.

Against this consistent set of judicial decisions protecting media content and rejecting media liability for copycat crimes, one court decision stands in opposition, having deemed the suit as meeting the Brandenburg test. *Rice v. Paladin Enterprises, Inc.* (128 F.3d 233, 265 [4th Cir. 1997]) involved a print book, *Hit Man: A Technical Manual for Independent Contractors* by Rex Feral (1983), that contained detailed instruction on how to commit assassinations. In the rare instance where media content creators and distributors were held liable for subsequent crimes, the courts held that the publisher of the manual was civilly liable for aiding and abetting a triple homicide by a hired assassin. An aspiring hitman used the book's step-by-step instructions on various methods for committing murder and escaping detection to commit three killings. The book was initially ruled as protected content in 1996, but in 1997 an appeals court reversed the lower court's decision, stating that aiding and abetting criminal conduct as outlined in the manual is not protected. The appeals court based its decision on the book's success in assisting others to commit crimes by providing detailed instructions. Paladin Press seriously weakened its own argument against its liability by admitting that its target market was murderers, that it intended for *Hit Man* to be used immediately by criminals in the solicitation, planning, and commission of murder, and that through publishing and selling *Hit Man*, it had assisted in a triple murder. The book's providing detailed instructions and targeting a specific audience were seen as keys for the appeals court to hold Paladin Press liable for the homicides committed based on the book's instructions.

As a group, these cases construct a high judicial bar for establishing media copycat crime liability. In most instances, the media creators and distributors of generator crimes are not held liable. This shield is not impenetrable, but its lowering requires a clear, overwhelming context, and to date all but the *Hit Man* instruction manual case have been unsuccessful. The courts have remained resistant to finding movie producers, song writers, video game programmers, and media production companies liable for copycat crime responses, even when acknowledging that a copycat crime occurred. The judicial position has evolved to the point that meeting the Brandenburg requirements requires plaintiffs to establish that the media directly promoted crime; indirect promotion, advocacy, or glamorization of crime would not be sufficient. The courts have further indicated that prior restraints against media creators, where content is barred based on the expectation of possible copycat effects, would not be constitutional. In sum, except in unusual and clearly linked circumstances such as the *Hit Man* case, where an instructional book was determined to be openly intended to help assassins (Gibeaut 1998), the US courts have not found media liable for copycat crimes.

Judging from the absence of cases over the last two decades, the courts see strong protection of media content as settled law. The bottom line is that as a route to policy changes regarding copycat crime, the courts should not be relied upon (Cooley 2003; Kunich 2000). In the absence of court support for liability or restrictions on media content, what copycat crime social policies might be pursued? Although copycat crimes have been historically shown to influence criminal justice policies (Davis 1980),[3] only a limited number of policies aimed at curtailing copycat crime have been championed, and voluntary recommendations more than legislative requirements dominate. Policy recommendations regarding media content are limited by both court postures and lack of research, but some recommendations aimed at media content creators do exist, most of which focus on the content of news coverage.

Copycat Crime Media Content Policy Recommendations

Recommendations for reducing suicide and school-shooting copycats are starting points. These recommendations focus on the content of news media and are therefore limited in their general effectiveness. Irrespective of their narrow focus, recommendations on news coverage of copycat suicides have been reported as effective for reducing suicides following changes in media content. The reduction in copycat suicides appears to emanate from providing less information in news reports rather than attempts to insert antisuicide messages into entertainment content, which is speculated to be an ineffective deterrent in the face of non-news-media images and narratives that romanticize suicide.

In addition, recommendations concerning news coverage of mass shootings have been forwarded (Chen 2018; Follman 2015; Hammerschlag 2005; Kambam et al. 2020, citing World Health Organization 2008; Majeed, Sudak, and Beresin 2019; Meindl and Ivy 2017). The following eight summary recommendations for the coverage of violent crimes are aimed at preventing some of the most feared copycat crimes, like mass and school shootings, and are applicable to reporting both generator crimes and copycat crimes:

1. Describe the perpetrator with dispassionate language; avoid stereo-types, oversimplified explanations, and terms like *lone wolf.*
2. Do not fixate on victim numbers or body counts as some copy-cats keep score and seek to outdo their predecessors. Focus on victims, survivors, and those who acted to end the crimes.
3. Avoid sensationalizing, glamourizing, and romanticizing cover-age. Do not emphasize crimes by prominent story placement.
4. Minimize the use of the criminal's name, especially in headlines.
5. Minimize the use of pictures of the criminal; avoid posed photos of the offender.
6. Do not publish the offender's videos or manifestos; instead, paraphrase, cite sparingly, and include debunking analysis and commentary.
7. Do not link a copycat crime to past generator crimes via names, photos, or comparison.
8. Discuss a generator and copycat crime's aftermath and empha-size failures. Stress the likelihood of failure, arrest, and punish-ment and the adverse consequences on the family, friends, and future of copycat offenders.

These now long-standing recommendations are herein endorsed but have limited impact on copycat crimes due to their focus on news con-tent and a small number of copycat crimes, as well as their voluntary nature. The news-content-related recommendations likely do no harm and are encouraged, but empirical evidence of their effectiveness remains absent. They are essentially reactions to copycat crime in the sense that they apply only to how news media should report generator and copycat crimes. They are not proposals for how to proactively reduce the creation of generator copycat crimes or the subsequent copycats. Proactive rec-ommendations along those lines are far less developed. Field-tested poli-cies geared for the criminal justice system are needed.

Criminal Justice System Copycat Crime Policy Recommendations

First, research suggesting the genesis role of media in the launching of juvenile criminal careers points to needed policies focused on at-risk juveniles (Surette and Chadee 2020; Surette and Maze 2015). Many per-sonality and attitude factors posited as related to the copying of crime suggest the feasibility of proactively identifying at-risk youth who have not yet attempted a copycat crime as appropriate for media-debunking efforts (Surette and Chadee 2020). The gist of these recommendations is reducing the number of potential copycat offenders produced by generator copycat crimes through policies aimed at target-hardening juveniles against media criminogenic effects. Copycat-at-risk youth need not be singled out, as debunking curricula could be widely beneficial and administered in media-literacy classes. Knowledge of how the media functions, how to evaluate content, and how content might influence is expected to have positive impacts on reducing the generation of copycat crime (Dill et al. 2011). It is strongly recommended that school-based curricula to reduce the influence of media crime models and debunk criminogenic media content be developed and tested.

Beyond recommendations geared for potential copycat offenders, suggestions for actions by criminal justice agencies exist. Although legacy media have not proven to be the best means to dampen copycat crime, an important role for law enforcement is possible (Surette 2020a). General deterrence and announcement effects from highly visible law enforcement actions, government prosecutions, and the imposition of fines and jail sentences can play a part in ending copycat crime waves and are recommended when appropriate. Additionally, like debunking curricula for juvenile precopycats, correctional programs for postcrime copycats that disconnect the effects of criminogenic media primes on decisionmaking and critique criminal scripts acquired from the media are recommended. Media-induced misconceptions about crime and punishment in offenders, particularly young-adult ones, should be directly addressed.

Lastly, projects are recommended that could be useful for reducing the traversing of the three copycat crime pathways shown in Figure 9.2. Commonly misrepresented in the media, accurate information about real-world likelihood of success and risks of arrest would help to decrease planned systematic crimes. Reducing real-world crime opportunities might help with heuristic, unplanned copycat crimes. And exposure to debunking curricula would assist in counteracting copycat priming from storybook generator crimes. At the inception of a copycat crime wave, effective ways to curtail its lifespan are to attack the crime's novelty, sever its connections to celebrity crime models, and undermine public perceptions of its harmlessness and acceptability (Surette 2020a). The use of celebrities who deliver copycat-crime-dampening messages is recommended in preventive efforts ("Shiggy" 2018).

Copycat Crime Policy Summary

Albeit without great optimism, a set of copycat crime policy actions are suggested. While potentially helpful, these policy recommendations are not panaceas, and their implementation should not be expected to erase media-prompted copycat crime effects. The voluntary restraint of news coverage of suicide has shown promise, but it is less likely that voluntarily restrictions will be widely adopted for crime news. More damning, copycat crime effects are significantly found in entertainment media, and given the judicial posture concerning media liability content, significant adoptions in entertainment media are unlikely. Policies from a target-hardening perspective—whereby high-risk individuals, teenagers in particular, are provided counterinformation to the misleading, dominant portrayals of crime associated with copycat generator crimes—show more promise. Exposure to generator crime content will likely remain widespread, but steps to insulate potential copycats from the pernicious effects of exposure should be pursued. Lastly, admittedly reactive rather than proactive, policies linked to the criminal justice system are important. After a copycat crime has been committed and publicized, high-visibility law enforcement and deterrence efforts should substantively shorten the life span of copycat crime waves.

More important than the policies that work around the edges of copycat crime, the reduction of real-world crime models as a policy goal would have a significant effect on copycat crime. Regardless of other policies, the number of at-risk copycat offenders will not be substantially reduced in crime-ridden neighborhood settings or crime-glamorizing cultures. The copycat offender's acceptance of media generator crimes as valid models to follow is tied to the overlap of generator crime portrayals with family, neighborhood, and real-world crime models. Crime in movies, the source most often cited for copycat crime ideas, becomes reality in cultures that support the validity of the media crime portraits and provide the opportunities to mimic them. A fictional criminal will remain fictional in infertile cultures and come to life in fertile ones.

In sum, the future likelihood of serious copycat-crime-dampening policies being instituted is low. Media generator crime content will only be marginally controlled, curtailed more in news content but uninhibited in entertainment content. Access to copycat-generator crime content will be increasingly difficult to control. Juvenile target-hardening and debunking curricula will require professional support from educators and resources not currently found. The necessary cultural shifts will be difficult to achieve in the social media age. The research points to policy steps that might help; the social trends point to predictions that they won't.

Rudders or Triggers?

Affecting copycat crime prevalence, policy, and research, the most important copycat crime issue yet to be determined is whether media generator crimes serve as triggers or rudders for ensuing copycat crimes. In the first model, criminogenic content is regarded as a direct cause of crime; in the second, the media are catalysts that shape criminality. The first model is represented by the general aggression model (Anderson, Gentile, and Buckley 2007), in which the media are perceived as triggering individuals to commit crimes and as a criminalizing influence on individuals who otherwise would be law abiding. In this manner, media portrayals of crimes increase both the number of offenders and their criminal motivation. In contrast, under the media-as-catalyst model, criminally disposed individuals conduct media searches for crime information (Ferguson et al. 2008; Rios and Ferguson 2020; Surette and Chadee 2020). The role that media crime content plays is significantly different in the two perspectives. In the trigger model, exposure to media crime models causes individuals to commit crimes that they would not have otherwise committed. In the rudder model, media molds criminal behavior that would have occurred in some fashion regardless. Media content has potential impact as both trigger and rudder, but it is much more important if its primary impact is as a crime trigger.

In the relevant research on media triggers versus rudders, media crime models and criminal behavior have more often been found to be instructional sources, crime rudders, rather than crime-generating triggers (Dill et al. 2011). Whether the media are triggering causes or catalyst rudders is important for which public policies to pursue (Rios and Ferguson 2020). If media content is a frequent direct causal trigger of crime, broad-based public policies on regulating content make sense. If the media are usually rudders for crime, a focus on at-risk potential copycat offenders to reduce imitations makes sense.

The strongest support for the media as rudder is found in a host of studies on copycat suicides.[4] The research on suicide supports a media-as-rudder mechanism where a detailed media description suggests suicide as a solution to personal problems. Examinations by Dunae (1979) and Springhall (1994) of the nineteenth-century penny dreadful publications show that support for the media providing crime techniques over motivations to copycat offenders has a long history. This early perception has been repeatedly backed in recent research.[5] The rudder model has also been supported in surveys of offenders in which the media are more often credited as sources of criminal techniques and less often as sources of criminal motivation (Pease and Love 1984b; Surette 2002).

From the research on terrorism, Brigitte Nacos (2009) additionally sees in the history of hijacking, embassy takeovers, beheadings, and suicide terrorism evidence of the media as a crime rudder. She does not see a significant trigger role for the media because terrorists exist before media attention, and therefore "inspirational contagion," where media might play a causal role, is rare for terrorists. Similarly, Viridiana Rios and Christopher Ferguson (2020) found evidence supporting a media-rudder over a media-trigger effect regarding media coverage of violent drug crime. In sum, assertion of the media as a copycat crime trigger is rarely found in the literature and is weakly supported in the research. The reality that most copycat criminals are likely to commit some sort of crime with or without exposure to media generator crime content leads to a policy focus on at-risk copycat offenders and their social settings. Changing media criminogenic content should change the form crime takes and perhaps lower copycat crime's harmfulness, but without broad social policies aimed at crime-generating environments, societal crime levels not connected to copycat crime will, at best, only be marginally reduced, and copycat crime will persist.

Conclusion

In closing, copycat crime is seen to encompass all types of crimes found across a broad range of media. Copycat criminals sometimes are motivated to commit their crimes by the media but more often have preestablished motivations and are influenced by media-provided crime instructions. Copycat crime needs to be studied and understood as both an individual act and an aggregate-level crime phenomenon. At the individual level, primed imitation emerges as the hypothesized short-term copycat crime mechanism and script acquisition as the most likely long-term mechanism. At the socially aggregated level, diffusion and social learning processes are thought to overlay social factors conducive to copycat crime, which determine copycat crime rates. Much of what is thought to be known about copycat crime, however, is hypothesized based upon anecdotal case studies and research on general crimes and noncriminal behavior not directly connected to copycat crime.

In addition, rigorous research of the understudied copycat crime research questions would benefit criminal justice policy formation. In the criminal justice system, knowledge about copycat crime would help law enforcement in the understanding, recognition, and prediction of crime trends and crime clusters. Recognition of incorrectly labeled copycat crimes would avoid unnecessary fear of crime and inappropriate news media reporting of crime waves. In the judicial system, confirmation of a copycat crime would be useful for prosecuting attorneys looking to establish premeditation or defense attorneys seeking extenuating considerations where pathological media immersion is evident. Understanding the mind-set of a convicted copycat offender would also enhance sentencing and rehabilitation. For example, restrictions on access to specific media content and internet sites would be a logical sentence condition for at-risk copycat offenders. Lastly, an appreciation of copycat crime and copycat offenders would improve media and criminal justice system relations. Specific knowledge would reduce calls for content restrictions and increase the release of nonproblematic information (Dill et al. 2011).

In the future, the media's copycat effects are expected to be enhanced as their current crime content contributes to an increased number of people at risk for negative media influences due to racial strife, income disparities, and criminogenic social conditions. Crime-prone persons who see themselves as having criminal self-efficacy will be at greater risk for emulating media-portrayed crime. As the media sensationalize crime and make celebrities of criminals, imitation will increase, and when successful crime is detailed, some innovative criminals will become copycat offenders.

As evidenced by the rise of political violence and the radicalization of citizens, the future of copycat crime will be heavily entwined with social media. Supported by a culture that intensely follows celebrities, generates a psychological need in consumers to share and participate, and enhances the perception that crimes are socially acceptable, copycat crime is expected to steadily increase over the twenty-first century. Understanding copycat crime dynamics will be crucial for understanding broader crime trends and the media's impact on society. A host of copycat crime research hypotheses await serious research and validation or rejection.

Notes

1. The discussion of copycat crime pathways draws upon Surette 2013b.

2. For a rendering of the multiple copycat waves generated by the Columbine shootings, see zyopp, "Columbine Iceberg," scifiaddicts.com, http://scifiaddicts.com /p/IcebergCharts/comments/owo44n/columbine_iceberg.

3. The London garroting panic of 1862, for example, documents a copycat crime wave changing criminal justice legislation and sentencing policy. The garroting panic involved a wave of copycat robberies in which victims were approached from behind, strangled with a cord, and robbed. Specifically aimed at garrotting offenders, the 1863 English Parliament Garrotters' Act imposed whipping with imprisonment for robberies with violence, thereby reversing a policy trend away from corporal punishment (Davis 1980). The garroting copycat crime wave also resulted in the extension of police powers and ultimately reversed the prior support for a more lenient penal system among the English ruling class to majority support for harsher policies (Davis 1980).

4. For suicide research that supports a media-as-rudder mechanism, see Ashton and Donnan 1981; Church and Philips 1984; Crosby, Rhee, and Holland 1977; Hawton et al. 1999; Hemenway 1911; Jonas 1992; Marzuk et al. 1993; Veysey, Kamanyire, and Volans 1999a, 1999b.

5. For discussion of the media as cause or catalyst, see Ferguson et al. 2008; Ferguson and Dyck 2012; Ferguson, San Miguel, and Hartley 2009; Grimes, Anderson, and Bergen 2008; Surette 2013a.

Bibliography

Adler, J. S. 1996. "The Making of a Moral Panic in 19th-Century America: The Boston Garroting Hysteria of 1865." *Deviant Behavior* 17, no. 3: 259–278.

Akers, R. 1973. *Deviant Behavior—a Social Learning Approach*. Belmont, CA: Wadsworth.

Akers, R. 2011. *Social Learning and Social Structure: A General Theory of Crime and Deviance*. New Brunswick, NJ: Transaction Publishers.

Akers, R., and Jensen, G. 2003. *Social Learning Theory and the Explanation of Crime*. New Brunswick, NJ: Transaction Publishers.

Akers, R. and Jensen, G. 2006. "The Empirical Status of Social Learning Theory of Crime and Deviance: The Past, Present, and Future." In *Taking Stock: The Status of Criminological Theory*, edited by F. Cullen, J. Wright, and K. Blevins, 37–76. New Brunswick, NJ: Transaction Publishers.

Akers, R., and Sellers, C. 2004. *Criminological Theories: Introduction, Evaluations, and Application*. 4th ed. Los Angeles, CA: Roxbury.

Alkiviadou, N. 2019. "Hate Speech on Social Media Networks: Towards a Regulatory Framework?" *Information and Communications Technology Law* 28, no. 1: 19–35.

Allport, F. 1924. *Social Psychology*. Boston: Houghton Mifflin Company.

Anderson, C., Carnagey, N., and Eubanks, J. 2003. "Exposure to Violent Media: The Effects of Songs with Violent Lyrics on Aggressive Thoughts and Feelings." *Journal of Personality and Social Psychology* 84, no. 5: 960–971.

Anderson, C., Carnagey, N., Flanagan, M., Benjamin, A., Arlin, J., and Eubanks, J. 2004. "Violent Video Games: Specific Effects of Violent Content on Aggressive Thoughts and Behavior." *Advances in Experimental Social Psychology* 36: 199–249.

Anderson, C. A., Gentile, D. A., and Buckley, K. E. 2007. *Violent Video Game Effects on Children and Adolescents: Theory, Research, and Public Policy*. London: Oxford University Press.

Aristotle. 350 BCE. *Poetics*.

Armstrong, E. G. 2001. "Sexism and Misogyny in Music Land." *Journal of Criminal Justice and Popular Culture* 8, no. 2: 96–126.

Arrington, R. L. 1982. "Advertising and Behavior Control." *Journal of Business Ethics* 1, no. 1: 3–12.

Asad, T. 2007. *On Suicide Bombing*. New York: Columbia University Press.

Ashton, J., and Donnan, S. 1981. "Suicide by Burning as an Epidemic Phenomenon: An Analysis of 82 Deaths and Inquests in England and Wales in 1978–9." *Psychological Medicine* 11: 735–739.

Atkin, D., and Abelman, R. 2009. "Assessing Social Concerns over the Impact of Popular Music and Music Video: A Review of Scholarly Research." *Open Social Science Journal* 2, no. 1: 37–49.

Aveni, A. 1977. "The Not-So-Lonely Crowd: Friendship Groups in Collective Behavior." *Sociometry* 40, no. 1: 96–99.

Baer, D., and Deguchi, H. 1985. "Generalized Imitation from a Radical-Behavioral Viewpoint." In *Theoretical Issues in Behavior Therapy*, edited by S. Reiss and R. Bootzin, 179–217. Orlando, FL: Academic Press.

Bai, Y., Wu, W. P., and Cheung, M. F. 2019. "How Personality Traits, Employee Incompetence and Consumer Similarity Influence Shoplifting Behavior." *Journal of Consumer Marketing* 3, no. 3: 379–392.

Bailey, S. 1993. "Fast Forward to Violence." *Criminal Justice Matters* 11, no. 1: 6–7.

Baker, W., and Faulkner, R. 2003. "Diffusion of Fraud: Intermediate Economic Crime and Investor Dynamics." *Criminology* 41, no. 4: 1173–1206.

Baldwin, J. 1899. *Social and Ethical Interpretations in Mental Development: A Study in Social Psychology*. New York: Macmillan. Reprinted New York: Arno Press, 1973.

Bandura, A. 1973. *Aggression: A Social Learning Analysis*. Englewood Cliffs, NJ: Prentice Hall.

Bandura, A. 1979. "Self-Referent Mechanisms in Social Learning Theory." *American Psychologist* 34, no. 5: 439–441.

Bandura, A. 1986. *Social Foundations of Thought and Action: A Social Cognitive Theory*. Englewood Cliffs, NJ: Prentice Hall.

Bandura, A. 1995. *Self-Efficacy in Changing Societies*. London: Cambridge University Press.

Bandura, A. 2001. "Social Cognitive Theory of Mass Communication." *Media Psychology* 3, no. 3: 265–299.

Bandura, A., and Walters, R. 1963. *Social Learning and Personality Development*. New York: Holt, Rinehart and Winston.

Barkan, S. 2001. *Criminology: A Sociological Understanding*. Upper Saddle River, NJ: Prentice Hall.

Bass, F. 1969. "A New Product Growth for Model Consumer Durables." *Management Science* 15, no. 5: 215–227.

Bass, F., Krishnan, R., and Jain, D. 1994. "Why the Bass Model Fits Without Decision Variables." *Marketing Science* 13, no. 3: 203–223.

Beaver, K., Eagle, M., Schutt, J., Boutwell, B., Ratchford, M., Roberts, K., and Barnes, J. 2009. "Genetic and Environmental Influences on Levels of Self-Control and Delinquent Peer Affiliation: Results from a Longitudinal Sample of Adolescent Twins." *Criminal Justice and Behavior* 36, no. 1: 41–60.

Berk, R. 1972. "The Controversy Surrounding Analyses of Collective Violence: Some Methodological Notes." In *Collective Violence*, edited by J. Short and M. Wolfgang, 112–118. Chicago: Aldine.

Berk, R. 1974. "A Gaming Approach to Crowd Behavior." *American Sociological Review* 39, no. 3: 355–373.

Berkowitz, L., and Macaulay, J. 1971. "The Contagion of Criminal Violence." *Sociometry* 34, no. 2: 238–260.

Biocca, F. 2013. "The Evolution of Interactive Media." In *Narrative Impact: Social and Cognitive Foundations*, edited by M. Green, J. Strange, and T. Brock, 97–130. New York: Psychology Press,

Blank, T., and McNeill, L. 2018. *Slender Man Is Coming: Creepypasta and Contemporary Legends on the Internet*. Boulder: University Press of Colorado.

Bleyer, W. 1927. *Main Currents in the History of American Journalism*. Boston: Houghton Mifflin.

Blood, R., and Pirkis, J. 2001. "Suicide and the Media." *Crisis* 22, no. 4: 163–169.

Blumer, H. 1939. "Collective Behavior." In *Principles of Sociology*, edited by R. Park, 219–288. New York: Barnes and Noble.

Bohm, R., and Surette, R. 2013. "Toward an Understanding of Aggregate Death Penalty Opinion Change: A Possible Role for Popular Music." *International Journal of Criminology and Sociology* 2: 32–56.

Bohstedt, J., and Williams, D. 1988. "The Diffusion of Riots: The Patterns of 1766, 1795, and 1801 in Devonshire." *Journal of Interdisciplinary History* 19, no. 1: 1–24.

Borg, G. 1995. "Subway Clerk Critically Burned as Life Imitates Violent Movie." *Chicago Tribune*. November 27. www.chicagotribune.com/news/ct-xpm-1995-11-27-9511270165-story.html.

Bosch, L., Bosch, B., De Boeck, K., Nawrot, T., Meyts, I., Vanneste, D., Le Bourlegat, C. A., Croda, J., and da Silva Filho, L. 2017. "Cystic Fibrosis Carriership and Tuberculosis: Hints Toward an Evolutionary Selective Advantage Based on Data from the Brazilian Territory." *BMC Infectious Diseases* 17, no. 1: 340.

Bowers, K., and Johnson, S. 2004. "Who Commits Near Repeats? A Test of the Boost Explanation." *Western Criminology Review* 5, no. 3: 12–24.

Bowers, K., and Johnson, S. 2005. "Domestic Burglary Repeats and Space-Time Clusters the Dimensions of Risk." *European Journal of Criminology* 2, no. 1: 67–92.

Brown, M., Bhadury, R., and Pope, N. 2010. "The Impact of Comedic Violence on Viral Advertising Effectiveness." *Journal of Advertising* 39, no. 1: 49–66.

Brown, S., Fuller, R., and Vician, C. 2004. "Who's Afraid of the Virtual World? Anxiety and Computer-Mediated Communication." *Journal of the Association for Information Systems* 5, no. 2: 79–107.

Brownstein, H., Fatton, R., Jr., and Fox, M. J. 1996. *The Rise and Fall of a Violent Crime Wave: Crack Cocaine and the Social Construction of a Crime Problem*. Boulder, CO: Lynne Rienner Publishers.

Bruinsma, G. 1992. "Differential Association Theory Reconsidered: An Extension and Its Empirical Test." *Journal of Quantitative Criminology* 8: 29–49.

Bryant, J., and Miron, D. 2002. "Entertainment as Media Effect." *Media Effects: Advances in Theory and Research* 2: 549–582.

Bushman, B., Jamieson, P., Weitz, I., and Romer, D. 2013. "Gun Violence Trends in Movies." *Pediatrics* 132, no. 6: 1014–1018.

Caplovitz, D., and Rogers, C. 1961. *Swastika 1960*. New York: Anti-Defamation League of B'nai B'rith.

Capote, T. 1966. *In Cold Blood*. New York: Random House.

Carlson, M., Marcus-Newhall, A., and Miller, N. 1998. "Effects of Situational Aggression Cues: A Quantitative Review." *Journal of Personality and Social Psychology* 38, no. 4: 622–633.

Carmo, J., Rumiati, R., and Vallesi, A. 2012. "Understanding and Imitating Unfamiliar Actions: Distinct Underlying Mechanisms." *PLoS One* 7, no. 10: e46939.

Carpenter, W. B. 1874. *Principles of Mental Physiology*. New York: Appleton.

Casey, C. 2010. "Common Misperceptions: The Press and Victorian Views of Crime." *Journal of Interdisciplinary History* 41, no. 3: 367–391.

Cavalli, E. 2008. "Jack Thompson Reaches Out to Take-Two Exec's Mother." *Wired*. April 24. www.wired.com/2008/04/jack-thompson-p.

Cavender, G., and Fishman, M. 1998. "Television Reality Crime Programs: Context and History." In *Entertaining Crime: Television Reality Programs*, edited by M. Fishman and G. Cavender, 3–15. New York: Aldine De Gruyter.

Chadee, D. 2010. "Copycat Crime Among Trinidad Low Risk Youth." St. Augustine, Trinidad, ANSA McAL Psychological Research Centre, Faculty of Social Sciences at the University of the West Indies.

Chae, S., and Flores, D. 1998. "Broadcasting Versus Narrowcasting." *Information Economics and Policy* 10, no. 1: 41–57.

Chan, S., Khader, M., Ang, J., Tan, E., Khoo, K., and Chin, J. 2012. "Understanding 'Happy Slapping.'" *International Journal of Police Science and Management* 14, no. 1: 42–57.

Cheatwood, D. 2010. "Images of Crime and Justice in Early Commercial Radio—1932 to 1958." *Criminal Justice Review* 35, no. 1: 32–51.

Chen, L. 2018. "The Effects of Media Coverage on Mass Shootings in the United States." *Pop Culture Intersections* 31 (September 12). https://scholarcommons.scu.edu/engl_176/31.

Chertoff, M. 2017. "A Public Policy Perspective of the Dark Web." *Journal of Cyber Policy* 2, no. 1: 26–38.

Chess, S., and Newsom, E. 2015. *Folklore, Horror Stories, and the Slender Man: The Development of an Internet Mythology.* New York: Palgrave MacMillan.

Chibnall, S. 1981. "The Production of Knowledge by Crime Reporters." In *The Manufacture of News,* edited by S. Cohen and J. Young, 75–97. Thousand Oaks, CA: Sage.

Church, I., and Philips, J. 1984. "Suggestion and Suicide by Plastic Bag Asphyxia." *British Journal of Psychiatry* 144: 100–101.

Clarke, R., and Felson, M., eds. 1993. *Routine Activity and Rational Choice.* Vol. 5. New Brunswick, NJ: Transaction Publishers.

Clarke, R., and McGrath, G. 1992. "Newspaper Reports of Bank Robberies and the Copycat Phenomenon." *Australian and New Zealand Journal of Criminology* 25: 83–88.

Claster, D. 1967. "Comparison of Risk Perception Between Delinquents and Nondelinquents." *Journal of Criminal Law, Criminology and Police Science* 58: 80–86.

Claxton, G. 2005. "Joining the Intentional Dance." In *Imitation, Human Development, and Culture.* Vol. 2 of *Perspectives on Imitation: From Neuroscience to Social Science,* edited by S. Hurley and N. Chater, 193–196. Cambridge: Massachusetts Institute of Technology Press.

Cohen, A. 2015. "To Know Their Names." *Daily Princetonian.* www.dailyprincetonian.com/category/opinion/columns.

Cohen, J., and Tita, G. 1999. "Diffusion in Homicide: Exploring a General Method for Detecting Spatial Diffusion Processes." *Journal of Quantitative Criminology* 15, no. 4: 451–493.

Cohn, G. 2018. "How Slender Man Became a Legend." *New York Times.* August 15. https://www.nytimes.com/2018/08/15/movies/slender-man-timeline.html.

Coleman, L. 1987. *Suicide Clusters.* London: Faber and Faber.

Coleman, L. 2004. *The Copycat Effect: How the Media and Popular Culture Trigger the Mayhem in Tomorrow's Headlines.* New York: Simon & Schuster.

Collins, R. 2011. "Content Analysis of Gender Roles in Media: Where Are We Now and Where Should We Go?" *Sex Roles* 64: 290–298.

Conklin, J. 1998. *Criminology.* Needham Heights, MA: Allyn and Bacon.

Conrad, J. 2009. *The Secret Agent.* Edited by T. Agathocleous. Toronto: Broadview Press.

Cook, P., and Goss, K. 1996. "A Selective Review of the Social-Contagion Literature." Working paper, Sanford Institute of Policy Studies, Duke University, Raleigh, North Carolina.

Cooley, A. 2003. "They Fought the Law and the Law (Rightfully) Won: The Unsuccessful Battle to Impose Tort Liability upon Media Defendants for Violent Acts of Mimicry Committed by Teenage Viewers." *Texas Review Entertainment and Sports Law* 6, no. 1: 203–236.

Couch, C. 1968. "Collective Behavior: An Examination of Some Stereotypes." *Social Problems* 15, no. 3: 310–322.

Coyne, S. 2007. "Does Media Violence Cause Violent Crime?" *European Journal of Criminal Policy Research* 13: 205–211.

Crosby, K., Rhee, J., and Holland, J. 1977. "Suicide by Fire: A Contemporary Method of Political Protest." *International Journal of Social Psychiatry* 23: 60–69.

Curtis, J. 1953. "Gabriel Tarde." In *Social Theorists*, edited by C. Mihanovich, 142–157. Milwaukee: Bruce Publishing.

Davidson, W. 1983. "The Third-Person Effect in Communication." *Public Opinion Quarterly* 47, no. 1: 1–15.

Davis, J. 1980. "The London Garroting Panic of 1862: A Moral Panic and the Creation of a Criminal Class in Mid-Victorian England." In *Crime and Law in Western Societies: Historical Essays*, edited by V. Gatrell, B. Lenman, and G. Parker, 190–213. London: Europa.

Day, T. 2007. "Bumfights and Copycat Crimes . . . Connecting the Dots: Negligent Publication or Protected Speech." *Stetson Law Review* 37: 825–853.

De Graaf, A., Hoeken, H., Sanders, J., and Beentjes, J. 2012. "Identification as a Mechanism of Narrative Persuasion." *Communication Research* 39, no. 6: 802–823.

De Vos, G. 2012. *What Happens Next?* Santa Barbara, CA: ABC-CLIO.

Dean, R. 2019. "Copycat Crime: *Dexter* TV Series." Unpublished research paper. Orlando: University of Central Florida, Department of Criminal Justice.

Decety, J., and Chaminade, T. 2005. "The Neurophysiology of Imitation and Intersubjectivity." In *Mechanisms of Imitation*. Vol. 1 of *Perspectives on Imitation: From Neuroscience to Social Science*, edited by S. Hurley and N. Chater, 119–140. Cambridge: Massachusetts Institute of Technology Press.

Delwiche, A., and Henderson, J. 2013. "Introduction: What Is Participatory Culture?" In *The Participatory Cultures Handbook*, edited by A. Delwiche and J. Henderson, 3–9. London: Routledge.

Deutsch, M. 1962. "The 1960 Swastika-Smearings: Analysis of the Apprehended Youth." *Merrill-Palmer Quarterly of Behavior and Development* 8, no. 2: 99–120.

Dewey, C. 2014. "The Complete History of 'Slender Man,' the Meme That Compelled Two Girls to Stab a Friend." *Washington Post*. June 3. www.washingtonpost.com/news/the-intersect/wp/2014/06/03/the-complete-terrifying-history-of-slender-man-the-internet-meme-that-compelled-two-12-year-olds-to-stab-their-friend.

Diekstra, R. 1974. "A Social Learning Theory Approach to the Prediction of Suicidal Behavior." In *Proceedings: 7th International Conference for Suicide Prevention, August 27–30, 1973*, edited by N. Speyer, R. Diekstra, and K. van de Loo, 55–86. Amsterdam: International Association for the Prevention of Suicide.

Diener, E., Beaman, A., Fraser, S., and Kelem, R. 1976. "Effects of Deindividuation Variables on Stealing Among Halloween Trick-or-Treaters." *Journal of Personality and Social Psychology* 33, no. 2: 178–183.

Dijksterhuis, A. 2005. "Why We Are Social Animals: The High Road to Imitation as Social Glue." In *Imitation, Human Development, and Culture*. Vol. 2 of *Perspectives on Imitation: From Neuroscience to Social Science*, edited by S. Hurley and N. Chater, 207–220. Cambridge: Massachusetts Institute of Technology Press.

Dijksterhuis, A., Aarts, H., Bargh, J., and van Knippenberg, A. 2000. "On the Relation Between Associative Strength and Automatic Behavior." *Journal of Experimental Social Psychology* 36: 531–544.

Dijksterhuis, A., and Bargh, J. 2001. "The Perception-Behavior Expressway: Automatic Effects of Social Perception on Social Behavior." In *Advances in Experimental Social Psychology*, edited by M. Zanna, 33:1–40. San Diego, CA: Academic Press.

Dijksterhuis, A., Bargh, J., and Miedema, J. 2000. "Of Men and Mackerels: Attention, Subjective Experience, and Automatic Social Behavior." In *The Message Within*, edited by H. Bless and J. Forgas, 37–51. Philadelphia: Psychology Press.

Dill, K., Redding, R., Smith, P., Surette, R., and Cornell, D. 2011. "Recurrent Issues in Efforts to Prevent Homicidal Youth Violence in Schools: Expert Opinions." *New Directions for Youth Development* 129: 113–128.

Doley, R., Ferguson, C., and Surette, R. 2013. "Copycat Firesetting: Bridging Two Research Areas." *Criminal Justice and Behavior* 40, no. 12: 1472–1491.

Dominick, J. 1978. "Crime and Law Enforcement in the Mass Media." In *Deviance and Mass Media*, edited by C. Winick, 105–128. Thousand Oaks, CA: Sage.

Drechsel, R. 1983. *News Making in the Trial Courts*. White Plains, NY: Longman.

Dressler, D. 1961. "Case of the Copycat Criminal." *New York Times Magazine*. December 10: 42–47.

Dunae, P. 1979. "Penny Dreadfuls: Late Nineteenth-Century Boys' Literature and Crime." *Victorian Studies* 22, no. 2: 133–150.

Egesdal, M., Fathauer, C., Louie, K., Neuman, J., Mohler, G., and Lewis, E. 2010. "Statistical and Stochastic Modeling of Gang Rivalries in Los Angeles." *SIAM Undergraduate Research Online* 3: 72–94.

Ehrlich, H. 1962. "The Swastika Epidemic of 1959–1960." *Social Problems* 9, no. 3: 264–272.

Eisenberg, L. 1986. "Does Bad News About Suicide Beget Bad News?" *New England Journal of Medicine* 315, no. 11: 705–707.

Engle, K. 2012. "Celebrity Diplomacy and Global Citizenship." *Celebrity Studies* 3, no. 1: 116–118.

Etzerdorfer, E., Sonneck, G., and Nagel-Kuess, S. 1992. "Newspaper Reports and Suicide." *New England Journal of Medicine* 327, no. 7: 502–503.

Etzioni, A., and Etzioni, O. 1997. "Communities: Virtual vs. Real." *Science* 277, no. 5324: 295–296.

Ezeihuoma, O. 2020. "Copycat Suicide Terrorism: The Case of Boko Haram in Nigeria." PhD diss., Texas Southern University.

Fagan, J., Wilkinson, D., and Davies, G. 2006. "Social Contagion of Violence." Columbia Public Law Research Paper No. 06-126. Columbia Law School Scholarship Archive. https//scholarship.law.columbia.edu/faculty_scholarship/1428.

Famoye, F., and Singh, K. 2006. "Zero-Inflated Generalized Poisson Regression Model with an Application to Domestic Violence Data." *Journal of Data Science* 4, no. 1: 117–130.

Farrar, K., and Krcmar, M. 2006. "Measuring State and Trait Aggression." *Media Psychology* 8, no. 2: 127–138.

Fennis, B., and Stroebe, W. 2016. *The Psychology of Advertising*. New York: Routledge.

Feral, R. 1983. *Hit Man: A Technical Manual for Independent Contractors*. Boulder, CO: Paladin Press.

Ferguson, C. 2015. "Do Angry Birds Make for Angry Children? A Meta-analysis of Video Game Influences on Children's and Adolescents' Aggression, Mental Health, Prosocial Behavior, and Academic Performance." *Perspectives on Psychological Science* 10, no. 5: 646–666.

Ferguson, C. 2018. "Strawberry Sabotage: What Are Copycat Crimes and Who Commits Them?" *The Conversation* (September): 1–3. https://eprints.qut.edu.au/127036.

Ferguson, C., and Dyck, D. 2012. "Paradigm Change in Aggression Research: The Time Has Come to Retire the General Aggression Model." *Aggression and Violent Behavior* 17, no. 3: 220–228.

Ferguson, C., and Kilburn, J. 2009. "The Public Health Risks of Media Violence: A Meta-analytic Review." *Journal of Pediatrics* 154, no. 5: 759–763.

Ferguson, C., Rueda, S., Cruz, A., Ferguson, D., Fritz, S., and Smith, S. 2008. "Violent Video Games and Aggression: Causal Relationship or Byproduct of Family Violence and Intrinsic Violence Motivation?" *Criminal Justice and Behavior* 35, no. 3: 311–332.

Ferguson, C., San Miguel, C., and Hartley, R. 2009. "A Multivariate Analysis of Youth Violence and Aggression: The Influence of Family, Peers, Depression, and Media Violence." *Journal of Pediatrics* 155, no. 6: 904–908.

Festinger, L., Pepitone, A., and Newcomb, T. 1952. "Some Consequences of Deindividuation in a Group." *Journal of Abnormal and Social Psychology* 47: 382–389.

Finklea, K. 2017. "Dark Web." Congressional Research Service Report. Federation of American Scientists. https://sgp.fas.org/crs/misc/R44101.pdf.

Fisch, S. 2002. "Vast Wasteland or Vast Opportunity? Effects of Educational Television on Children's Academic Knowledge, Skills, and Attitudes." In *Media Effects: Advances in Theory and Research*, edited by J. Bryant and D. Zillmann, 397–426. Mahwah, NJ: Lawrence Erlbaum.

Flanders, J. 1968. "A Review of Research on Imitative Behavior." *Psychological Bulletin* 69, no. 3: 316–337.

Fletcher, D. 2009. "A Brief History of the Tylenol Poisonings." *Time Magazine*. February 9. http://content.time.com/time/nation/article/0,8599,1878063,00.html.

Fletcher, W. 1908. "Latah and Crime." *The Lancet* 172, no. 4430: 254–255.

Flew, T. 2002. *New Media: An Introduction*. South Melbourne, Australia: Oxford University Press.

Flichy, P. 2008. "New Media History." In *Handbook of New Media*, edited by L. Lievrouw and S. Livingstone, 136–150. Thousand Oaks, CA: Sage.

Folkvord, F., Anschütz, D., Boyland, E., Kelly, B., and Buijzen, M. 2016. "Food Advertising and Eating Behavior in Children." *Current Opinion in Behavioral Sciences* 9: 26–31.

Follman, M. 2015. "How the Media Inspires Mass Shooters." *Mother Jones*. October 6. www.motherjones.com/politics/2015/10/media-inspires-mass-shooters-copycats.

Fortes, M. 1938. "Social and Psychological Aspects of Education in Taleland." International Institute of African Languages and Cultures, Memorandum XVII. London: Oxford University Press.

Fox, J., Sanders, N., Fridel, E., Duwe, G., and Rocque, M. 2021. "The Contagion of Mass Shootings: The Interdependence of Large-Scale Massacres and Mass Media Coverage." Statistics and Public Policy. https://doi.org/10.1080/2330443X.2021.1932645.

Freedman, E. 2011. "Crimes Which Startle and Horrify: Gender, Age and the Racialization of Sexual Violence in White American Newspapers, 1870–1900." *Journal of the History of Sexuality* 20, no. 3: 465–497.

Freedman, J. 1982. "Theories of Contagion as They Relate to Mass Psychogenic Illness In *Mass Psychogenic Illness*, edited by M. Colligan, J. Pennebaker, and L. Murp' 171–182. Hillsdale, NJ: Erlbaum.

Freedman, J. 1984. "Effect of Television Violence on Aggressiveness." *Psycholo Bulletin* 96, no. 2: 227.

Freedman, J. 2002. *Media Violence and Its Effect on Aggression: Assessing the Sc fic Evidence*. Toronto: University of Toronto Press.

Freeman, M. 1912. "The Copy Cat." *Harpers Monthly* 125: 179–190.

Friis, S. 2015. "Beyond Anything We Have Ever Seen: Beheading Videos and the Visibility of Violence in the War Against ISIS." *International Affairs* 91, no. 4: 725–746.

"From 1966 Comes *The Battle of Algiers*." 2007. *The Toronto Star*. https://www.thestar .com/entertainment/2007/03/04/battle_of_algiers.htmlgiers.

Frosch, D., and Johnson, K. 2012. "12 Are Killed at Showing of Batman Movie in Colorado." *New York Times*. July 20. http://www.nytimes.com/2012/07/21/us/shooting -at-colorado-theater-showing-batman-movie.html.

Galef, B. 2005a. "Breathing New Life into the Study of Imitation by Animals: What and When Do Chimpanzees Imitate?" In *Mechanisms of Imitation*. Vol. 1 of *Perspectives on Imitation: From Neuroscience to Social Science*, edited by S. Hurley and N. Chater, 295–297. Cambridge: Massachusetts Institute of Technology Press.

Galef, B. 2005b. "How to Analyze Learning by Imitation." In *Mechanisms of Imitation*. Vol. 1 of *Perspectives on Imitation: From Neuroscience to Social Science*, edited by S. Hurley and N. Chater, 218–220. Cambridge: Massachusetts Institute of Technology Press.

Gauntlett, D. 2005. *Moving Experiences: Media Effects and Beyond*. Vol. 13. Bloomington: Indiana University Press.

Gentile, D., and Bushman, B. 2012. "Reassessing Media Violence Effects Using a Risk and Resilience Approach to Understanding Aggression." *Psychology of Popular Media Culture* 1, no. 3: 138–151.

Gergen, K. 1985. "Social Constructionist Inquiry: Context and Implications." In *The Social Construction of the Person*, edited by K. Gergen and K. Davis, 3–18. New York: Springer-Verlag.

"Ghost Riding the Whip." N.d. Urban Dictionary. https://www.urbandictionary.com /define.php?term=ghost+riding+the+whip.

Gibeaut, J. 1998. "Deadly Advice Targeted: Decision Allows Suit Against Publisher of Murder Manual." *ABA Journal* 84, no. 7: 24–25.

Gillis, C. 2005. "New Crime Shows Educate Criminals." *Maclean's Magazine*. November 7. https://www.thecanadianencyclopedia.ca/en/article/new-crime-shows-educate-criminals.

Glaser, D. 1956. "Criminality Theories and Behavioral Images." *American Journal of Sociology* 61, no. 5: 433–444.

Goethe, Johann von. 1989. *The sorrows of young Werther*. Translated by M. Hause. London: Penguin Books.

Goldman, A. 2005. "Imitation, Mind Reading, and Simulation." In *Imitation, Human Development, and Culture*. Vol. 2 of *Perspectives on Imitation: From Neuroscience to Social Science*, edited by S. Hurley and N. Chater, 79–94. Cambridge: Massachusetts Institute of Technology Press.

Gorn, E. 1992. "The Wicked World: The National Police Gazette and Gilded-Age America." *Media Studies Journal* 6: 3–4.

Gottfredson, M., and Hirschi, T. 1990. *A General Theory of Crime*. Stanford, CA: Stanford University Press.

Gould, M., Jamieson, P., and Gould, M. 2003. "Media Contagion and Suicide Among the Young." *American Behavioral Scientist* 46, no. 9: 1269–1284.

Gould, M., and Olivares, M. 2017. "Mass Shootings and Murder-Suicide: Review of the Empirical Evidence for Contagion." In *Media and Suicide*, edited by T. Niederkrotenthaler and S. Stack, 41–65. New Brunswick, NJ: Transaction Publishers.

Gould, M., and Shaffer, D. 1986. "The Impact of Suicide in Television Movies." *New England Journal of Medicine* 315, no. 11: 690–694.

Green, B., Horel, T., and Papachristos, A. 2017. "Modeling Contagion Through Social Networks to Explain and Predict Gunshot Violence in Chicago, 2006 to 2014." *JAMA Internal Medicine* 177, no. 3: 326–333.

Green, M. 2004. "Transportation into Narrative Worlds: The Role of Prior Knowledge and Perceived Realism." *Discourse Processes* 38: 247–266.

Green, M., and Brock, T. 2000. "The Role of Transportation in the Persuasiveness of Public Narratives." *Journal of Personality and Social Psychology* 79: 701–721.

Green, M., Garst, J., Brock, T., and Chung, S. 2006. "Fact Versus Fiction Labeling: Persuasion Parity Despite Heightened Scrutiny of Fact." *Media Psychology* 8, no. 3: 267–285.

Green, S. 2017. "10 Real-Life Murderers Who Were Influenced by Dexter Morgan." Listverse. https://listverse.com/2017/11/08/10-real-life-murderers-who-were-influenced -by-dexter-morgan.

Greene, J. 2018. "Slender Man Is Still Making People Uneasy—but Now for New Reasons." *Vulture*. August 7. http://www.vulture.com/2018/08/is-slender-man-capitalizing -on-a-real-life-tragedy.html.

Greitemeyer, T. 2011. "Effects of Prosocial Media on Social Behavior: When and Why Does Media Exposure Affect Helping and Aggression?" *Current Directions in Psychological Science* 20, no. 4: 251–255.

Grimes, T., Anderson, J., and Bergen, L. 2008. *Meta Violence and Aggression: Science and Ideology.* Thousand Oaks, CA: Sage.

Grochowski, T. 2006. "Running in Cyberspace: OJ Simpson Web Sites and the (De)construction of Crime Knowledge." *Television and New Media* 7, no. 4: 361–382.

Grodal, T. 2003a. "Stories for Eye, Ear and Muscles." In *The Video Game Theory Reader*, edited by M. Wolf and B. Perron, 129–155. New York: Routledge.

Grodal, T. 2003b. "Video Games and the Pleasures of Control." In *Media Entertainment*, edited by D. Zillmann and P. Vorderer, 197–212. Mahwah, NJ: Erlbaum.

Gundlach, J., and Stack, S. 1990. "The Impact of Hyper Media Coverage on Suicide: New York City, 1910–1920." *Social Science Quarterly* 71, no. 3: 619–627.

Hamblin, R., Jacobsen, R., and Miller, J. 1973. *A Mathematical Theory of Social Change.* New York: Wiley-Interscience.

Hammerschlag, M. 2005. "The Copycat Effect." *Hammernews.* http://hammernews.com /copycateffect.htm.

Haridakis, P. 2002. "Viewer Characteristics, Exposure to Television Violence, and Aggression." *Media Psychology* 4, no. 4: 323–352.

Harmsworth, A. 1893. "The Editor Speaks." Halfpenny Marvel Library. November 11.

Harrington, R. 1992. "Time for a Crackdown?" *Washington Post.* July 29. www .washingtonpost.com/archive/lifestyle/1992/07/29/time-for-a-crackdown/9e83fd64 -0029-4b5c-8d7e-34aa82070f92.

Harris, J., Bargh, J., and Brownell, K. 2009. "Priming Effects of Television Food Advertising on Eating Behavior." *Health Psychology* 28, no. 4: 404–413.

Harris, P., and Want, S. 2005. "On Learning What Not to Do: The Emergence of Selective Imitation in Tool Use by Young Children." In *Imitation, Human Development, and Culture.* Vol. 2 of *Perspectives on Imitation: From Neuroscience to Social Science*, edited by S. Hurley and N. Chater, 149–162. Cambridge: Massachusetts Institute of Technology Press.

Hassan, R. 1995. "Effects of Newspaper Stories on the Incidence of Suicide in Australia: A Research Note." *Australian and New Zealand Journal of Psychiatry* 29, no. 3: 480–483.

Hawton, K., Simkin, S., Deeks, J., O'Connor, S., Keen, A., Altman, D., Philo, G., and Bulstrode, C. 1999. "Effects of a Drug Overdose in a Television Drama on Presentations to Hospital for Self Poisoning: Time Series and Questionnaire Study." *British Medical Journal* 318, no. 7189: 972–977.

Hayes, B. 2002. "Statistics of Deadly Quarrels." *American Scientist* 90: 10–15.

Hays, W. 1932. *President's Report to the Motion Picture Producers and Distributors' Association.* Washington, DC: US Government Printing Office.

Helfgott, J. 2008. *Criminal Behavior: Theories, Typologies, and Criminal Justice.* Thousand Oaks, CA: Sage.

Helfgott, J. 2015. "Criminal Behavior and the Copycat Effect: Literature Review and Theoretical Framework for Empirical Investigation." *Aggression and Violent Behavior* 22: 46–64.

Helfgott, J. Forthcoming. *Copycat Crime: How Media, Technology, and Digital Culture Influence Criminal Behavior and Violence.* Santa Barbara, CA: Praeger/ABC-CLIO.

Heller, M., and Polsky, S. 1976a. "Project III: Television Studies with Youthful and Violent Offenders (Pilot)." In *Studies in Violence and Television*, edited by M. Heller and S. Polsky, 80–95. New York: American Broadcasting Company.

Heller, M., and Polsky, S. 1976b. "Project IV: Television Viewing, Anti-social Development and Violent Behavior—an Examination of One Hundred Young Male Offenders." In *Studies in Violence and Television*, edited by M. Heller and S. Polsky, 96–152. New York: American Broadcasting Company.

Hemenway, H. 1911. "To What Extent Are Suicide and Other Crimes Against the Person Due to Suggestion from the Press?" *Bulletin of the American Academy of Medicine* 12, no. 5: 253–263.

Hendrick, G. 1977. "When TV Is a School for Criminals." *TV Guide*. January 29: 10–14.

Hennigan, K., Del Rosario, M., Heath, L., Cook, T., Wharton, J., and Calder, B. 1982. "Impact of the Introduction of Television on Crime in the United States: Empirical Findings and Theoretical Implications." *Journal of Personality and Social Psychology* 42, no. 3: 461–477.

Heyes, C. 2005. "Imitation by Association." In *Mechanisms of Imitation*. Vol. 1 of *Perspectives on Imitation: From Neuroscience to Social Science*, edited by S. Hurley and N. Chater, 157–176. Cambridge: Massachusetts Institute of Technology Press.

Hinds-Aldrich, M. 2009. "The Seductions of Arson: Ritualized Political Violence and the Revelry of Arson." *Journal of Criminal Justice and Popular Culture* 16: 103–135.

Hittner, J. B. 2005. "How Robust Is the Werther Effect? A Re-examination of the Suggestion-Imitation Model of Suicide." *Mortality* 10, no. 3: 193–200.

Holden, R. 1986. "The Contagiousness of Aircraft Hijacking." *American Journal of Sociology* 91, no. 4: 874–904.

Holding, R. 1975. "Suicide and 'The Befrienders.'" *British Medical Journal* 27, no. 5986: 751–752.

Holloway, L. 1995. "Token Booth Fire Attack Seems Unrelated to Movie." *New York Times*. December 16. www.nytimes.com/1995/12/16/nyregion/token-booth-fire-attack-seems-unrelated-to-movie.html.

Horton, D., and Wohl, R. 1956. Mass Communication and Para-social Interaction: Observations on Intimacy at a Distance. *Psychiatry* 19: 215–229.

Houen, A. 2002. *Terrorism and Modern Literature: From Joseph Conrad to Ciaran Carson*. Oxford: Oxford University Press.

Hourigan, B. 2008. "The Moral Code of Grand Theft Auto." *IPA Review*. July 21–22.

Huesmann, L. R. 1986. "Psychological Process Promoting the Relation Between Exposure to Media Violence and Aggressive Behavior by the Viewer." *Journal of Social Issues* 42, no. 3: 125–139.

Huesmann, L. R. 1998. "The Role of Social Information Processing and Cognitive Schema in the Acquisition and Maintenance of Habitual Aggressive Behavior." In *Human Aggression*, edited by R. Geen and E. Donnerstin, 73–109. New York: Academic Press.

Hughes, H. 1940. *News and the Human Interest Story*. Chicago: University of Chicago Press.

Hurley, S., and Chater, N. 2005. *Imitation, Human Development, and Culture*. Vol. 2 of *Perspectives on Imitation: From Neuroscience to Social Science*. Boston: Massachusetts Institute of Technology Press.

Iacoboni, M., and Geffen, D. 2013. "The Potential Role of Mirror Neurons in the Contagion of Violence." In *National Research Council Contagion of Violence: Workshop Summary*, 73–78. Washington, DC: National Academies Press.

Isaacs, N. 1961. "The Crime of Crime Reporting." *Crime and Delinquency* 7: 312–320.

Jackson, L., and Dougall, C. 1998. "English Grad Student Plays Detective in Unabomber Case." *Brigham Young Magazine* (Fall): https://magazine.byu.edu/article/english-grad-student-plays-detective-in-unabomber-case.

James, W. 1890. "The Perception of Reality." *Principles of Psychology* 2: 283–324.

Jeter, M. 2014. "Terrorism and the Media." IZA Discussion Paper no. 8497. Institute for the Study of Labor, Bonn, Germany.

Jeter, M. 2017. "Terrorism and the Media: The Effect of US Television Coverage on al-Qaeda Attacks." IZA Discussion Paper no. 10708. Institute for the Study of Labor, Bonn, Germany.

Ji, N., Lee, W., Noh, M., and Yip, P. 2014. "The Impact of Indiscriminate Media Coverage of a Celebrity Suicide on a Society with a High Suicide Rate: Epidemiological Findings on Copycat Suicides from South Korea." *Journal of Affective Disorders* 156: 56–61.

Johnson, S. D. 2008. "Repeat Burglary Victimisation: A Tale of Two Theories." *Journal of Experimental Criminology* 4, no. 3: 215–240.

Johnson, S. D., Bernasco, W., Bowers, K., Elffers, H., Ratcliffe, J., Rengert, G., and Townsley, M. 2007. "Space-Time Patterns of Risk: A Cross National Assessment of Residential Burglary Victimization." *Journal of Quantitative Criminology* 23, no. 3: 201–219.

Johnson, S. D., and Bowers, K. 2004. "The Burglary as Clue to the Future: The Beginnings of Prospective Hot-Spotting." *European Journal of Criminology* 1, no. 2: 237–255.

Jonas, K. 1992. "Modelling and Suicide: A Test of the Werther Effect." *British Journal of Social Psychology* 31: 295–306.

Jones, M. 1998. "Behavioral Contagion and Official Delinquency: Epidemic Course in Adolescence." *Social Biology* 45, no. 12: 134–142.

Kahneman, D. 2011. *Thinking, Fast and Slow*. New York: MacMillan.

Kambam, P., Pozios, V., Bond, K., and Ostermeyer, B. 2020. "The Influence of Media Related to Mass Shootings." *Psychiatric Annals* 50, no. 9: 393–398.

Kasten, R. 2020. "The Role of Mirror Neurons from the Emergence of Empathy to Criminal Behavior." *International Journal of Innovative Studies in Medical Sciences* 4, no. 3. https://ijisms.com/storage/Volume4/Issue3/IJISMS-040304.pdf.

Kesling, K. 2013. "Tylenol Killings Remain Unsolved and Unforgotten After 30 Years." *Wall Street Journal*. October 11. https://www.wsj.com/articles/SB1000142405270 2303492504579115573613137300.

Kifner, J. 1995. "McVeigh's Mind: A Special Report." *New York Times*. December 13. www.nytimes.com/1995/12/31/us/mcveigh-s-mind-special-report-oklahomabombing -suspect-unraveling-frayed-life.html.

Kinard, B., and Webster, C. 2010. "The Effects of Advertising, Social Influences, and Self-Efficacy on Adolescent Tobacco Use and Alcohol Consumption." *Journal of Consumer Affairs* 44, no. 1: 24–43.

King, D. 2002. "Accused Says Alter Ego Vamp Was the Killer." *The Scotsman*. http://news .scotsman.com/topics,cfm?tid=722&id=1097142003.

King, D., and Jacobson, S. 2017. "Random Acts of Violence? Examining Probabilistic Independence of the Temporal Distribution of Mass Killing Events in the United States." *Violence and Victims* 32, no. 6: 1014–1023.

King, L., Burton, C., Hicks, J., and Drigotas, S. 2007. "Ghosts, UFOs, and Magic: Positive Affect and the Experiential System." *Journal of Personality and Social Psychology* 92, no. 5: 905–919.

King, P. 1987. "Newspaper Reporting, Prosecution Practice and Perceptions of Urban Crime: The Colchester Crime Wave of 1765." *Continuity and Change* 2, no. 3: 423–454.

Kinsbourne, M. 2005. "Imitation as Entrainment: Brain Mechanisms and Social Consequences." In *Imitation, Human Development, and Culture*. Vol. 2 of *Perspectives on Imitation: From Neuroscience to Social Science*, edited by S. Hurley and N. Chater, 163–172. Cambridge: Massachusetts Institute of Technology Press.

Kiousis, S. 2002. "Interactivity: A Concept Explication." *New Media and Society* 4, no. 3: 355–383.

Kirch, M., and Lester, D. 1986a. "Clusters of Suicide." *Psychological Reports* 59: 1126.

Kirch, M., and Lester, D. 1986b. "Suicide from the Golden Gate Bridge: Do They Cluster Over Time?" *Psychological Reports* 59: 1314.

Kissner, J. 2016. "Are Active Shootings Temporally Contagious? An Empirical Assessment." *Journal of Police and Criminal Psychology* 31, no. 1: 48–58.

Koch, A. 2018. "Jihadi Beheading Videos and Their Non-Jihadi Echoes." *Perspectives on Terrorism* 12, no. 3: 24–34.

Kostinsky, S., Bixler, E. O., and Kettl, P. A. 2001. "Threats of School Violence in Pennsylvania After Media Coverage of the Columbine High School Massacre: Examining the Role of Imitation." *Archives of Pediatrics & Adolescent Medicine* 155, no. 9: 994–1001.

Kotowitz, Y., and Mathewson, F. 1979. "Informative Advertising and Welfare." *American Economic Review* 69, no. 3: 284–294.

Krohn, M., Skinner, W., Massey, J., and Akers, R. 1985. "Social Learning Theory and Adolescent Cigarette Smoking: A Longitudinal Study." *Social problems* 32, no. 5: 455–473.

Kunich, J. 2000. "Natural Born Copycat Killers and the Law of Shock Torts." *Washington University Law Quarterly* 78: 1157–1267.

Kymissis, E., and Poulson, C. 1990. "The History of Imitation in Learning Theory: The Language Acquisition Process." *Journal of the Experimental Analysis of Behavior* 54, no. 2: 113–127.

Lambert, D. 1992. "Zero-Inflated Poisson Regression, with an Application to Defects in Manufacturing." *Technometrics* 34, no. 1: 1–14.

Landsbaum, C. 2016. "Are the New York Slashings Copycat Crimes? Maybe." *The Cut*. February 18. www.thecut.com/2016/02/new-york-slashings-could-be-copycat-crimes.html.

Langman, P. 2017. "Role Models, Contagions, and Copycats: An Exploration of the Influence of Prior Killers on Subsequent Attacks." SchoolShooters.info. June 22. https://schoolshooters.info/sites/default/files/role_models_3.1.pdf.

Langman, P. 2018. "Different Types of Role Model Influence and Fame Seeking Among Mass Killers and Copycat Offenders." *American Behavioral Scientist* 62, no. 2: 210–228.

Lanier, M., and Henry, S. 2004. *Essential Criminology*. Boulder, CO: Westview Press.

Lankford, A. 2016. "Fame-Seeking Rampage Shooters: Initial Findings and Empirical Predictions." *Aggression and Violent Behavior* 27: 122–129.

Lankford, A. 2021. "A Close Examination of the 2016 Dallas and Baton Rouge Police Killers: Identifying Potential Risk Factors and Influences for Copycat Violence." *International Criminal Justice Review,* 10575677211061257: 1–18.

Lankford, A., and Tomek, S. 2018. "Mass Killings in the United States from 2006 to 2013: Social Contagion or Random Clusters?" *Suicide and Life-Threatening Behavior* 48, no. 4: 459–467.

Larkin, R. 2009. "The Columbine Legacy: Rampage Shootings as Political Acts." *American Behavioral Scientist* 52, no. 9: 1309–1326.

Lawrence, J., and Jewett, R. 2002. *The Myth of the American Superhero*. Grand Rapids, MI: William. B. Eerdmans Publishing.

Le Bon, G. 1895 (2000). *Psychology of Crowds*. Edited by A. Cuffaro and D. Kauders. Exeter, UK: Sparkling Books Ltd.

Lee, K., Peng, W., and Klein, J. 2010. "Will the Experience of Playing a Violent Role in a Video Game Influence People's Judgments of Violent Crimes?" *Computers in Human Behaviors* 26: 1019–1023.

Lentini, P., and Bakashmar, M. 2007. "Jihadist Beheading: A Convergence of Technology, Theology, and Teleology?" *Studies in Conflict and Terrorism* 30, no. 4: 303–325.

Leung, R. 2005. "Can a Video Game Lead to Murder?" *60 Minutes*. March 4. www.cbsnews.com/news/can-a-video-game-lead-to-murder-04-03-2005.

Levy, D., and Nail, P. 1993. "Contagion: A Theoretical and Empirical Review and Reconceptualization." *Genetic, Social and General Psychology Monographs* 119, no. 2: 235–288.

Lewis, E., Mohler, G., Brantingham, P., and Bertozzi, A. 2012. "Self-Exciting Point Process Models of Civilian Deaths in Iraq." *Security Journal* 25, no. 3: 244–264.

Li, R., and Thompson, W. 1975. "The 'Coup Contagion' Hypothesis." *Journal of Conflict Resolution* 19: 63–88.

Ling, R., and Campbell, S. 2010. *The Reconstruction of Space and Time: Mobile Communication Practices*. Piscataway, NJ: Transaction Press.

Lister, M., Dovey, J., Giddings, S., Grant, I., and Kelly, K. 2003. *New Media: A Critical Introduction*. New York: Routledge.

Livingstone, N. 1982. *The War Against Terrorism*. Washington, DC: Heath.

Lochner, D. 2002. "Social Contagion Theory." In *Collective Behavior*, edited by D. A. Lochner, 11–23. Upper Saddle River, NJ: Pearson Education.

Loeffler, C., and Flaxman, S. 2018. "Is Gun Violence Contagious? A Spatiotemporal Test." *Journal of Quantitative Criminology* 34: 999–1017.

Loftin, C. 1986. "Assaultive Violence As a Contagious Social Process." *Bulletin New York Academy of Medicine* 62, no. 5: 550–555.

Lotze, R. 1852. *Medical Psychology or the Physiology of the Soul*. Liepzig: Weidmann'sche Buchhandlung.

Ludwig, J., and Kling, J. 2007. "Is Crime Contagious?" *Journal of Law and Economics* 50, no. 3: 491–518.

Mackay, C. 1841 (2012). *Extraordinary Popular Delusions and the Madness of Crowds*. New York: Simon & Schuster.

Mahajan, V., Muller, E., and Bass, F. 1995. "Diffusion of New Products: Empirical Generalizations and Managerial Uses." *Marketing Science* 14, no. 3: 79–88.

Majeed, M., Sudak, D., and Beresin, E. 2019. "Mass Shootings and the News Media: What Can Psychiatrists Do?" *Academic Psychiatry* 43, no. 4: 442–446.

Malernee, J., and Haas, B. 2006. "Viciousness Confounds All Reasoning." *South Florida Sun-Sentinel*. January 15: 13a.

"Man Convicted in Seaside Slayings." 1999. *AP News*. May 22. https://apnews.com/article/1b06d2fb18cded253048497dc725bf5d.

Markel, H. 2014. "How the Tylenol Murders of 1982 Changed the Way We Consume Medication." *PBS News Hour*. September 29. www.pbs.org/newshour/health/tylenol-murders-1982.

Markey, P., Markey, C., and French, J. 2015. "Violent Video Games and Real-World Violence: Rhetoric Versus Data." *Psychology of Popular Media Culture* 494: 277–295.

Marsden, P. 2000. "Forefathers of Memetics: Gabriel Tarde and the Laws of Imitation." *Journal of Memetics—Evolutionary Models of Information Transmission* 4, no. 1: 61–66.

Marsh, I., and Melville, G. 2014. *Crime, Justice, and the Media*. New York: Routledge.

Martin, D. 1993. "The Music of Murder." *William and Mary Bill of Rights Journal* 2: 159–164.

Marzuk, P., Hirsch, C., Leon, A., Stajic, M., Hartwell, N., and Portera, L. 1993. "Increase in Suicide by Asphyxiation in New York City After the Publication of *Final Exit*." *New England Journal of Medicine* 329: 1508–1510.

Massey, J. N.d. "Bum Fights." Unpublished research paper. Orlando: University of Central Florida, Department of Criminal Justice.

Mathew, B., Dutt, R., Goyal, P., and Mukherjee, A. 2019. "Spread of Hate Speech in Online Social Media." In *WebSci '18: Proceedings of the 10th ACM Conference on Web Science*, ed. WebSci, 173–182. New York: Association for Computing Machinery.

Mazur, A. 1982. "Bomb Threats and the Mass Media: Evidence for a Theory of Suggestion." *American Sociological Review* 47: 407–411.

Mazur, J. M. 2002. *Learning and Behavior*. Upper Saddle River, NJ: Prentice Hall.

McIntosh, W., and Schmeichel, B. 2004. "Collectors and Collecting: A Social Psychological Perspective." *Leisure Sciences* 26, no. 1: 85–97.

McPhail, C. 2017. *The Myth of the Madding Crowd*. New York: Routledge.

Meade, N., and Islam, T. 2006. "Modelling and Forecasting the Diffusion of Innovation—a 25-Year Review." *International Journal of Forecasting* 22: 519–545.

Megens, K., and Weerman, F. 2012. "The Social Transmission of Delinquency: Effects of Peer Attitudes and Behavior Revisited." *Journal of Research in Crime and Delinquency* 49, no. 3: 420–443.

Meindl, J., and Ivy, J. 2017. "Mass Shootings: The Role of the Media in Promoting Generalized Imitation." *American Journal of Public Health* 107, no. 3: 368–370.

Meltzoff, A. N. 2005. "Imitation and Other Minds: The 'Like Me' Hypothesis." In *Imitation, Human Development, and Culture*. Vol. 2 of *Perspectives on Imitation: From Neuroscience to Social Science*, edited by S. Hurley and N. Chater, 55–77. Cambridge: Massachusetts Institute of Technology Press.

Mercy, J., Kresnow, M., O'Carroll, P., Lee, R., Powell, K., Potter, L., Swann, A., Frankowski, R., and Bayer. T. 2001. "Is Suicide Contagious? A Study of the Relation Between Exposure to the Suicidal Behavior of Others and Nearly Lethal Suicide Attempts." *American Journal of Epidemiology* 154, no. 2: 120–127.

Meyrowitz, J. 1986. *No Sense of Place: The Impact of Electronic Media on Social Behavior*. Oxford: Oxford University Press.

Midlarsky, M. 1970. "Mathematical Models of Instability and a Theory of Diffusion." *International Studies Quarterly* 14: 60–84.

Milgram, S. 1977. "Crowds." In *The Individual in a Social World*, edited by S. Milgram, 206–274. Reading, MA: Addison-Wesley.

Miller, D. 2000. *Introduction to Collective Behavior and Collective Action*. Prospect Heights, IL: Waveland Press.

Miller, N., and Dollard, J. 1941. *Social Learning and Imitation*. New Haven, CT: Yale University Press.

Minois, G. 1999. *History of Suicide: Voluntary Death in Western Culture*. Baltimore: Johns Hopkins University Press.

Mintz, M. 1978. "Who's Liable if Life Imitates TV Violence." *Washington Post*. April 24. www.washingtonpost.com/archive/politics/1978/04/24/whos-liable-if-life-imitates-tv-violence/f27981b9-2d29-443e-ba30-7338c4c7a1f6.

Mohler, G., Short, M., Brantingham, P., Schoenberg, F., and Tita, G. 2012. "Self-Exciting Point Process Modeling of Crime." *Journal of the American Statistical Association* 106, no. 493: 100–108.

Montet, V. 2009. "Videos of US Homeless Beatings Spike Online." *Sidney Morning Herald*. August 27. www.smh.com.au/technology/videos-of-us-homeless-beatings-spike-online-20090827-ezxy.html.

Morgan, C. L. 1896. *Habit and Instinct*. London: E. Arnold Publishers.

Mulry, D. 2000. "Popular Accounts of the Greenwich Bombing and Conrad's *The Secret Agent*." *Rocky Mountain Review of Language and Literature* 54, no. 2: 43–64.

Mundorf, N., and Laird, K. 2002. "Social and Psychological Effects of Information Technologies and Other Interactive Media." In *Media Effects: Advances in Theory and Research*, edited by J. Bryant and D. Zillmann, 583–602. Mahwah, NJ: Lawrence Erlbaum Associates.

"Murdered Man's Diary Found: 'Copycat' Inquiry." 1961. *Daily Telegraph*. April 1: A16.

Myers, D. 2000. "The Diffusion of Collective Violence: Infectiousness, Susceptibility, and Mass Media Networks." *American Journal of Sociology* 106, no. 1: 173–208.

Nacos, B. 2007. *Mass-Mediated Terrorism*. Lanham, MD: Rowan & Littlefield.

Nacos, B. 2009. "Revisiting the Contagion Hypothesis: Terrorism, News Coverage, and Copycat Attacks." *Perspectives on Terrorism* 3, no. 3 (September): 3–13. https://www.jstor.org/stable/26298412.

National Research Council. 2013. *Contagion of Violence: Workshop Summary*. Washington, DC: National Academies Press.

Nedim, U., and Holmes, Z. 2018. "The Influence of the Media on Copycat Crimes." Sidney Criminal Lawyers. October 31. https://www.sydneycriminallawyers.com.au/blog/the-influence-of-the-media-on-copycat-crimes.

Nelson, P. 1974. "Advertising as Information." *Journal of Political Economy* 82, no. 4: 729–754.

Newburn, T. 1994. *Young Offenders and the Media: Viewing Habits and Preferences*. London: Policy Studies Institute.

Niederkrotenthaler, T. 2017. "Papageno Effect: Its Progress in Media Research and Contextualization with Findings on Harmful Media Effects." In *Media and Suicide*, edited by T. Niederkrotenthaler and S. Stack, 159–170. New Brunswick, NJ: Transaction Publishers.

Niederkrotenthaler, T., Braun, M., Pirkis, J., Till, B., Stack, S., Sinyor, M., Tran, U., et al. 2020. "Association Between Suicide Reporting in the Media and Suicide: Systematic Review and Meta-analysis." *British Medical Journal* 368 (March 18): m575. www.bmj.com/content/368/bmj.m575.

Niederkrotenthaler, T., and Stack, S. 2017. "Introduction." In *Media and Suicide*, edited by T. Niederkrotenthaler and S. Stack, 1–13. New Brunswick, NJ: Transaction Publishers.

Notredame, C., Pauwels, N., Walter, M., Danel, T., Nandrino, J., and Vaiva, G. 2017. "Why Media Coverage of Suicide May Increase Suicide Rates: An Epistemological Review." In *Media and Suicide*, edited by T. Niederkrotenthaler and S. Stack, 133–158. New Brunswick, NJ: Transaction Publishers.

Nyberg. A. 1998. "Comic Books and Juvenile Delinquency: A Historical Perspective." In *Popular Culture, Crime and Justice*, edited by F. Bailey and D. Hale, 71–90. Belmont, CA: Wadsworth.

O'Carroll, P., and Potter, L. 1994. "Suicide Contagion and the Reporting of Suicide: Recommendations from a National Workshop." CDC. www.cdc.gov/mmwr/preview /mmwrhtml/00031539.htm.

O'Kane, J. 2017. *Wicked Deeds: Murder in America*. New York: Routledge.

O'Keefe, G., Rosenbaum, D., Lavrakas, P., Reid, K., and Botta, R. 1996. *Taking a Bite Out of Crime*. Thousand Oaks, CA: Sage.

Oppenheimer, D. 1910. "On Suicide with Particular Reference to Suicide Among Young Students." In *Symposium: Revised papers*, edited by P. Friedman. New York: International Universities Press.

Ornstein, J., and Hammond, R. 2017. "The Burglary Boost: A Note on Detecting Contagion Using the Knox Test." *Journal of Quantitative Criminology* 33, no. 1: 65–75.

Oswell, D. 2007. *The Unabomber and the Zodiac*. Lulu.com/Douglas Oswell Publisher.

Panee, C., and Ballard, M. 2002. "High Versus Low Aggressive Priming During Video-Game Training: Effects on Violent Action During Game Play, Hostility, Heart Rate, and Blood Pressure." *Journal of Applied Social Psychology* 32: 2458–2474.

Papachristos, A., Braga, A., Piza, E., and Grossman, L. 2015. "The Company You Keep: The Spillover Effects of Gang Membership on Individual Gunshot Victimization in a Co-offending Network." *Criminology* 53, no. 4: 624–649.

Pape, R. 2006. *Dying to Win: The Strategic Logic of Suicide Terrorism*. New York: Random House.

Papke, D. 1987. *Framing the Criminal*. Hamden, CT: Archon Books.

Park, J., Essex, M., Zahn-Waxler, C., Armstrong, J., Klein, M., and Goldsmith, H. 2005. "Relational and Overt Aggression in Middle Childhood: Early Child and Family Risk Factors." *Early Education and Development* 16, no. 2: 233–258.

Park, R. 1904 1982. *The Crowd and the Public and Other Essays*. Chicago: University of Chicago Press.

Parks, M., and Robers, L. 1998. "'Making MOOsic': The Development of Personal Relationships Online and a Comparison to Their Off-Line Counterparts." *Journal of Social and Personal Relationships* 15, no. 4: 517–537.

Patel, D., Simon, M., and Taylor, R. 2013. *Contagion of Violence: Workshop Summary*. Washington, DC: National Academies Press.

Paternoster, R., Jaynes, C. M., and Wilson, T. 2017. "Rational Choice Theory and Interest in the 'Fortune of Others.'" *Journal of Research in Crime and Delinquency* 54, no. 6: 847–868.

Pease, S., and Love, C. 1984a. "The Copycat Crime Phenomenon." In *Justice and the Media: Issues and Research*, edited by R. Surette, 199–211. Springfield, IL: Charles C. Thomas.

Pease, S., and Love, C. 1984b. "The Prisoner's Perspective of Copycat Crime." Paper presented at the Annual Meeting of the American Society of Criminology, Cincinnati, Ohio, November 7–11.

Peck, A. 2015. "Tall, Dark, and Loathsome: The Emergence of a Legend Cycle in the Digital Age." *Journal of American Folklore* 128, no. 509: 333–348.

Peck, A. 2017. "Capturing the Slender Man: Online and Offline Vernacular Practice in the Digital Age." *Cultural Analysis* 16: 30–48.

Penfold-Mounce, R. 2010. *Celebrity Culture and Crime: The Joy of Transgression*. New York: Springer.

Pepler, D., and Slaby, R. 1994. "Theoretical and Developmental Perspectives on Youth and Violence." In *Reason to Hope: A Psychosocial Perspective on Violence and Youth*, edited by L. Eron, J. Gentry, and P. Schlegel, 27–58. Washington, DC: American Psychological Association.

Peres, R., Muller, E., and Mahajan, V. 2010. "Innovation Diffusion and New Product Growth Models: A Critical Review and Research Directions." *International Journal of Research in Marketing* 27: 91–106.

Perloff, R. 2002. "The Third-Person Effect." In *Mass Effects: Advances in Theory and Research*, edited by J. Bryant and D. Zillmann, 489–506. Mahwah, NJ: Lawrence Erlbaum.

Persky, S., and Blascovich, J. 2008. "Immersive Virtual Video Game Play and Presence: Influences on Aggressive Feelings and Behavior." *Presence: Teleoperators and Virtual Environments* 17, no. 1: 57–72.

Petty, R., Priester, J., and Brinol, P. 2002. "Mass Media Attitude Change: Implications of the Elaboration Likelihood Model of Persuasion." In *Media Effects: Advances in Theory and Research*, edited by J. Brant and D. Zillmann, 155–198. Mahwah, NJ: Lawrence Erlbaum.

Pevere, G. 2004. "Polarizing Film on Terrorism Gets a Tragic, Real-Life Sequel." *Toronto Star*. July 2. C07.

Pevere, G. 2007. "Battle of Algiers." *Toronto Star*. March 4. https://www.thestar.com/entertainment/2007/03/04/battle_of_algiers.html.

Phelps, E. 1911. "Neurotic Books and Newspapers as Factors in the Mortality of Suicide and Crime." *Journal of Social Medicine* 12: 264–306.

Phillips, D. 1974. "The Influence of Suggestion on Suicide: Substantive and Theoretical Implications of the Werther Effect." *American Sociological Review* 39: 340–54.

Phillips, D. 1979. "Suicide, Motor Vehicle Fatalities, and the Mass Media: Evidence Toward a Theory of Suggestion." *American Journal of Sociology* 84, no. 5: 1150–1174.

Phillips, D. 1982. "The Impact of Fictional Television Stories on U.S. Adult Fatalities." *American Journal of Sociology* 87, no. 6: 1340–1359.

Phillips, D., Lesyna, K., and Paight, D. 1992. "Suicide and the Media." In *Assessment and Prediction of Suicide*, edited by R. Maris and A. Berman, 499–519. New York: Guilford Press.

Phillips, N. 2017. "Violence, Media Effects and Criminology." In Oxford Research Encyclopedias: Criminology and Criminal Justice. July 27. oxfordre.com/criminology/view/10.1093/acrefore/9780190264079.001.0001/acrefore-9780190264079-e-189.

Phillips, N., and Strobl, S. 2013. *Comic Book Crime: Truth, Justice, and the American Way*. New York: New York University Press.

Phillips, P. 2013. "Imitation Processes and Lone Wolf Terrorism: Who Will the Copycat Copy?" SSRN. December 5. http://ssrn.com/abstract=2364195.

Piaget, J. 1928. *The Child's Conception of the World.* London: Routledge and Kegan Paul.

Piersa, J. 2009. "Ghost Riding and Its Spread via the Internet." Unpublished manuscript. Orlando: University of Central Florida, Department of Criminal Justice.

Pirkis, J., and Blood, R. 2001. "Suicide and the Media: Part I. Reportage in Nonfictional Media." *Crisis: The Journal of Crisis Intervention and Suicide Prevention* 22, no. 4: 146–154.

Pirkis, J., Blood, R., Beautrais, A., Burgess, P., and Skehan, J. 2006. "Media Guidelines on the Reporting of Suicide." *Crisis: The Journal of Crisis Intervention and Suicide Prevention* 27, no. 2: 82–87.

Pirkis, J., Burgess, P., Blood, R., and Francis, C. 2007. "The Newsworthiness of Suicide." *Suicide and Life-Threatening Behavior* 37, no. 3: 278–283.

Pirkis, J., Burgess, P., Francis, C., Blood, R., and Jolley, D. 2006. "The Relationship Between Media Reporting of Suicide and Actual Suicide in Australia." *Social Science and Medicine* 62: 2874–2886.

Poland, J. 1988. *Understanding Terrorism.* Englewood Cliffs, NJ: Prentice Hall.

Polichak, J., and Gerrig, R. 2002. "Get Up and Win! Participatory Responses to Narrative." In *Narrative Impact*, edited by M. Green, J. Strange, and T. Brock, 71–95. Mahwah, NJ: Lawrence Erlbaum Associates.

Porter, C. 2004. "A Typology of Virtual Communities: A Multi-disciplinary Foundation for Future Research." *Journal of Computer-Mediated Communication* 10, no. 1: JCMC1011.

Porter, M., and White, G. 2012. "Self-Exciting Hurdle Models for Terrorist Activity." *Annals of Applied Statistics* 6, no. 1: 106–124.

Pratt, T., and Cullen, F. 2005. "Assessing Macro-Level Predictors and Theories of Crime: A Meta-analysis." *Crime and Justice* 32: 373–450.

Pratt, T., Cullen, F., Sellers, C., Winfree, T., Madensen, T., Daigle, L., and Gau, J. 2010. "The Empirical Status of Social Learning Theory: A Meta-analysis." *Justice Quarterly* 27, no. 6: 765–802.

Pratt, T. C. 2008. "Rational Choice Theory, Crime Control Policy, and Criminological Relevance." *Criminology & Public Policy* 7: 43.

Prinz, W. 2005. "An Ideomotor Approach to Imitation." In *Mechanisms of Imitation.* Vol. 1 of *Perspectives on Imitation: From Neuroscience to Social Science*, edited by S. Hurley and N. Chater, 141–156. Cambridge: Massachusetts Institute of Technology Press.

Proctor, K., and Niemeyer, R. 2020. "Retrofitting Social Learning Theory with Contemporary Understandings of Learning and Memory Derived from Cognitive Psychology and Neuroscience." *Journal of Criminal Justice* 66, no. 12: 108–122.

Pusey, A. 2017. "Sept. 29, 1982: 7 Deaths Point to Cyanide-Laced Pain Reliever." *ABA Journal.* September 1. www.abajournal.com/magazine/article/chicago_tylenol_murders.

Ramsland, K. 2011. "Movies Made Me Murder." Tru TV Crime Library. http://www.trutv.com/library/crime/criminal_mind/psychology/movies_made_me_kill/1_index.html (accessed February 13, 2015).

Ramsland, K. 2013. "Murder Mentors for Copycat Killers." *Psychology Today.* July 23. https://www.psychologytoday.com/us/blog/shadow-boxing/201307/murder-mentors-copycat-killers.

Ramsland, K. 2014. "The 'Dexter' Murders." *Psychology Today.* January 18. www.psychologytoday.com/us/blog/shadow-boxing/201401/the-dexter-murders.

Ratcliffe, J., and Rengert, G. 2008. "Near-Repeat Patterns in Philadelphia Shootings." *Security Journal* 21: 58–76.

Redl, F. 1949. "The Phenomenon of Contagion and 'Shock Effect' in Group Therapy." In *Searchlights on Delinquency: New Psychoanalytic Studies*, edited by K. R. Eissler, 315–328. Washington, DC: International Universities Press.

Reilly, P. 2018. *The Dark Landscape of Modern Fiction.* New York: Routledge.

Reiss, A. 1988. Co-offending and Criminal Careers. *Crime and Justice, 10:* 117–170.

Rennie, Y. 1978. *The Search for Criminal Man: A Conceptual History of the Dangerous Offender.* Lexington, MA: Lexington Books.

Rice, R., and Atkin, C. 2002. "Theory, Design, Implementation, and Evaluation." In *Media Effects: Advances in Theory and Research*, edited by J. Bryant and D. Zillmann, 427–451. Mahwah, NJ: Lawrence Erlbaum.

Rios, V., and Ferguson, C. 2020. "News Media Coverage of Crime and Violent Drug Crime: A Case for Cause or Catalyst?" *Justice Quarterly* 37, no. 6: 1012–1039.

Ritterband, P., and Silberstein, R. 1973. "Group Disorders in Public Schools." *American Sociological Review* 37: 461–467.

Rizzolatti, G. 2005. "The Mirror Neuron System and Imitation." In *Mechanisms of Imitation.* Vol. 1 of *Perspectives on Imitation: From Neuroscience to Social Science*, edited by S. Hurley and N. Chater, 55–76. Cambridge: Massachusetts Institute of Technology Press.

Rizzolatti, G., and Fogassi, L. 2014. "The Mirror Mechanism: Recent Findings and Perspectives." *Philosophical Transactions of the Royal Society B: Biological Sciences* 369, no. 1644 (April 28). https://royalsocietypublishing.org/doi/full/10.1098/rstb .2013.0420.

Rlindlof, T. 1988. "Media Audiences as Interpretive Communities." *Annals of the International Communication Association* 11, no. 1: 81–107.

Robertson, J. 2003a. "Murder Accused Blames Attack on Vampire Film." *The Scotsman.* October 3: b1.

Robertson, J. 2003b. "Vampire Case Man Jailed for Eighteen Years." *The Scotsman.* October 9. www.scotsman.com/news/vampire-case-man-jailed-for-18-years-2480367 (accessed February 13, 2015).

Rogers, E. 2003. *Diffusion of Innovations.* New York: Free Press.

Romano, Aja. 2012. "The Definitive Guide to Creepypasta—the Internet's Urban Legends." Daily Dot. October 31. www.dailydot.com/unclick/definitive-guide-creepy pasta-slender-man.

Rosekrans, M., and Hartup, W. 1967. "Imitative Influences of Consistent and Inconsistent Response Consequences to a Model on Aggressive Behavior in Children." *Journal of Personality and Social Psychology* 7: 429–434.

Roskos-Ewoldsen, D., Roskos-Ewoldsen, B., and Dillman, C. F. 2002. "Media Priming: A Synthesis." In *Media Effects: Advances in Theory and Research*, edited by B. Jennings and D. Zillmann, 97–120. Mahwah, NJ: Lawrence Erlbaum.

Roskos-Ewoldson, D., Roskos-Ewoldsen, B., and Dillman, C. F. 2009. "Media Priming: An Updated Synthesis." In *Media Effects: Advances in Theory and Research*, edited by J. Bryant and M. Oliver, 74–93. New York: Routledge.

Rost, H. 1912. *Der Selbstmord in den deutschen Städten.* Paderborn: Schoningh.

Rowe, D., and Farrington, D. 1997. "The Familial Transmission of Criminal Convictions." *Criminology* 35: 177–201.

Rubin, A. 2002. "The Uses-and-Gratifications Perspective of Media Effects." In *Media Effects: Advances in Theory and Research*, edited by J. Bryant and D. Zillmann, 525–548. Mahwah, NJ: Lawrence Erlbaum.

Rubinstein, D. 1983. "Epidemic Suicide Among Micronesian Adolescents." *Social Science and Medicine* 17: 657–665.

Ryan, B., and Gross, N. 1943. "The Diffusion of Hybrid Seed Corn in Two Iowa Communities." *Rural Sociology* 8: 15–24.

Sacco, V. 2005. *When Crime Waves.* Thousand Oaks, CA: Sage.

Savage, J. 2004. "Does Viewing Violent Media Really Cause Criminal Violence? A Methodological Review." *Aggression and Violent Behavior* 10: 99–128.

Savage, J. 2008. "The Role of Exposure to Media Violence in the Etiology of Violent Behavior." *American Behavioral Scientist* 51, no. 8: 1123–1136.

Scherr, S., and Steinleitner, A. 2017. "Between Werther and Papageno Effects: A Propositional Meta-analysis of Ambiguous Findings for Helpful and Harmful Media Effects on Suicide Contagion." In *Media and Suicide*, edited by T. Niederkrotenthaler and S. Stack, 193–206. New Brunswick, NJ: Transaction Publishers.

Schlesinger, P., Tumber, H., and Murdock, G. 1991. "The Media Politics of Crime and Criminal Justice." *British Journal of Sociology* 42: 397–420.

Schmid, A., and de Graaf, J. 1982. *Violence as Communication*. Thousand Oaks, CA: Sage.

Schmidtke, A., and Hafner, H. 1988. "Imitation Effects After Fictional Television Suicides." In *Current Issues of Suicidology*, edited by H. Moller, A. Schmidtke, and R. Welz, 341–348. Heidelberg: Springer.

Schmidtke, A., and Schaller, S. 2000. "The Role of Mass Media in Suicide Prevention." In *The International Handbook of Suicide and Attempted Suicide*, edited by K. Hawton and K. van Heeringen, 675–697. New York: John Wiley and Sons.

Schmidtke, A., Schaller, S., and Müller, I. 2002. "Imitation of Amok and Amok-Suicide." *Kriz Dergisi* 10, no. 2: 49–60.

Schorn, D. 2006. "'Bumfight' Videos Inspired Joy-Killing." *60 Minutes*. September 28. www.cbsnews.com/news/bumfight-videos-inspired-joy-killing.

Schramm, W., Lyle, J., and Parker, E. 1961. *Television in the Lives of Our Children*. Stanford, CA: Stanford University Press.

Sellers, C., Cochran, J., and Winfree, L. 2003. "Social Learning Theory and Courtship Violence: An Empirical Test." *Social Learning Theory and the Explanation of Crime* 1: 109–127.

Sharpe, J. 1999. *Crime in Early Modern England, 1550–1750*. London: Longman.

Sherif, M. 1936. *The Psychology of Social Norms*. New York: Harper and Brothers.

Sherizen, S. 1978. "Social Creation of Crime News." In *Deviance and Mass Media*, edited by C. Winick, 203–224. Thousand Oaks, CA: Sage.

"Shiggy, Comedian Behind 'In My Feelings' Challenge, Warns Against Jumping Out of Cars." 2018. *CBS News*. August 3. www.cbsnews.com/news/shiggy-comedian-behind -in-my-feelings-challenge-warns-kids-against-jumping-out-of-cars.

Short, M., D'Orsogna, M., Brantingham, P., and Tita, G. 2009. "Measuring and Modeling Repeat and Near-Repeat Burglary Effects." *Journal of Quantitative Criminology* 25, no. 3: 325–339.

Showalter, E. 1997. *Hystories: Hysterical Epidemics and Modern Culture*. New York: Columbia University Press.

Shrum, L. 2002. "Media Consumption and Perceptions of Social Reality: Effects and Underlying Processes." In *Media Effects: Advances in Theory and Research*, edited by J. Brant and D. Zillmann, 69–95. Mahwah, NJ: Lawrence Erlbaum.

Shulevitz, J. 2001. "Chasing After Conrad's Secret Agent." *Slate*. September 27. https:// slate.com/culture/2001/09/chasing-after-conrad-s-secret-agent.html.

Siegelberg, B. 2011. "Copycat: Where Does the Term Come From?" *Slate*. August 12. www.slate.com/articles/news_and_politics/explainer/2011/08/what_a_copycat.html.

Silver, N. 2012. *The Signal and the Noise*. New York: Penguin Press.

Simon, A. 2007. "Application of Fad Theory to Copycat Crimes: Quantitative Data Following the Columbine Massacre." *Psychological Reports* 100 (3 suppl): 1233–1244.

Sindall, R. 1987. "The London Garotting Panics of 1856 and 1862." *Social History* 12, no. 3: 351–359.

Singhal, A., and Rogers, E. 2012. *Entertainment-Education: A Communication Strategy for Social Change*. New York: Routledge.

Skinner, B. F. 1988. *The Selection of Behavior: The Operant Behaviorism of BF Skinner*. Cambridge: Cambridge University Press Archive.

Slater, M., and Rouner, D. 2002. "Entertainment-Education and Elaboration Likelihood: Understanding the Processing of Narrative Persuasion." *Communication Theory* 12, no. 2: 173–191.

Slutkin, G. 2013. "Violence Is a Contagious Disease." In *Contagion of Violence: Workshop Summary*, ed. National Research Council, 94–110. Washington, DC: National Academies Press. www.ncbi.nlm.nih.gov/books/NBK207245.

Smith, S., and Boyson, A. 2002. "Violence in Music Videos: Examining the Prevalence and Context of Physical Aggression." *Journal of Communication* 52, no. 1: 61–83.

Smith, S., and Donnerstein, E. 1998. "Harmful Effects of Exposure to Media Violence: Learning of Aggression, Emotional Desensitization, and Fear." In *Human Aggression*, edited by R. Geen and E. Donnerstin, 167–202. New York: Academic Press.

Solis, M. 2020. "How Human Brains Are Different." *Scientific American.* July 7. www.scientificamerican.com/article/how-human-brains-are-different-it-has-a-lot-to-do-with-the-connections.

Sparks, G., and Sparks, C. 2002. "Effects of Media Violence." In *Media Effects: Advances in Theory and Research*, edited by B. Jennings and D. Zillmann, 269–285. Mahwah, NJ: Lawrence Erlbaum.

Spector, M., and Kitsuse, J. 1987. *Constructing Social Problems*. Hawthorne, NY: Aldine de Gruyter.

Spilerman, S. 1970. "The Causes of Racial Disturbance: A Comparison of Alternative Explanations." *American Sociological Review* 35: 627–629.

Springhall, J. 1994. "Pernicious Reading? The Penny Dreadful as Scapegoat for Late-Victorian Juvenile Crime." *Victorian Periodicals Review* 27, no. 4: 326–349.

Stack, S. 1987. "Celebrities and Suicide: A Taxonomy and Analysis, 1948–1983." *American Sociological Review* 52: 401–412.

Stack, S. 2000. "Media Impacts on Suicide: A Quantitative Review of 293 Findings." *Social Science Quarterly* 814: 957–972.

Stovel, K. 2001. "Local Sequential Patterns: The Structure of Lynching in the Deep South, 1882–1930." *Social Forces* 79, no. 3: 843–880.

Strahan, S. 1893. *Suicide and Insanity*. London: Swan Sonnenschein.

Strange, J. 2002. "How Fictional Tales Wag Real-World Beliefs." In *Narrative Impact*, edited by M. Green, J. Strange, and T. Brock, 236–286. Mahwah, NJ: Lawrence Erlbaum.

Sullivan, T. 1977. "The Critical Mass in Crowd Behavior: Crowd Size, Contagion and the Evolution of Riots." *Humboldt Journal of Social Relations* 4, no. 2: 46–59.

Surette, R. 1998. "Some Unpopular Thoughts About Popular Culture." In *Popular Culture, Crime and Justice*, edited by F. Bailey and D. Hale, xiv–xxiv. Belmont, CA: Wadsworth.

Surette, R. 2002. "Self-Reported Copycat Crime Among a Population of Serious and Violent Juvenile Offenders." *Crime and Delinquency* 48: 46–69.

Surette, R. 2012. "21st Century Crime and Justice, New Media, and Maximizing Audience Participation." *Pop Culture Universe: Icons, Idols, Ideas.* Santa Barbara, CA: ABC-CLIO.

Surette, R. 2013a. "Cause or Catalyst: The Interaction of Real World and Media Crime Models." *American Journal of Criminal Justice* 38, no. 3: 392–409.

Surette, R. 2013b. "Pathways to Copycat Crime." In *Criminal Psychology*, edited by J. Helfgott, no. 2: 251–273. Santa Barbara, CA: Praeger Publishers.

Surette, R. 2014. "Estimating the Prevalence of Copycat Crime: A Research Note." *Criminal Justice Policy Review* 25, no. 6: 703–718.

Surette, R. 2015a. *Media, Crime and Criminal Justice*. Stamford, CT: Cengage.

Surette, R. 2015b. "Thought Bite: A Case Study of the Social Construction of a Crime and Justice Concept." *Crime Media Culture* 11, no. 2: 105–135.

Surette, R. 2016a. "Copycat Crime and Copycat Criminals: Concepts and Research Questions." *Journal of Criminal Justice and Popular Culture* 18, no. 1: 49–78.

Surette, R. 2016b. "Measuring Copycat Crime." *Crime Media Culture* 12, no. 1: 37–64.
Surette, R. 2016c. "Performance Crime and Justice." *Current Issues in Criminal Justice* 27, no. 2: 195–216.
Surette, R. 2017. "Copycat Crime." Oxford Research Encyclopedia of Criminology: Crime, Media, and Popular Culture. September 26. https://doi.org/10.1093/acrefore/9780190264079.013.33.
Surette, R. 2020a. "A Copycat Crime Meme: Ghost Riding the Whip." *Crime Media Culture* 16, no. 2: 239–264.
Surette, R. 2020b. "Female Copycat Crime: An Exploratory Analysis." *Violence and Gender*. October 27. https://doi.org/10.1089/vio.2020.0046.
Surette, R., and Chadee, D. 2020. "Copycat Crime Among Non-incarcerated Adults." *Current Issues in Criminal Justice* 32, no. 1: 59–75.
Surette, R., Hansen, K., and Noble, G. 2009. "Measuring Media Oriented Terrorism." *Journal of Criminal Justice* 37, no. 4: 360–370.
Surette, R., Helfgott, J., Parkin, W., and O'Toole, M. 2021. "The Social Construction of Copycat Crime in Open Access Media." *Journal of Criminal Justice and Popular Culture* 21, no. 1: 104–127.
Surette, R., and Maze, A. 2015. "Video Game Play and Copycat Crime: An Exploratory Analysis of an Inmate Population." *Psychology of Popular Media Culture* 4, no. 2: 360–374.
Sutherland, E. 1947. *Principles of Criminology*. New York: Harper & Row.
Sutherland, E., Cressey, D., and Luckerbill, D. 1992. *Principles of Criminology*. Dix Hills, NY: General Hall.
Sykes, G., and Matza, D. 1957. "Techniques of Neutralization: A Theory of Delinquency." *American Sociological Review* 22, no. 6: 664–670.
Tarde, G. (1898) 1969. "Opinion and Conversation." In *On Communication and Social Influence: Selected Papers*, edited by T. Clark, 295–324. Chicago: University of Chicago Press.
Tarde, G. (1901) 1969. "The Public and the Crowd." In *On Communication and Social Influence: Selected Papers*, edited by T. Clark, 277–294. Chicago: University of Chicago Press.
Tarde, G. (1912) 1968. *Penal Philosophy*. Translated by Rapelje Howell. Montclair, NJ: Patterson Smith.
Thompson, A. 1997. "Why 14-Year-Old Michael Carneal Went On a Shooting Spree at Heath High School in Paducah, Kentucky." *CNBC*. December 4. www.cnbc.com/cctv-transcripts (accessed December 4, 2014).
Thorndike, E. 1898. "Animal Intelligence." *Nature* 58, no. 1504: 390.
Thorpe, W. 1963. *Learning and Instinct in Animals*. London: Methuen.
Thorson, J., and Oberg, P. 2003. "Was There a Suicide Epidemic After Goethe's Werther?" *Archives of Suicide Research* 7, no. 1: 69–72.
Tillotson, M. 1997. "Paducah Murders: DA Explains 'Confession' Tape." *CNN*. December 4. www.cnn.com (accessed December 5, 2014).
Tilly, C. 1978. *From Mobilization to Revolution*. Reading, MA: Addison-Wesley.
Tomasello, M., and Carpenter, M. 2005. "Intention Reading and Imitative Learning." In *Imitation, Human Development, and Culture*. Vol. 2 of *Perspectives on Imitation: From Neuroscience to Social Science*, edited by S. Hurley and N. Chater, 133–148. Cambridge: Massachusetts Institute of Technology Press.
Torrecilla, J., Quijano-Sánchez, L., Liberatore, F., López-Ossorio, J., and González-Álvarez, J. 2019. "Evolution and Study of a Copycat Effect in Intimate Partner Homicides: A Lesson from Spanish Femicides." *PloS One* 14, no. 6: e0217914.
Tosti, G. 1897. "The Sociological Theories of Gabriel Tarde." *Political Science Quarterly* 12, no. 3: 490–511.

Towers, S., Gomez-Lievano, A., Khan, M., Mubayi, A., and Castillo-Chavez, C. 2015. "Contagion in Mass Killings and School Shootings." *PLoS One* 10, no. 7.

Townsley, M., Homel, R., and Chaseling, J. 2003. "Infectious Burglaries: A Test of the Near Repeat Hypothesis." *British Journal of Criminology* 43, no. 3: 614–633.

Tresniowski, A. 2005. "Driven to Kill." *People Magazine* 64, no. 13. https://people.com/archive/driven-to-kill-vol-64-no-13/.

Tuman, J. 2010. *Communicating Terror.* Thousand Oaks, CA: Sage.

Turner, R. 1964. "Collective Behavior." In *Handbook of Modern Sociology*, edited by R. Faris, 382–425. Chicago: Rand McNally.

Turner, R., and Killian, L. 1957. *Collective Behavior.* Englewood Cliffs, NJ: Prentice Hall.

Tuten, T. 2008. *Advertising 2.0: Social Media Marketing in a Web 2.0 World.* Santa Barbara, CA: ABC-CLIO.

Ueda, M., Mori, K., and Matsubayashi, R. 2014. "The Effects of Media Reports of Suicides by Well-Known Figures Between 1989 and 2010 in Japan." *International Journal of Epidemiology* 43, no. 2: 623–629.

Ugander, J., Backstrom, L., Marlow, C., and Kleinberg, J. 2012. "Structural Diversity in Social Contagion." *Proceedings of the National Academy of Sciences* 109, no. 16: 5962–5966.

Unus, M. 1910. "Kapitel I." In *Über den Selbstmord insbescondere den Schülerselbstmord*, ed. Vereinsleitung des Wiener psychoanalytischen Vereins, 5–18. Wiesbaden: Bergmann.

Valente, T., and Saba, W. 1998. "Mass Media and Interpersonal Influence in a Reproductive Health Communication Campaign in Bolivia." *Communication Research* 25, no. 1: 96–124.

Vaughn, R. 1980. "How Advertising Works: A Planning Model." *Journal of Advertising Research* 20, no. 5: 27–33.

Vernallis, C. 2013. *Unruly Media: YouTube, Music Video, and the New Digital Cinema.* Oxford: Oxford University Press.

Veysey, M., Kamanyire, R., and Volans, G. 1999a. "Antifreeze Poisonings Give More Insight into Copycat Behavior. Effects of Drug Overdose in Television Drama on Presentations for Self Poisoning." *British Journal of Medicine* 319, no. 7217: 1131–1132.

Veysey, M., Kamanyire, R., and Volans, G. 1999b. "Effects of Drug Overdose in Television Drama on Presentations for Self Poisoning." *British Medical Journal* 319, no. 7217: 1131.

Vidmar, N., and Rokeach, M. 1974. "Archie Bunker's Bigotry: A Study in Selective Perception and Exposure." *Journal of Communication* 24, no. 1: 36–47.

Vine, M. 1973. "Gabriel Tarde." In *Pioneers in Criminology*, edited by H. Mannheim, 292–304. Montclair, NJ: Patterson Smith.

Ward, J., and Fox, J. 1977. "A Suicide Epidemic on an Indian Reserve." *Canadian Psychiatric Association Journal* 22: 423–426.

Warr, M. 1993. "Age, Peers, and Delinquency." *Criminology* 31: 17–40.

Warr, M. 2002. *Companions in Crime: The Social Aspects of Criminal Conduct.* Cambridge: Cambridge University Press.

Wasserman, I. 1984. "Imitation and Suicide: A Reexamination of the Werther Effect." *American Sociological Review* 49, no. 3: 427–436.

Watts, J. 2008. "Cop Killer: A Copy Cat Crime." Unpublished research paper. Orlando: University of Central Florida, Department of Criminal Justice.

Weimann, G., and Winn, C. 1994. *The Theater of Terror: Mass Media and International Terrorism.* New York: Longman.

Weintraub, A., and Knaus, C. 2000. "Predicting the Potential for Risky Behavior Among Those 'Too Young' to Drink as the Result of Appealing Advertising." *Journal of Health Communication* 5, no. 1: 13–27.

Weitzer, R., and Kubrin, C. 2009. "Misogyny in Rap Music: A Content Analysis of Prevalence and Meanings." *Men and Masculinities* 12, no. 1: 3–29.

Wells, W., Burnett, J., Moriarty, S., Pearce, R., and Pearce, C. 1989. *Advertising: Principles and Practice*. Englewood Cliffs, NJ: Prentice Hall.

Wells, W., Wu, L., and Ye, X. 2012. "Patterns of Near-Repeat Gun Assaults in Houston." *Journal of Research in Crime and Delinquency* 49, no. 2: 186–212.

Wertham, F. 1954. *Seduction of the Innocent*. New York: Rinehart.

Wessely, S. 1994. "The History of Chronic Fatigue Syndrome." In *Chronic Fatigue Syndrome*, edited by S. Straus, 29–40. New York: Marcel Dekker.

Westermeyer, J. 1973. "On the Epidemicity of Amok Violence." *Archives of General Psychiatry* 28, no. 6: 873–876.

Wheeler, L. 1966. "Toward a Theory of Behavioral Contagion." *Psychological Review* 73, no. 2: 179–192.

Whiten, A., Horner, V., and Marshall-Pescini, S. 2005. "Selective Imitation in Child and Chimpanzee: A Window on the Construal of Others' Actions." In *Mechanisms of Imitation*. Vol. 1 of *Perspectives on Imitation: From Neuroscience to Social Science*, edited by S. Hurley and N. Chater, 263–284. Cambridge: Massachusetts Institute of Technology Press.

Wilkinson, D., and Carr, P. 2008. "Violent Youths' Responses to High Levels of Exposure to Community Violence: What Violent Events Reveal About Youth Violence." *Journal of Community Psychology* 36, no. 8: 1026–1051.

Williams, J., Lawton, C., Ellis, S., Walsh, S., and Reed, J. 1987. "Copycat Suicide Attempts." *The Lancet* 2: 102–103.

Wilson, B., Colvin, C., and Smith, S. 2002. "Engaging in Violence on American Television: A Comparison of Child, Teen, and Adult Perpetrators." *Journal of Communication* 52, no. 1: 36–60.

Wilson, J., and Kelling, G. 1982. "Broken Windows." *The Atlantic*. March. https://www.theatlantic.com/magazine/archive/1982/03/broken-windows/304465.

Wilson, J. Q., and Herrnstein, R. 1985. *Crime and Human Behavior*. New York: Simon & Schuster.

Wilson, P. 1987. "Stranger Child-Murder: Issues Relating to Causes and Controls." *International Journal of Offender Therapy and Comparative Criminology* 31, no. 1: 49–59.

Wilson, W., and Hunter, R. 1983. "Movie-Inspired Violence." *Psychological Reports* 53, no. 2: 435–441.

Withrock, I., Anderson, S., Jefferson, M., McCormack, G., Mlynarczyk, G., Nakama, A., Lange, J., et al. 2015. "Genetic Diseases Conferring Resistance to Infectious Diseases." *Genes and Diseases* 2, no. 3: 247–254.

"Woman Convicted of Killing Two in Excedrin Tampering." 1988. History.com. May 8. https://www.history.com/this-day-in-history/woman-convicted-for-tampering-with-excedrin.

Woodard, D. 2006. *The America That Reagan Built*. New Haven, CT: Greenwood Publishing.

Wooditch, A., and Weisburd, D. 2016. "Using Space-Time Analysis to Evaluate Criminal Justice Programs: An Application to Stop-Question-Frisk Practices." *Journal of Quantitative Criminology* 32, no. 2: 191–213.

World Health Organization (WHO). 2008. *Preventing Suicide: A Resource for Media Professionals. World Health Organization and International Association for Suicide Prevention*. Geneva: WHO Document Production Services.

Wyant, B. R., Taylor, R. B., Ratcliffe, J. H., and Wood, J. 2012. "Deterrence, Firearm Arrests, and Subsequent Shootings: A Micro-Level Spatio-temporal Analysis." *Justice Quarterly* 29, no. 4: 524–545.

Wyer, R., and Srull, T. 1989. *Memory and Cognition in Its Social Context*. Hillsdale, NJ: Lawrence Erlbaum.

Yar, M. 2012. "Crime, Media and the Will-to-Representation: Reconsidering Relationships in the New Media Age." *Crime Media Culture* 8, no. 3: 245–260.

Yi, Y. 1990. "Cognitive and Affective Priming Effects of the Context for Print Advertisements." *Journal of Advertising* 19: 40–48.

Young, J., Rebellion, C., Barnes, J., and Weeman, R. 2013. "Unpacking the Black Box of Peer Similarity in Deviance: Understanding the Mechanisms Linking Personal Behavior, Peer Behavior, and Perceptions." *Criminology* 52, no. 1: 60–86.

Youstin, T., Nobles, M., Ward, J., and Cook, C. 2011. "Assessing the Generalizability of the Near Repeat Phenomenon." *Criminal Justice and Behavior* 38, no. 10: 1042–1063.

Zhang, Y., Zhao, J., Ren, L., and Hoover, L. 2015. "Space-Time Clustering of Crime Events and Neighborhood Characteristics in Houston." *Criminal Justice Review* 40, no. 3: 340–360.

Zhu, Q., Skoric, M., and Shen, F. 2017. "I Shield Myself from Thee: Selective Avoidance on Social Media During Political Protests." *Political Communication* 34, no. 1: 112–131.

Zillmann, D. 2002. "Exemplification Theory of Media Influence." In *Media Effects: Advances in Theory and Research*, edited by J. Bryant and D. Zillmann, 19–41. Mahwah, NJ: Lawrence Erlbaum.

Zillmann, D., and Weaver, J. 1997. "Psychoticism in the Effect of Prolonged Exposure to Gratuitous Media Violence on the Acceptance of Violence as a Preferred Means of Conflict Resolution." *Personality and Individual Differences* 22, no. 5: 613–627.

Index